Teen Finance Series

Earning Information For Teens,
First Edition

Earning Information For Teens, First Edition

Tips For a Successful Financial Life

Including Facts about Child Labor Laws, Teen Jobs, Résumé Preparation, Job Search, Workplace Skills, Workers' Rights, Workplace Safety, and Workplace Stress

OMNIGRAPHICS
615 Griswold, Ste. 901
Detroit, MI 48226

Earning Information For Teens

Library of Congress Cataloging in Publication Control Number: 2018042236

Table of Contents

Preface

Part One: When and How Can You Work?

Part Two: First Steps—Résumé Preparation and Job Search

Part Three: On the Job

Part Four: Managing Your Earnings

Part Five: Smart Spending

Part Six: Saving and Protecting Your Earnings

Part Seven: Looking Ahead

Part Eight: If You Need More Information

Preface

About This Book

The U.S. Bureau of Labor Statistics (BLS) reports the number of youth working, from the age of 16–24 years has increased from 2 million to 20.9 million from April to July 2018. With technology and information at their fingertips, teens today earn, shop, and live in new ways and want the financial independence to do so. One way to achieve that independence is a job. Employment can offer financial security. However, the challenge for any teen is to find the right job and choose a career path that would benefit them in the future.

Earnings Information for Teens, First Edition provides insights into the world of work for teens. It offers the reader information on labor laws, teen workforce participation, age requirements, and various kinds of employment available in the market. Other featured topics include self-assessment, résumé preparation, job searches, apprenticeships, internships, networking, and how to recognize a job scam. The book also explains the organizational skills that are expected of teens in the workplace and outlines basic workers' rights and ways to maintain work–life balance. Sections on managing earnings wisely and spending smartly are included as well as are explanations about the usage of credit and debit cards, online payments, and electronic banking. The book also explains how to build a financially secure future and includes sections on credit history, credit reports, and investing wisely. The book concludes with a list of online money management tools and a directory of resources for financial information.

How to Use This Book

This book is divided into parts and chapters. Parts focus on broad areas of interest; chapters are devoted to single topics within a part.

Part One: When and How Can You Work? opens with child labor laws, including the Fair Labor Standards Act (FLSA) and the Occupational Safety and Health Act (OSHA). This part talks about how teens have become a prominent part of the labor force, and progresses to rules and regulations established by the government for teens as to when and where they may work, specific age requirements, and work hazards involved. The part also talks about the different kinds of job opportunities for teens and employment during different seasons.

Part Two: First Steps—Résumé Preparation and Job Search begins with the topic of self-assessment for teens, which helps them discover a career path they would like to take in the future. Preparations that would steer them in their career choice include creating a résumé, researching a job, and networking. The part also provides basic information about apprenticeships, internships, and types of job scams.

Part Three: On the Job talks about how teens can ensure success on the job. The part details how young teens can prepare themselves for work with adequate skills for a job. It also provides information on workplace ethics, safety, rights, stress, and a chapter on work–life balance.

Part Four: Managing Your Earnings enhances youth financial knowledge and capability. A job provides income, but also requires teens to understand how to manage those earnings. Since teens may not have much knowledge in making basic choices for their finances once they have a job, this part explains effective money management and developing a financial plan, and the benefits of savings and investments. Financial checkups are also a must for teens who want to manage their earnings well. The part also includes tax education for teens, electronic banking, and financial empowerment.

Part Five: Smart Spending discusses cashless transactions. Basic knowledge about debit and credit cards is necessary in today's modern world. Tips on how teens can spend smartly and be safe are included in chapters about managing money, online shopping, safety about mobile wallets, and late payments.

Part Six: Saving and Protecting Your Earnings begins with information on savings and investing, banking basics, and stolen debit or credit cards. Cybercrimes, identity theft and fraud, and telemarketing scams are on the rise, so this part also teaches teens how not to become a victim of financial fraud.

Part Seven: Looking Ahead discusses self-employment, credit history, the credit scoring system, improving credit scores, credit reports, credit report errors, ways to maintain a healthy credit score, and why credit scores matter. The part concludes with advice on investing wisely.

Part Eight: If You Need More Information offers online money management tools and resources for financial information.

Bibliographic Note

This volume contains documents and excerpts from publications issued by the following government agencies: Administration for Children and Families (ACF); Board of

Governors of the Federal Reserve System; Centers for Disease Control and Prevention (CDC); Consumer Financial Protection Bureau (CFPB); Federal Bureau of Investigation (FBI); Federal Communications Commission (FCC); Federal Deposit Insurance Corporation (FDIC); Financial Literacy and Education Commission (FLEC); Federal Student Aid; Federal Trade Commission (FTC); Internal Revenue Service (IRS); Occupational Safety and Health Administration (OSHA); U.S. Bureau of Labor Statistics (BLS); U.S. Department of Justice (DOJ); U.S. Department of Labor (DOL); U.S. Department of the Interior (DOI); U.S. Department of the Treasury; U.S. Securities and Exchange Commission (SEC); U.S. Small Business Administration (SBA); USA.gov; and Youth.gov.

The photograph on the front cover is © Dean Drobot.

Part One
When and How Can You Work?

Chapter 1

Child Labor Laws in the United States

If you are under 18, there are rules regarding your employment, but generally, you have the same rights as other workers. Being familiar with the rules that have to do with pay, safety, and health, and discrimination will help you have a positive work experience.

Fair Labor Standards Act (FLSA)

The Fair Labor Standards Act (FLSA) establishes rules regarding the employment of individuals under the age of 18. In addition to rules for young workers, the FLSA contains provisions on minimum wage, overtime, and recordkeeping.

Occupational Safety and Health Act (OSHA)

The Occupational Safety and Health Act (OSHA) establishes federal workplace safety rules and requires that employers provide a safe and healthful work environment and comply with occupational safety and health standards for all employees, regardless of their age. On the OSHA website (www.osha.gov), you can find information on potential hazards you may be exposed to on the job, read about actual accidents and tragedies involving your peers, and find out about special OSHA safety campaigns for young workers.

About This Chapter: Text in this chapter begins with excerpts from "Child Labor Laws in the US," *YouthRules!*, U.S. Department of Labor (DOL), May 8, 2012; Text under the heading "Wage and Hour Division (WHD)" is excerpted from "Wage and Hour Division (WHD)," U.S. Department of Labor (DOL), September 2016; Text under the heading "Occupational Safety and Health Act—Safety in the Workplace" is excerpted from "Workers," Occupational Safety and Health Administration (OSHA), January 21, 2014.

Hazardous Occupations Regulations

The FLSA contains restrictions on employing workers under the age of 18 in hazardous occupations. Among these occupations are excavation, manufacturing explosives, mining, and operating many types of power-driven equipment. There are different hazardous occupations for agricultural work that are prohibited only for children under age 16.

Discrimination

Employment discrimination on the basis of race, color, religion, national origin, sex, disability, age, and retaliation are prohibited under the federal Equal Employment Opportunity Commission (EEOC) laws. Visit the Equal Employment Opportunity Commission (EEOC) Youth@Work website (www.eeoc.gov/youth) to learn about different types of discrimination affecting young workers and what you can do to help prevent discrimination in the workplace.

Wage and Hour Division (WHD)

The Fair Labor Standards Act (FLSA) establishes minimum wage, overtime pay, record-keeping, and child labor standards affecting full- and part-time workers in the private sector and in federal, state, and local governments.

The Wage and Hour Division (WHD) of the U.S. Department of Labor (DOL) administers and enforces the FLSA with respect to private employment, state and local government employment, and federal employees of the Library of Congress (LOC), U.S. Postal Service (USPS), Postal Rate Commission (PRC), and the Tennessee Valley Authority (TVA). The FLSA is enforced by the U.S. Office of Personnel Management (OPM) for employees of other Executive Branch agencies, and by the U.S. Congress for covered employees of the Legislative Branch.

Special rules apply to state and local government employment involving fire protection and law enforcement activities, volunteer services, and compensatory time off instead of cash overtime pay.

Basic Wage Standards

Covered, nonexempt workers are entitled to a minimum wage of $7.25 per hour effective July 24, 2009. Special provisions apply to workers in American Samoa and the Commonwealth of the Northern Mariana Islands. Nonexempt workers must be paid overtime pay at a rate of not less than one and one-half times their regular rates of pay after 40 hours of work in a workweek.

Wages required by the FLSA are due on the regular payday for the pay period covered. Deductions made from wages for such items as cash or merchandise shortages, employer-required uniforms, and tools of the trade, are not legal to the extent that they reduce the wages of employees below the minimum rate required by the FLSA or reduce the amount of overtime pay due under the FLSA.

The FLSA contains some exemptions from these basic standards. Some apply to specific types of businesses; others apply to specific kinds of work.

While the FLSA does set basic minimum wage and overtime pay standards and regulates the employment of minors, there are a number of employment practices which the FLSA does not regulate.

For example, the FLSA does not require:

1. Vacation, holiday, severance, or sick pay

2. Meal or rest periods, holidays off, or vacations

3. Premium pay for weekend or holiday work

4. Pay raises or fringe benefits

5. A discharge notice, reason for discharge, or immediate payment of final wages to terminated employees

The FLSA does not provide wage payment or collection procedures for an employee's usual or promised wages or commissions in excess of those required by the FLSA. However, some states do have laws under which such claims (sometimes including fringe benefits) may be filed.

Also, the FLSA does not limit the number of hours in a day or days in a week an employee may be required or scheduled to work, including overtime hours, if the employee is at least 16 years old.

The above matters are for agreement between the employer and the employees or their authorized representatives.

Occupational Safety and Health Act—Safety in the Workplace

Know Your Rights

Under federal law, you are entitled to a safe workplace. Your employer must provide a workplace free of known health and safety hazards. If you have concerns, you have the right to speak up about them without fear of retaliation. You also have the right to:

- be trained in a language you understand

- work on machines that are safe

- be provided required safety gear, such as gloves or a harness and lifeline for falls

- be protected from toxic chemicals

- request an OSHA inspection, and speak to the inspector

- report an injury or illness, and get copies of your medical records

- see copies of the workplace injury and illness log

- review records of work-related injuries and illnesses

- get copies of test results done to find hazards in the workplace

---

What Are My Safety Responsibilities on the Job?

To work safely you should:

- follow all safety rules and instructions
- use safety equipment and protective clothing when needed
- look out for coworkers
- keep work areas clean and neat
- know what to do in an emergency
- report any health and safety hazard to your supervisor

(Source: "Are You a Working Teen?" Centers for Disease Control and Prevention (CDC).)

When to File a Complaint

- **Safety and health complaint:** If you believe working conditions are unsafe or unhealthful, you may file a confidential complaint with OSHA and ask for an inspection. If possible, bring the conditions to your employer's attention.

- **Protection from retaliation:** It is illegal for an employer to fire, demote, transfer, or otherwise retaliate against a worker for using their rights under the law. If you believe you have been retaliated against in any way, file a whistleblower complaint within 30 days of the alleged retaliation.

What If I Need Help?

- Talk to your boss about the problem

- Talk to your parents or teachers

- For a Hazard Alert on preventing injuries and deaths of adolescent workers or for information on specific workplace hazards, contact:

  NIOSH at 800-35-NIOSH (800-356-4674) and ask for Report #95-125 or visit the NIOSH homepage (www.cdc.gov/niosh).

  (Source: "Are You a Working Teen?" Centers for Disease Control and Prevention (CDC).)

Chapter 2

Age Requirements for Getting Employed

The Fair Labor Standards Act (FLSA) sets wage, hours worked, and safety requirements for minors (individuals under the age of 18) working in jobs covered by the statute. The rules vary depending upon the particular age of the minor and the particular job involved. As a general rule, the FLSA sets 14 years of age as the minimum age for employment, and limits the number of hours worked by minors under the age of 16.

Also, the FLSA generally prohibits the employment of a minor in work declared hazardous by the U.S. Secretary of Labor (for example, work involving excavation, driving, and the operation of many types of power-driven equipment). The FLSA contains a number of requirements that apply only to particular types of jobs (for example, agricultural work or the operation of motor vehicles) and many exceptions to the general rules (for example, work by a minor for his or her parents). Each state also has its own laws relating to employment, including the employment of minors. If state law and the FLSA overlap, the law which is more protective of the minor will apply.

Posting requirements: Nonagricultural employers must also post the U.S. Department of Labor (DOL)-issued minimum wage poster listing minimum age requirements in a prominent place at the worksite.

What Is the Youngest Age at Which a Person Can Be Employed?

The Fair Labor Standards Act (FLSA) sets 14 as the minimum age for most nonagricultural work. However, at any age, youth may deliver newspapers; perform in radio, television,

About This Chapter: This chapter includes text excerpted from "Age Requirements," U.S. Department of Labor (DOL), February 1, 2002.

movie, or theatrical productions; work in businesses owned by their parents (except in mining, manufacturing or hazardous jobs); and perform babysitting or minor chores around a private home. Also, at any age, youth may be employed as homeworkers to gather evergreens and make evergreen wreaths.

Different age requirements apply to the employment of youth in agriculture. Many states have enacted child labor laws, some of which may have a minimum age for employment which is higher than the FLSA. Where both the FLSA and state child labor laws apply, the higher minimum standard must be obeyed.

What Hours Can Youth Work?

Under the Fair Labor Standards Act (FLSA), the minimum age for employment in nonagricultural employment is 14. Hours worked by 14- and 15-year-olds are limited to:

- Nonschool hours
- 3 hours on a school day
- 18 hours in a school week
- 8 hours on a nonschool day
- 40 hours in a nonschool week
- The hours between 7 a.m. and 7 p.m. (except from June 1 through Labor Day, when evening hours are extended to 9 p.m.)

Youth who are 14 and 15 years old enrolled in an approved Work Experience and Career Exploration Program (WECEP) may be employed for up to 23 hours in a school week and 3 hours on school days (including during school hours).

The FLSA does not limit the number of hours or times of day for workers 16 years and older.

(Source: "Know the Rules—Frequently Asked Questions," YouthRules!, U.S. Department of Labor (DOL).)

Chapter 3

Teen Labor Participation

In the changing economy of the United States, the pull of education is a key factor in how teens are fitting into the labor force. Back in 1979, about 58 percent of teens (16–19) were in the labor force, but by 2000, only 52 percent were. By 2011, after the recession, about 34 percent of teens were in the labor force. What's behind this change? Most teens who do not participate in the labor force cite school as the reason. Consider these factors:

- **Higher attendance:** In 2015, about three in four teens were enrolled in school. This proportion has trended up from about 60 percent in 1985.

- **Time-consuming classes:** After sleeping, school activities take up more time than anything else in a teenager's week day. And high-school coursework has become more strenuous. High schoolers today are taking tougher and more advanced courses, including those specifically designed for college preparation and credit. And most start college the fall after graduating from high school. In October 2015, about 70 percent of recent high-school graduates were enrolled in college, compared with less than half of recent graduates in October 1959.

- **More summer students:** Summer has always been the most common time for teens to work, but fewer teens are holding summer jobs: about 4 in 10 teens were in the labor force last July, compared with about 7 in 10 in July 1978. At the same time, school attendance in summer is on the rise. The proportion of teens enrolled in July 2016 (42%) was more than four times higher than in July 1985.

About This Chapter: Text in this chapter begins with excerpts from "Teens Trends," U.S. Department of Labor (DOL), March 9, 2017; Text beginning with the heading "Teen Labor Force Participation before and after the Great Recession and Beyond" is excerpted from "Teen Labor Force Participation before and after the Great Recession and Beyond," U.S. Bureau of Labor Statistics (BLS), U.S. Department of Labor (DOL), February 2017.

- **Higher education costs:** College tuition costs have risen dramatically in real (inflation-adjusted) terms, so a part-time job is generally not sufficient to cover costs. Teens enrolled in college, therefore, are more likely to cover costs through loans and grants: 84 percent of full-time undergraduates received financial aid in 2011–12, compared with 58 percent in 1992–93.

Teens who want to work face competition, of course. Labor force participation for those ages 55 and older has been growing; their labor force participation rate surpassed the rate for teens in 2009.

What does the future hold? U.S. Bureau of Labor Statistics (BLS) projects that the teen labor participation rate could drop further in 2024, to 26.4 percent.

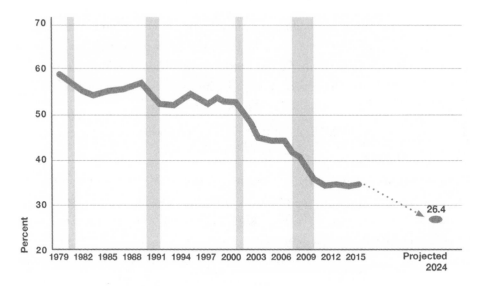

Figure 3.1. Teen Labor Force

Teen Labor Force Participation before and after the Great Recession and Beyond

Teen labor force participation has been on a long-term downward trend, and the decline is expected to continue to 2024, the latest year for which projections are available. A number of factors are contributing to this trend: an increased emphasis toward school and attending college among teens, reflected in higher enrollment; more summer school attendance; and more strenuous coursework. Parental emphasis on the rewards of education has contributed to the decline in teen labor force participation. Tuition costs have continued to rise dramatically, as has borrowing to pay for college. Taxpayers can qualify for tax credits to help defray tuition costs. Teen earnings are low and pay little toward the costs of college. In a teenager's 24-hour day, except for sleeping, school activities take up the largest amount of time. Teens who do in fact want jobs face competition from older workers, young college graduates, and foreign-born workers. This chapter examines labor force participation trends for teens ages 16–19, using data from the Current Population Survey (CPS). The chapter also examines labor force projections data from the Employment Projections program the U.S. Bureau of Labor Statistics (BLS).

Teen labor force participation has been on a long-term downward trend. Since reaching a peak of 57.9 percent in 1979, the rate fell to 52.0 percent in 2000, just prior to the 2001 recession. The rate then dropped rapidly during and after the 2007–09 recession to reach 34.1 percent in 2011, and since then, it has stayed within a narrow range. The latest projection of labor force participation from the U.S. Bureau of Labor Statistics (BLS) points toward an even lower teen participation rate by 2024.

Why has teen labor force participation declined and remained low? A growing proportion of people ages 16 and 19 years old are in school, and school enrollment has an impact on labor force participation. Other factors besides education affect the participation rate as well. This study will concentrate on labor force participation rates for the 16-to-19 age group, using not seasonally adjusted historical data from BLS, along with projected data. The historical participation rate data are annual averages, except for an analysis of the July rate that is used for evaluating teen labor force participation during the summer.

Trends in Teen Labor Force Participation

Labor force participation for teens trended down from 52.5 percent in 1948 to 44.5 percent in 1964. The rate moved upward until it reached its high point of 57.9 percent in 1979. Several recessions occurred since 1979, including those of 1981–82, 1990–91, 2001, and the most recent recession, often called the "Great Recession" of 2007–09. Over the past several decades, the rate exhibited a similar pattern; it fell just before, during, and for a short time after recessions ended, followed by little change during most of the recovery. The overall drop in the rate was especially steep, however, during the two most recent recessions. In 2000, just before the 2001 recession, a little more than one-half of teenagers (52.0%) were in the labor force. By 2003, the rate had fallen to 44.5 percent. In 2006 (just before the 2007–09 recession), the rate was 43.7 percent. The participation rate declined during that recession and immediately after, falling to 34.1 percent in 2011. It has changed little since 2011.

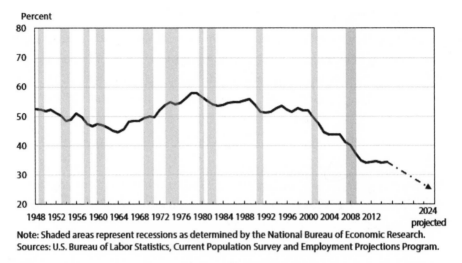

Note: Shaded areas represent recessions as determined by the National Bureau of Economic Research.
Sources: U.S. Bureau of Labor Statistics, Current Population Survey and Employment Projections Program.

Figure 3.2. Labor Force Participation for Teens Ages 16–19, 1948–2015 and Projected 2024

Traditionally, teens held summer jobs even if they did not work during the school year, and labor force participation is higher during the summer than during the school year. Even though some teens still have summer jobs, the proportion of teens who participate in the labor force during the summer has dropped dramatically. The summer break typically includes July. In July 2016, the teen labor force participation rate was 43.2 percent, down almost 30 percentage points from the high point of 71.8 percent in July 1978.

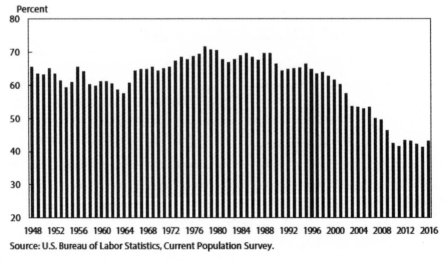

Source: U.S. Bureau of Labor Statistics, Current Population Survey.

Figure 3.3. Labor Force Participation for Teens Ages 16–19, 1948–2016

Summer Youth Labor Force in July 2017

From April to July 2017, the labor force of 16- to 24-year-olds grew by 2.4 million, or 11.6 percent, to 23.1 million. Over the same period, the number of employed 16- to 24-year-olds increased by 1.9 million to 20.9 million. The youth labor force—those working or actively looking for work—grows sharply between April and July each year. During these months, large numbers of high-school and college students search for or take summer jobs, and many graduates enter the labor market to look for or begin permanent employment.

The labor force participation rate for 16- to 24-year-olds was 60.6 percent in July, little different from a year earlier. (The labor force participation rate is the proportion of the civilian noninstitutional population that is working or available and looking for work.) The summer labor force participation rate of 16- to 24-year-olds has held fairly steady since July 2010, after trending downward for the prior two decades. The summer youth labor force participation rate peaked at 77.5 percent in July 1989.

The July 2017 labor force participation rate for young men, at 62.3 percent, continued to be higher than the rate for young women, at 58.8 percent. The rate for young women edged up from last July, while the rate for young men was essentially unchanged.

(Source: "TED: The Economics Daily," U.S. Bureau of Labor Statistics (BLS).)

Education Impacts

Educators, parents, policymakers, and other stakeholders are paying more attention to the value of education. Workers with more education tend to have higher pay and lower unemployment. Indeed, data from BLS illustrate this relationship. As stakeholders pay more attention to the value of education, teen school enrollment has continued to grow and labor force participation to decline.

Teen School Enrollment

In 2015, about three out of four teens were enrolled in school. Despite dipping in 2013, this proportion trended up from 58.7 percent in 1985, which is the first year of data.

More teens attend school during the summer now than in previous years. The proportion of teenagers enrolled in July 2016 was more than 4 times higher than it was in July 1985—42.1 percent versus 10.4 percent.

According to the Annual Social and Economic Supplement (ASEC) of the current population survey (CPS), the major reason teens give for not being in the labor force is that they are attending school. The supplement includes a question for those who did not work at all in the previous year: "What was the main reason (you/she/he) did not work in (year)?" In 2014, 92 percent of 16- to 19-year-olds who did not participate in the labor force cited "going to school" as the main reason. In 2004, this percentage was 89 percent. The percentage of teens who did not work at all during the year because they were going to school was 59.5 percent in 2014 versus 46.1 percent 10 years earlier.

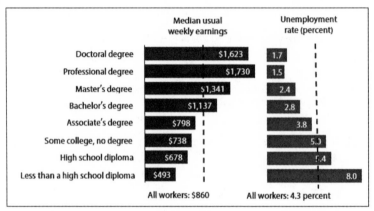

Note: Data are for people ages 25 and over. Earnings are for full-time wage and salary workers.
Source: U.S. Bureau of Labor Statistics, Current Population Survey.

Figure 3.4. Earnings and Unemployment Rates by Educational Attainment, 2015

Labor force participation rates are available by enrollment status. The participation for enrolled teens is much lower than for nonenrolled teens. Both rates were at their highest points in 1989. Both rates began to decline sharply before the 2001 recession and continued to descend until 2011; since then, both have stayed within a narrow range. The decline for enrolled teens has been sharper than the decline for teens not in school. About one-quarter of enrolled teens participated in the labor force in 2015, whereas the rate was 42.8 percent in 2000. The rate for teens who are not enrolled fell from 71.6 percent in 2000 to 58.9 percent in 2015.

1. Reasons for the dip in teen enrollment in 2013 are not clear. A corresponding increase in labor force participation for this age group did not occur in 2013. Many researchers point toward cyclical trends in school enrollment; that is, people tend to return to school during recessionary periods and to the labor force during recoveries. This factor likely affects young adults more than teenagers, however. Other researchers point toward the high cost of college and concerns about debt. Indeed, tuition costs and college debt have been rising. Despite the dip in enrollment in 2013, the proportion enrolled still remains high by historical standards.

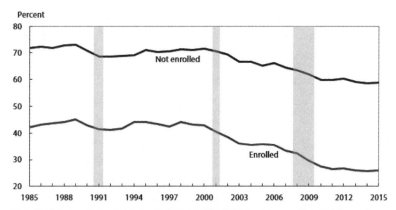

Note: Shaded areas represent recessions as determined by the National Bureau of Economic Research.
Source: U.S. Bureau of Labor Statistics, Current Population Survey.

Figure 3.5. Labor Force Participation Rates by Enrollment Status for Teens Ages 16–19, 1948–2015

High School Coursework

Pressures to increase achievement and to better prepare high school students for college have grown, as shown by changes in coursework. High schoolers are taking tougher and more advanced courses, including those specifically designed for college preparation and credit—Advanced Placement (AP) courses. Dedicating more time to studies may leave less time for participation in the labor force.

The National Commission on Excellence in Education (NCEE) recommended in 1983 that all college-bound students take the following as a minimum during four years of high school: four years of English; three years each of social studies, science, and mathematics; two years of a foreign language; and one-half year of computer science. The National Center for Education Statistics (NCES) has data on combinations of courses taken by high school graduates, including the combination recommended by the Commission, minus computer science. The proportion of high school graduates completing the previous combination of years, at a minimum, was 9.5 percent in 1982. It grew to 61.8 percent of 2009 high school graduates, or more than 6 times higher than the proportion for 1982 high school graduates.

The National Center for Education Statistics (NCES) also has data on selected courses taken by high school graduates by area of study for selected years from 1982–2009. As for mathematics, the proportion of graduates who have taken advanced math courses in high school has grown. Notably, the proportion taking algebra II grew from 39.9 percent in 1982

17

to 75.5 percent in 2009. The proportion with a semester in analysis/precalculus was just 6.2 percent of graduates in 1982, and it climbed to a little more than 35 percent of graduates in 2009. Coursework in statistics/probability and calculus also rose over the period.

More high school graduates have been taking science, including multiple science courses. Nearly all 2009 graduates earned at least one year in biology (95.6%), 70.4 percent earned one year in chemistry, and 36.1 percent earned at least one year in physics. The proportion of graduates earning multiple years in the sciences has grown. In 2009, 68.3 percent of graduates earned years in both biology and chemistry, and 30.1 percent earned years in biology, chemistry, and physics. By comparison, 29.3 percent of 1989 graduates earned years in biology and chemistry and 11.2 percent in biology, chemistry, and physics.

As for foreign languages, 86.4 percent of 2009 graduates had taken a foreign language, compared with 54.4 percent in 1982. The proportion of graduates taking one year or less of a foreign language declined since 1982. Those having taken a minimum of two years in foreign languages was 19.5 percent in 1982 and 35.3 percent in 2009, having dipped from 2005. The proportion earning three or more years has more than doubled since 1982. In 2009, nearly 40 percent of graduates had three or more years of a foreign language.

The proportion of graduates with credits in AP courses has increased as well. AP courses allow students to take college-level courses in high school, and they can earn college credit for the courses if they achieve a minimum score on an AP examination. In 2009, 36.3 percent of public high school graduates had taken an AP course, compared with 26.9 percent in 2000.

College after High School

BLS data show that the proportion of high school graduates who go to college immediately following graduation has trended up, despite dipping slightly in recent years. In October 2015, the proportion of 2015 high school graduates enrolled in college was 69.2 percent, close to the high point of 70.1 percent in October 2009. Although this proportion dipped from 2009 through 2013 (from 70.1 to 65.9%), it has trended up since. By comparison, less than half of recent high school graduates were enrolled in college in October 1959. As noted earlier, students are less likely to participate in the labor force.

Time Spent on School Activities

The time that teens spend on school-related activities can take away from any hours left in the day for a job. According to the BLS American Time Use Survey (ATUS), participation in educational activities consumes a large amount of time in a young person's day. Educational activities in ATUS include attending class, doing homework and research, and other activities, including related travel. Estimates are available for youth who are ages 15–19 years old and enrolled in high school. According to ATUS, enrolled youth who participated in educational activities spent 7.72 hours a day on the activities for the combined years 2010–14. This measure is up slightly from 2003–07 when it was 7.59 hours. Only sleeping, at 8.63 hours in 2003–07 and 8.68 hours in 2010–14, accounted for more time in a 24-hour period than educational activities.

Some high schools require prospective graduates to spend time volunteering to graduate. The CPS has a supplementary survey on volunteering. The data show that the proportion of the 16-to-19-year-old population who volunteer has been a little more than one-quarter of the teenage population. This proportion has moved little since the CPS supplement started in 2002. Teenagers do volunteer at higher rates than several other age groups, including 20-to-24-year-olds. Data from ATUS on time use also indicate that among teens who volunteer, the time spent on volunteering has not risen. According to ATUS, 15-to-19-year-old volunteers enrolled in high school spent 1.65 hours volunteering during school weekdays in 2010–14 versus 2.1 hours in 2003–07. Still, hours spent during the day on volunteering take time from other activities, including working.

Earlier School Start Dates

School terms have become less likely to start after Labor Day. The school starting dates for many school districts have moved earlier into the summer, oftentimes to extend the school year so that students have more time to prepare for standardized tests. For example, schools in Cleveland, Ohio, have moved their starting dates up about one week for the past two summers and moved up another week in 2016 to a start date of August 8, 2016. In Texas, many school districts want to change the state law on when school starts (which is late August) to allow more time for test preparation and to better balance school days with school breaks. Last school year, just three states (Virginia, Minnesota, and Michigan) had state laws that prohibited schools from starting before Labor Day unless they received a waiver; some school systems, such as those in Hawaii, started at the end of July. With a shorter summer off from school, students may be less inclined to get a summer job, and employers may be less inclined to hire them.

Paying for College

The price of college tuition has continued to rise. The average cost for undergraduate tuition, fees, room, and board for the school year 2014–15 (in constant 2014–15 dollars) was nearly $22,000, more than double the amount experienced 30 years earlier. Tuition for both public and private colleges has risen. The average public school tuition was about $16,000 in 2014–15, compared with about $7,600 for the 1984–85 school year. The increase in private (both for-profit and nonprofit) tuition was even greater, from approximately $18,000 to about $37,000 over the same period.

As tuition costs have risen, so has the proportion of students receiving financial aid. During the 2011–12 school year, 84.4 percent of full-time, full-year undergraduates received financial aid (grants, loans, and work study), up from 58.2 percent in 1992–93. The proportion receiving grants grew from nearly one-half to close to three-fourths, and the share with loans from about 3 in 10 to almost 6 in 10. In addition, parents are borrowing more, through Parent Plus loans. The average per borrower of a Parent Plus loan for an undergraduate was $11,999 for the 2015–16 school year, up from $3,231 (in constant 2015 dollars) for the 1995–96 school year.

Taxpayers also can take advantage of tax credits or deductions to assist with tuition costs. As of tax year 2009, the American Opportunity Credit replaced the former Hope Scholarship Credit. The American Opportunity Credit is for students in their first four years of school who are attending school at least halftime. It allows taxpayers to qualify for a credit for education expenses when they file their taxes, up to $2,500 (depending on income). The amount of education tax credits was $17.8 billion in 2014, up from 4.3 billion in 1998 (in 2014 dollars).

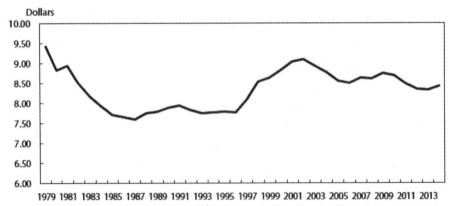

Note: The Consumer Price Index research series is used to convert current dollars into constant 2014 dollars.
Source: U.S. Bureau of Labor Statistics, *BLS Reports*, report 1058, "Highlights of women's earnings in 2014," table 20: "Inflation-adjusted median hourly earnings, by age, for wage and salary workers paid hourly rates, 1979–2014 annual averages," November 2015.

Figure 3.6. Median Hourly Earnings for Teens Ages 16–19 Paid Hourly Rates in Constant 2014 Dollars, 1979–2014

Since college is so costly, teen earnings may not make much of a dent in the tuition bill. Moreover, with available financial aid and tax credits, teens still in school may not have to work as much to pay for college. In fact, teens' buying power has declined in recent years. In 2014, median hourly earnings for teens paid hourly rates was $8.43 (in constant 2014 dollars), down from $9.09 in 2002.

Parental Emphasis on School-Related Activities

Anecdotal evidence points toward parents preferring that their children do not work and that they instead use their time for school-related activities. This preference is more apparent among highly educated families and those with the highest incomes according to analyses using CPS and ATUS data. Shirley L. Porterfield and Anne E. Winkler analyzed teen employment rates using CPS data and found that declines in employment from 1995–96 to 2003–04 were greatest for teens in the most educated families. The same study analyzed ATUS data, and results showed that teens in families with the highest incomes spent more time on the "traditional activities" of extracurricular pursuits, plus hobbies, reading, and writing.

Another study of time use data found a large increase in time that parents with college education spend in "childcare," meaning time spent with children. Garey Ramey and Valerie A. Ramey studied time use data from 1965–2007 and found that the increase in time spent with children was twice as great for college-educated parents, and the increase was mainly time spent on activities of older children. The authors state, "...the increase in time spent in childcare, particularly among the college educated, may be a response to an increase in the perceived return to attending a good college, coupled with an increase in competition in college admissions."

Competition for Jobs

Are teens competing with other workers for jobs? Older workers looking for jobs, perhaps after retiring from their careers; young, underemployed college graduates; and immigrants are among those who may compete with teens for low-wage jobs. Competition with other workers could affect the labor force participation of all teens, whether enrolled or not.

Older Workers and Young College Graduates

While teens have seen reductions in their labor force participation rates, participation among the 55-and-over age group has been growing. The labor force participation rate for people ages 55 and over surpassed the rate for teens in 2009. By 2015, the participation rate for the older age group was 39.9 percent versus 34.3 percent for teenagers. In 2015, the number of employed people ages 55 and over was about seven times greater than the number of employed 16- to 19-year-olds. Older people are staying in the labor force longer than ever before. In addition, even though older workers may officially "retire" from their career jobs, many do not officially exit the labor force; instead, they increasingly take on "bridge" jobs, usually part-time or part-year and lower wage jobs.

Foreign-Born Workers

Overall, the percentage of the total labor force held by the foreign-born was 16.7 percent in 2015, whereas it was 14.8 percent in 2005 (the first year of CPS published foreign-born data). These foreign-born workers may compete directly with teens for the types of jobs teens would typically hold, which would be those with low educational requirements. The educational attainment of foreign-born workers is lower than that of native-born workers. According to the CPS, about one-quarter of the foreign-born labor force ages 25 and over had less than a high school diploma as their highest level of educational attainment in 2015, while that proportion was about 5 percent for the native-born labor force ages 25 and over. An analysis by Christopher L. Smith of the Federal Reserve Board (FRB) found that immigrant employment has a greater effect on employment of native-born 16- to 17-year-olds than it does on native-adult employment. According to Smith, ". . . a 10-percent increase in the number of immigrants with a high-school degree or less is estimated to reduce the average total number of hours worked in a year by 3–3½ percent for native teens and by less than one percent for less educated adults."

Fewer Teens Not in the Labor Force Actually "Want a Job"

Do those teens who are not in the labor force want to be working? According to the CPS, in 2015, just 8.8 percent of 16-to-19-year-olds not in the labor force wanted a job. In 1994, this proportion was 20.0 percent. It declined to 9.8 percent in 2007 and has ranged from about 9–10 percent since then.

What about 2024?

BLS projects declining teen labor force participation in the next decade—the rate is projected to drop from 34.0 percent in 2014 to 26.4 percent in 2024. BLS links the projected decline to increased school enrollment. Overall labor force participation (for all ages) is projected to fall. This projection for the overall rate is partly due to declines among youth, but mainly, it is due to the baby-boom generation moving into the older age groups who have lower labor force participation rates. At the same time, the participation rates for cohorts ages 55 and over are projected to increase over the projection period. In fact, the projected participation rate for the ages 65-to-74 cohort, at 29.9 percent in 2024, is greater than the rate projected for teenagers.

Overall, labor force participation of teens has been declining since 1979, and their low rates of labor force participation continued into the recovery period following the latest recession. In particular, teen participation during the summer has dropped dramatically. School enrollment has increased, especially during the summer months, and enrollment affects the participation of teenagers in the labor force. Along with the increased emphasis toward college, coursework has also become more strenuous in high school. In addition, teens spend much of their time on school activities—only sleeping accounts for more time in a teenager's day. Teens who do want jobs may face competition from others for the types of jobs they typically hold. As for the future, the labor force participation rate for teens is projected to decline further in 2024, according to the latest BLS projections.

Chapter 4

When and Where Is a Teen Allowed to Work?

Every year, millions of teens work in part-time or summer jobs. Early work experiences can be rewarding for young workers, providing great opportunities to learn important skills. However, the jobs that teens are hired to do should not jeopardize their health or well-being. The U.S. Department of Labor (DOL) launched the *YouthRules!* initiative. This initiative promotes positive and safe work experiences for young workers by educating parents, teens, employers, and educators about the types of jobs teens can hold and the number of hours they can work.

14- and 15-Year-Olds Can Work

- Outside school hours
- After 7 a.m. and until 7 p.m. (hours are extended to 9 p.m. June 1 through Labor Day)
- Up to 3 hours on a school day
- Up to 18 hours in a school week
- Up to 8 hours on a nonschool day
- Up to 40 hours in a nonschool week

Jobs Teens Can Perform

- Teens 13 or younger can babysit, deliver newspapers, or work as an actor or performer.

About This Chapter: Text in this chapter begins with excerpts from "When and Where Is Your Teen Allowed to Work?" *YouthRules!*, U.S. Department of Labor (DOL), July 31, 2004; Text beginning with the heading "I Am under 14" is excerpted from "Know the Rules," *YouthRules!*, U.S. Department of Labor (DOL), October 3, 2016.

- Fourteen- and 15-year-olds may work in a variety of jobs including those located in offices, grocery stores, retail stores, restaurants, movie theaters, amusement parks, baseball parks, or gasoline service stations. However, they are prohibited from working in jobs declared hazardous by the U.S. Secretary of Labor.

- Sixteen- and 17-year-olds can work in any job that hasn't been declared hazardous. There are 17 hazardous jobs young workers under the age of 18 are prohibited from doing.

- Some of these jobs include mining, meat packing or processing, using power-driven bakery machines or paper-product machines, roofing, and excavation operations. Most driving is also prohibited.

- Once a youth reaches 18 years of age, she or he is no longer subject to the federal youth employment laws. Different rules apply to youth employed in agriculture. States may also have different laws.

Through the *YouthRules!* initiative, the U.S. Department of Labor (DOL) wants to ensure that all teens have positive work experiences that help prepare them for the demands of the workforce.

After all, today's youth will be the workforce of tomorrow.

I Am under 14

Kids under 14 can gain valuable experience working, but there are limits to what jobs you can do.

What Jobs Can I Do?

If you are under 14 you are only allowed to:

- deliver newspapers to customers

- babysit on a casual basis

- work as an actor or performer in movies, TV, radio, or theater

- work as a homeworker gathering evergreens and making evergreen wreaths

- work for a business owned entirely by your parents as long as it is not in mining, manufacturing, or any of the 17 hazardous occupations

There are different rules for children under age 14 working in agriculture. States also have rules, and employers must follow both.

I Am 14 or 15

Fourteen- and 15-year-olds are limited in what hours they can work and what jobs they can do.

What Hours Can I Work?

All work must be performed outside school hours and you may not work:

- more than 3 hours on a school day, including Friday

- more than 18 hours per week when school is in session

- more than 8 hours per day when school is not in session

- more than 40 hours per week when school is not in session

- before 7 a.m. or after 7 p.m. on any day, except from June 1st through Labor Day, when night-time work hours are extended to 9 p.m.

If you are homeschooled, attend a private school, or no school, a "school day" or "school week" is any day or week when the public school where you live while employed is in session. There are some exceptions to the hours' standards for 14- and 15-year-olds—if you have graduated from high school, you are excused from compulsory school attendance; or if you are enrolled in an approved Work Experience or Career Exploration Program or Work-Study Program, then you are excused.

What Jobs Can I Do?

There are certain jobs you are allowed to do, including:

- Retail occupations

- Intellectual or creative work such as computer programming, teaching, tutoring, singing, acting, or playing an instrument

- Errands or delivery work by foot, bicycle, and public transportation

- Clean-up and yard work which does not use power-driven mowers, cutters, trimmers, edgers, or similar equipment

- Works in connection with cars and trucks, such as dispensing gasoline or oil and washing or hand polishing

- Some kitchen and food service work, including reheating food, washing dishes, cleaning equipment, and limited cooking

- Cleaning vegetables and fruits; wrapping sealing, labeling, weighing, pricing, and stocking of items when performed in areas separate from a freezer or meat cooler

- Loading or unloading objects for use at a worksite, including rakes, handheld clippers, and shovels

Fourteen- and 15-year-olds who meet certain requirements can perform limited tasks in sawmills and woodshops. 15-year-olds who meet certain requirements can perform lifeguard duties at traditional swimming pools and water amusement parks. If an occupation is not specifically permitted, it is prohibited for youth ages 14 and 15.

How Much Should I Be Paid?

Although some exceptions may apply, in most circumstances you must be paid at least the federal minimum wage, which is currently $7.25 per hour. Your eligibility for the federal minimum wage depends on what you do and where you work.

If you are younger than 20 and eligible for the minimum wage, your employer may pay you as little as $4.25 per hour for the first 90 consecutive calendar days of your employment. This is not limited to your first employer. Each time you change jobs, your new employer can pay you this youth minimum wage.

There are different rules for 14- and 15-year-olds working in agriculture and states also have rules; employers must follow both.

I Am 16 or 17

Although there are no federal rules limiting the hours 16- and 17-year-olds may work, there are restrictions on the types of jobs you can do.

What Hours Can I Work?

At 16 and 17 you may work unlimited hours.

What Jobs Can I Do?

Any job that has not been declared hazardous by the U.S. Secretary of Labor is permissible for 16- and 17-year olds.

How Much Should I Be Paid?

Although some exceptions may apply, in most circumstances you must be paid at least the federal minimum wage, which is currently $7.25 per hour. Your eligibility for the federal minimum wage depends on what you do and where you work.

If you are younger than 20 and eligible for the minimum wage, your employer may pay you as little as $4.25 per hour for the first 90 consecutive calendar days of your employment. This is not limited to your first employer. Each time you change jobs, your new employer can pay you this youth minimum wage.

There are different rules for 16- and 17-year-olds working in agriculture. States also have rules, and employers must follow both.

No worker under 18 may:

- Drive a motor vehicle as a regular part of the job or operate a forklift at any time
- Operate any types of powered equipment like a circular saw, box crusher, meat slicer, or bakery machine
- Work in wrecking, demolition, excavation, or roofing
- Work in mining, logging, or a sawmill
- Work in meat-packing or slaughtering
- Work where there is exposure to radiation
- Work where explosives are manufactured or stored

(Source: "Are You a Working Teen?" Centers for Disease Control and Prevention (CDC).)

I Am 18

Once you turn 18, most youth work rules do not apply.

What Hours Can I Work?

There are no limits to the number of hours 18-year-olds can work.

What Jobs Can I Do?

Once you turn 18, you can perform any job for which you are qualified.

How Much Should I Be Paid?

Although some exceptions may apply, in most circumstances you must be paid the federal minimum wage, $7.25 per hour. Your eligibility for the federal minimum wage depends on what you do and where you work.

If you are younger than 20 and eligible for the minimum wage, your employer may pay you as little as $4.25 per hour for the first 90 consecutive calendar days of your employment. This is not limited to your first employer. Each time you change jobs, your new employer can pay you this youth minimum wage. States also have rules, and employers must follow both.

Chapter 5

Part-Time Employment

Part-Time Concepts

A voluntary part-time worker:

- Works 1–34 hours a week

- Does not want to work 35 or more hours a week OR is not available to do so

An involuntary part-time worker:

- Works 1–34 hours a week

- Wants to work 35 or more hours a week

- Is available to work 35 or more hours a week

- Is called an involuntary part-time worker

In this chapter, these part-time concepts refer specifically to a person's usual work hours, but they are more often presented on the basis of the number of hours a person actually worked during the survey reference week regardless of his or her usual full- or part-time status.

A key metric used for comparisons in this chapter is the voluntary part-time rate, or the percentage of all employed people who work part-time voluntarily. In this analysis, the term "part-time" includes workers who usually work part-time hours, regardless of whether their actual hours at work during the reference week were full- or part-time. However, part-time workers who did not work during the reference week are not included in this rate because

About This Chapter: This chapter includes text excerpted from "Who Chooses Part-Time Work and Why?" U.S. Bureau of Labor Statistics (BLS), U.S. Department of Labor (DOL), March 2018.

they are not asked about the reason they work part-time, and therefore, cannot be classified as either voluntary or involuntary.

Holiday Pay

A part-time employee is entitled to be paid for a federal holiday when the holiday falls on a day when she or he would otherwise be required to work or take leave. This does not include overtime work. Part-time employees who are excused from work on a holiday receive their rate of basic pay for the hours they are regularly scheduled to work on that day. Employees must be in a pay status or a paid-time-off status category (i.e., leave, compensatory time off, compensatory time off for travel, or credit hours) on their scheduled workdays either before or after a holiday in order to be entitled to their regular pay for that day. Employees who are in a nonpay status for the workdays immediately before and after a holiday may not receive compensation for that holiday.

(Source: "Factsheet—Part-Time Employment," U.S. Bureau of Labor Statistics (BLS).)

Who Works Part-Time Voluntarily?

Historically, women have been more likely than men to work part-time voluntarily. However, the voluntary part-time rate for women trended down modestly from 1994 through 2013, driving the trend in the overall voluntary part-time rate. In 2016, about one in five working women worked part-time on a voluntary basis. The proportion of employed men voluntarily working part-time varied little over much of the last two decades. However, their voluntary part-time rate has trended upward reaching nearly 1 in 10 in 2016. Voluntary part-time rates for women were higher than those for men regardless of age, race, or ethnicity.

By age, teenagers and older workers are more likely to choose part-time work than people of prime working age (25–54 years old). Employed teenagers have the highest voluntary part-time rates of any age group. Given school schedules, some states' restrictions on hours for those younger than age 18, and shifting labor–leisure preferences of young people, it is no surprise that many employed 16- to 17-year-olds work part-time. For instance, in 2016, about four out of five employed 16- to 17-year-olds worked part-time voluntarily. Older teenagers, ages 18 and 19, also were inclined to work part-time—slightly more than half of those employed worked part-time voluntarily in 2016, a modest increase from the rate in 1994. Although teenagers and young adults (20–24 years old) have become less likely to work since 2000—as evidenced by downward-trending employment-population ratios—older teens and young adults who worked became increasingly likely to work part-time on a voluntary basis over the timeframe studied and were the only age groups to do so.

Older workers (those 65 years of age and older) also have an above-average tendency to work part-time. However, this tendency toward voluntary part-time work, unlike that of younger workers, subsided over the period studied. The high voluntary part-time rate of older workers, at 34.6 percent in 2016, may reflect provisions in the social safety net that become available to Americans in their mid-60s. Namely, Medicare could affect labor–leisure preferences of older workers by divorcing the provision of health insurance from full-time employment, and Social Security could affect the preferred length of workweeks by reducing the earnings recipients need to maintain their living standards.

Before the Social Security earnings test was eliminated, it restricted the amount of money a beneficiary could earn without penalties. This test could have affected older workers' preferred work hours by limiting the amount they could earn, which effectively restricted the number of hours they could work. The earnings test was eliminated for beneficiaries of full retirement age in 2000. In fact, the voluntary part-time rate of older workers began to fall in 2000, perhaps partially reflecting the elimination of this test. In 1994, nearly half of older workers chose to work part-time, a proportion that remained fairly stable through 1999. This rate began a steady decline in 2000, and by 2016, only about one-third of older workers were working part-time voluntarily. Shifting preferences toward full-time employment among older workers could reflect other social or economic phenomena as well. Improvements in healthcare over the past two decades have contributed to better health among older Americans, possibly enabling older workers to work longer hours than previous generations. In addition, over this period, older workers (like all workers) became more heavily concentrated in less physically arduous occupations, such as management, professional, and technical occupations, and less concentrated in more physically demanding occupations, such as natural resource, construction, and maintenance occupations.

This occupational shift could have contributed to a change in the number of hours older workers are willing or able to work. Older workers could also prefer more hours today than in the past in pursuit of retirement security. Today's older workers may have inadequate savings to support a nearly 20-year retirement, possibly because of lingering effects of the Great Recession, lower overall savings, or a structural shift in employee retirement benefits from defined benefit plans to defined contribution plans.

Why Do People Work Part-Time Voluntarily?

The reasons people voluntarily work less than 35 hours a week vary. School attendance is the primary reason that people choose part-time hours, which correlates with the large number of youth working part-time voluntarily. In 2016, 6.0 million people, or 29 percent of all voluntary part-time workers, worked part-time to attend school, reflecting that nearly one-third of voluntary part-time workers were between the ages of 16 and 24. The second most common reason people choose part-time work is family or personal obligations (other than childcare problems). In 2016, family or personal obligations were the reason that 4.3 million people, or 21 percent of all voluntary part-time workers, worked part-time, and women accounted for an overwhelming majority of them. This finding is supported by American Time Use Survey data, which show that women are more likely to both engage in eldercare than men (18% compared with 15%) and spend more time caring for children than men (2.1 hours a day compared with 1.6 hours a day).

A full-time workweek of less than 35 hours, which has become more common over time, is the third most common reason for voluntary part-time work. The number of voluntary part-time workers who maintained that their hours were full time more than doubled since 1994, reaching 3.8 million in 2016. These workers accounted for about 18 percent of all voluntary part-time workers in 2016, up from 11 percent in 1994.

The growth in the number and share of overall voluntary part-time workers who work short full-time work weeks was evident across all age groups and both genders. Furthermore, this growth was at the expense of the most common reason for each group. Since 1994, school attendance has been the most common reason men had for voluntary part-time work. However, the share of men who worked part-time for this reason shrank from about one-half in 1994 to just over one-third in 2016, and the share of men working short full-time work weeks nearly doubled to 20 percent in 2016. Similarly, family or personal obligations have been the most common reason women worked part-time hours since 1994. However, the share of women choosing part-time hours, for this reason, shrank by 10 percentage points to 28 percent in 2016, while the share working short full-time weeks grew by 8 percentage points, to 18 percent. Likewise, in 2016, smaller shares of teenagers and young adults worked part-time to attend school than those who did so in 1994, a smaller share of prime-age workers worked part-time because of family obligations, and smaller shares of workers ages 55 and older worked part-time because they were retired. Meanwhile, the share of each of these groups that had short full-time work weeks grew—either because fewer workers were reporting the most common reason for their group or because the growth in the number reporting short full-time workweeks was larger than overall growth, or both.

This phenomenon has several plausible explanations. The rise of the short full-time workweek could be a byproduct of the decades-long shift away from industries that have a traditional 40-hour workweek toward those with shorter average weeks, such as retail or leisure and hospitality. It could also possibly reflect employers offering work schedules that more closely match their workers' preferences for shorter work hours, productivity gains reducing the number of labor hours that employers need, or even a shift in workers' perceptions of a full-time schedule. The dynamics behind these reported short "full-time" workweeks are not readily evident because of limitations in the data. Presumably, different situations could lead people to describe their work hours as full-time, even though they do not meet the 35-hour threshold that has been used for statistical purposes since the 1940s. All that these data can reveal is that a growing number of people consider their hours to be full time even though they meet the statistical definition of a part-time worker.

The remaining reasons people voluntarily work part-time combined—childcare problems, health or medical limitations, and other reasons—apply to about 20 percent of all voluntary part-time workers. Notably, among all voluntary part-time workers, only about 5 percent worked part-time because they could not find adequate or affordable childcare in 2016, relatively unchanged since 1994. As expected, women were more likely to work part-time for this reason than were men (7% versus 1% in 2016). Nevertheless, relative to other reason categories, few women chose their work hours for this reason.

Where Do Voluntary Part-Time Workers Work?

The majority of voluntary part-time workers, much like most workers in the United States, are wage and salary workers—that is, they are not self-employed but are employees of others. However, wage and salary workers are less likely to work part-time voluntarily than the self-employed (13.6% versus 19.2% in 2016). Among wage and salary workers, nearly half of those who chose part-time work were employed in just three industries in 2016: retail trade (18%), food services and drinking places (15%), and private educational services (12%). However, these industries accounted for about one-fourth of all wage and salary workers. These industries employ disproportionately large shares of youth and women, groups that have high voluntary part-time rates.

Among the self-employed, voluntary part-time rates were higher for those whose businesses were unincorporated than for those with incorporated businesses in 2016 (the majority of the self-employed have unincorporated businesses). Voluntary part-time rates of the incorporated and unincorporated self-employed could differ because there are differences in the nature of their work. The incorporated self-employed are more likely to own firms providing creative, business, or analytical services, as opposed to the unincorporated, whose firms are more likely to provide physical services such as cleaning or landscaping.

Self-employed women were particularly likely to work part-time voluntarily in 2016. The voluntary part-time rate for self-employed women was high even when compared with that of self-employed men or that of women who worked as employees. In 2016, 31.7 percent of self-employed women worked part-time voluntarily, compared with 12.5 percent of self-employed men and 18.9 percent of women who were wage and salary workers.

How Much Do Voluntary Part-Time Workers Earn?

In 2016, the median weekly earnings of all voluntary part-time workers were $245. Notably, women working part-time on a voluntary basis earned about 10 percent more than their male counterparts ($252 compared with $230). This overall earnings advantage for women does not hold however when comparing the earnings of women and men in the same age groups. The earnings difference between male and female voluntary part-time workers is opposite that of full-time workers, which is more widely reported—female full-time workers had weekly earnings about 18 percent less than their male counterparts in 2016.

Although the median for all women working part-time voluntarily is higher than the median for all men, this earnings discrepancy is largely due to their different age profiles. In other words, women who voluntarily work part-time are disproportionately of prime working age (25–54 years) compared with men. Among voluntary part-time workers, nearly half of all women were of prime working age in 2016, compared with about one-fourth of all men. For both men and women, earnings of prime-age voluntary part-time workers are higher than earnings of both youth and older workers. Median weekly earnings of female and male voluntary part-time workers in the same age group were not statistically different, with one exception: older workers. For voluntary part-time workers ages 65 and older, men outearned women ($272 versus $238).

Workers by Educational Attainment

In 2016, voluntary part-time rates for workers ages 25 and older differed little by educational attainment, ranging from 10.0 percent for college graduates to 12.3 percent for workers with some college or an associate's degree. Although voluntary part-time rates showed little difference across educational attainment categories for all workers, differences persisted between men and women. Rates for men ranged from 5.4 percent for workers with a bachelor's degree to 8.0 percent for those with a professional degree. Rates for women ranged from 12.8 percent for those with a professional degree to 21.0 percent for those with less than a high school diploma. In general, voluntary part-time rates were highest among women with less education—those who did not have a high school diploma. This pattern of higher rates among women with less education held across race and ethnicity groups. Among men, however, rates were higher for White male college graduates with advanced degrees than their counterparts with less education; Black and Asian men with advanced degrees, on the other hand, had lower rates than Black and Asian men who had less than a high school diploma.

Chapter 6

Working during College

More than 70 percent of college students work while they are enrolled in school. Although most colleges recommend that full-time students limit part-time jobs to between 10 and 15 hours per week, 40 percent of undergraduates work more than 30 hours per week, and 25 percent are employed full-time. Some students have on-campus, work-study jobs that are part of a financial aid package. Others work at part-time, off-campus jobs to earn extra spending money. About one-third of students continue working at the same job they held before enrolling in college. Many companies offer tuition assistance to help cover the cost of higher education for employees who want to increase their skills.

The biggest drawback to working during college is that jobs take time that you might otherwise spend studying, participating in extracurricular or social activities, or even sleeping. After all, working at a job for 10–20 hours per week is the equivalent of taking one to two additional classes. If the time commitment prevents you from taking a full load of classes, staying healthy, enjoying your college experience, or graduating on time, then working during college may not be worth it.

However, employment during college also offers benefits that may outweigh the costs. Some of the advantages you may gain by working include the following:

Better Academic Performance

Studies have shown that college students who work between 1 and 12 hours per week have higher graduation rates than students who do not work. The working students tend to perform

About This Chapter: "Working during College," © 2017 Omnigraphics.

as well or even better academically than their nonworking peers. Many students find that the business challenges and workplace issues they face in their jobs apply directly to their college classes and enhance the learning experience. Some students also use ideas from their college classes to solve problems in the workplace.

Time Management Skills

Keeping up with the demands of college and a job forces you to manage your time effectively. You learn to stay organized, stick to a schedule, prioritize tasks, and develop good work and study habits. Building these critical time-management skills in college helps prepare you for a fast-paced, demanding career after graduation.

Less Student-Loan Debt

Most students who work during college do so in order to help pay for their education. Although many still need student loans to cover the costs of tuition and room and board, employment income can reduce the amount they need to borrow. By paying for books and basic living expenses out of their earnings, working students may be able to graduate with less student-loan debt than nonworking students.

More Independence

Some students must work to help cover education-related expenses. Others choose to work because they want to have cash available to spend on clothes, travel, eating out, entertainment, and other treats. If your parents are already paying for your education, you may feel guilty asking them for more funds. Earning your own spending money can give you greater independence. In addition, you can avoid the financial trap of applying for student credit cards to cover your extra expenses.

Money Management Skills

Students who work during college gain valuable knowledge of personal finance. Earning an income allows you to take responsibility for establishing a budget, keeping track of expenses, paying bills, and managing your money. These skills will prove valuable once you graduate from college and launch your career.

Career Experience

Part-time jobs—even ones that may seem menial or meaningless—offer valuable work experience that can help you gain skills, build self-confidence, and meet potential references or networking contacts. Students who find part-time jobs or internships within their field of study also have an opportunity to clarify their career goals and add to the list of qualifications on their résumés. During job interviews, you can provide real-world examples of your ability to solve problems, work independently, and take responsibility. For many employers, work experience during college sets you apart from other recent graduates and improves your chances of landing a full-time job after graduation.

References

1. Dumbauld, Beth. "Six Things You Should Know about Working While Going to College," Straighter Line, October 20, 2016.

2. Higuera, Valencia. "Five Benefits of Working a Job While in College," Money Crashers, 2017.

3. Levy, David. "The Benefits of Working While in College," Edvisors, 2017.

4. "Pros and Cons of Work-Study in College," The Prospect, 2014.

Chapter 7

Seasonal Jobs

For many retailers, the holiday shopping season is a "make or break" period which can define their bottom lines for the entire year. Temporary and part-time employment spikes as retailers and other businesses increase staffing to accommodate their seasonal increase in business. Workers not familiar with this sort of employment, and employers unaccustomed to hiring part-time and/or seasonal employees, may not be fully aware of the regulations surrounding such employment. The chapter offers the following information to help guide both employers and employees in an informed manner.

Frequently Asked Questions Regarding Part-Time or Seasonal Employment
How Many Hours Is Full-Time Employment? How Many Hours Is Part-Time Employment?

The Fair Labor Standards Act (FLSA) does not define full-time employment or part-time employment. This is a matter generally to be determined by the employer. Whether an employee is considered full-time or part-time does not change the application of the FLSA.

About This Chapter: Text in this chapter begins with excerpts from "Seasonal Employment/Part-Time Information," U.S. Department of Labor (DOL), December 13, 2011; Text under the heading "Employment Spikes in Retail Trade around the Holidays" is excerpted from "Employment Spikes in Retail Trade around the Holidays," U.S. Bureau of Labor Statistics (BLS), U.S. Department of Labor (DOL), December 2017.

How Many Hours per Day or per Week Can an Employee Work?

The FLSA does not limit the number of hours per day or per week that employees aged 16 years and older can be required to work. However, as noted above, overtime compensation requirements can apply for hours worked over 40 in a work week.

When Can an Employee's Hours of Work Be Changed?

The FLSA imposes no restrictions on the scheduling of employees, with the exception of the Child Labor provisions. Therefore, the FLSA does not limit an employer's ability to change an employee's work hours without giving prior notice or obtaining the employee's consent (of course, such changes may be limited by prior agreements between the employer and employee and the employee's representative).

Youth Employment

Many students experience an increase both in their free time and their need for extra cash around the holidays. As many retailers have an increased need for seasonal/part-time help at that same time, many employers will fill their seasonal and/or part-time positions with young workers. It is often a good fit for both parties.

Wage and Hour Division (WHD) is committed to helping young workers find those positive and early employment experiences that can be so important to their development, but the work must be safe. The youth employment provisions of the FLSA were enacted to ensure that when young people work, the work does not jeopardize their health, well-being, or educational opportunities.

Children 14 and 15 years of age may be employed outside of school hours in a variety of nonmanufacturing and nonhazardous jobs for limited periods of time and under specified conditions. It is important to keep in mind that any work that is not specifically permitted for these 14- and 15-year-old youth, as listed in the department's child labor regulations, is strictly prohibited.

Sixteen- and seventeen-year-olds may be employed for unlimited hours in any occupation other than those declared hazardous by the U.S. Secretary of Labor. Once a youth reaches 18 years of age, she or he is no longer subject to the federal youth employment provisions.

Employment Spikes in Retail Trade around the Holidays

In retail trade, the holiday season is the most wonderful time of the year. And preparing for extra business usually means increased hiring, according to data from the U.S. Bureau of Labor Statistics (BLS).

Employment in the retail trade industry typically rises in the final months of the year, a time when businesses expect a surge of holiday customers. The chart illustrates a pattern in retail: Employment gains from October through December are followed by losses in January and February. Also, increases in summer employment are surpassed by the spikes that accompany the holiday shopping season.

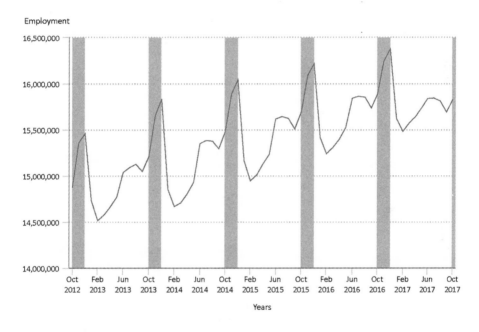

Figure 7.1. Employment Spikes in Retail Trade around the Holidays

The data presented are from the BLS Current Employment Statistics (CES) program, a monthly survey of businesses. CES produces estimates like those in this chart for the nation and for states and metropolitan areas.

45

Chapter 8

Summer Employment: A Snapshot of Teen Workers

Summer jobs offer teens the opportunity to explore the work environment. Although teens may work all year in different part-time jobs, the summer months provide an opportunity for teens to work on a full-time basis. Hence, summer is the right time for teens to earn more money, get introduced to the 40-hour-work weeks, and gain valuable experience, responsibility, and skills through summer employment.

Finding a Summer Job

Teens can identify job leads for summer employment through various sources:

- Internet

- Classified ads section in the local newspaper

- Job boards

- School counselors

- Recommendations from friends and family members

If you are interested in working at a specific place, then do not hesitate to contact the manager and inquire about possible job openings. Although there will likely be plenty of job openings for teens during the summer months, the competition will also be very high, so try to be the early bird. It is better to begin your job search well before the onset of summer.

About This Chapter: "Summer Employment: A Snapshot of Teen Workers," © 2019 Omnigraphics.

Common Summer Jobs for Teens

There will be many openings in minimum-wage service industries for teenagers during the summer months. Before you jump into the process of job hunting, make a list of your likes and dislikes and try to find a job that suits you the best. Choosing the right summer job often sets you on the right career path in adulthood. Some common summer employment opportunities available for teens are as follows:

- **Camp counseling:** A camp counselor guides and mentors kids during outdoor camp programs and events. This job will suit older teens who are natural leaders and those who wish to spend more time outdoors.

- **Tutoring:** Some students use the summer months to catch up on school work and prepare for tests. Academically inclined teens can use this opportunity to teach such kids.

- **Golf caddying:** The game of golf picks up in the summer and there will be plenty of openings for golf caddying. This job involves a lot of walking and carrying heavy bags of golf clubs.

- **Swimming pools or amusement parks:** Swimming pools and amusement parks are in action during the summer months. They provide job opportunities for teens in many areas, including ticket sales, park tours, swimming pool cleaning, food stalls, and so on.

- **Babysitting:** Working parents often look for safe, secure, and reliable child care for their young children during the months when schools are not in session. Teens who enjoy spending time with children can consider babysitting or working at daycare centers.

- **Gardening:** Some people may not have the time or may be physically incapable of taking care of their lawns. Teens can assist them with planting, fertilizing, lawn mowing, and repairing irrigation systems. Gardening is in high demand during the summer months and may extend into the fall.

- **Retail sales:** Teens can find a great deal of opportunity as retail salespeople in fast-food restaurants, malls, grocery stores, etc.

- **House sitting:** Many people travel during the summer vacation months and will be looking for responsible house sitters to look after their homes in their absence. The responsibilities of a house sitter include keeping the house clean, collecting mail and newspapers, watering plants, taking care of the safety of the house, and so on.

Don't Give Up!

Some teens tend to give up too easily when they don't receive a reply from a potential employer after applying for a job. Persistent and polite follow-ups can be an effective tool in such situations. However, due to heavy competition, not all teens end up getting a job. If you don't find a suitable job, you can consider volunteering or internships.

- **Volunteering:** Volunteering means providing a service without getting paid. Teens can volunteer at schools, hospitals, and welfare organizations. Like paid jobs, you can find volunteering opportunities online.

- **Internships:** Internships are short-term, hands-on training opportunities offered by companies and businesses to bright students. Some internships may pay their interns a nominal salary, but most of them do not. However, if you perform well during the internship, then there is a good chance that you may be offered a full-time job.

Although most of the volunteering jobs and internships do not pay you a salary, they serve as a great way to build your knowledge and experience and look good on a résumé. They can be helpful to grab a high-paying job in the future.

References

1. "Teen Summer Jobs," Houston Chronicle, August 7, 2018.

2. "Finding a Summer Job or Internship," TeensHealth from Nemours, June 2017.

3. "15 Great Summer Jobs for Teens," Investopedia, May 12, 2017.

4. "Mistakes Teens Make In Looking for Summer or Part-Time Jobs," LiveCareer, January 4, 2013.

Chapter 9

Hazardous Occupations for Teens

The Hazardous Occupations Orders (HOs)

The Fair Labor Standards Act (FLSA) establishes an 18-year minimum age for those non-agricultural occupations that the U.S. Secretary of Labor finds and declares to be particularly hazardous for 16- and 17-year-old minors, or detrimental to their health or well-being. In addition, Child Labor Regulation No. 3 also bans 14- and 15-year-olds from performing any work proscribed by the Hazardous Occupations (HOs). There are 17 HOs which include a partial or total ban on the occupations or industries they cover.

HO 1. Manufacturing or storing explosives—bans minors working where explosives are manufactured or stored, but permits work in retail stores selling ammunition, gun shops, trap and skeet ranges, and police stations.

HO 2. Driving a motor vehicle or work as an outside helper on motor vehicles—bans operating motor vehicles on public roads and working as outside helpers on motor vehicles, except 17-year-olds may drive cars or small trucks during daylight hours for limited times and under strictly limited circumstances.

HO 3. Coal mining—bans most jobs in coal mining.

HO 4. Occupations in forest fire fighting, forest fire prevention, timber tract, forestry service, and occupations in logging and sawmilling operations—bans most jobs in: forest

About This Chapter: Text under the heading "The Hazardous Occupations Orders (HOs)" is excerpted from "Child Labor Provisions of the Fair Labor Standards Act (FLSA) for Nonagricultural Occupations," U.S. Department of Labor (DOL), December 2016; Text under the heading "Common Violations Regarding Youth Employment" is excerpted from "Seasonal Employment/Part-Time Information," U.S. Department of Labor (DOL), December 13, 2011.

fire fighting; forest fire prevention that entails extinguishing an actual fire; timber tract management; forestry services; logging; and sawmills.

HO 5. Power-driven woodworking machines—bans the operation of most power-driven woodworking machines, including chainsaws, nailing machines, and sanders.*

HO 6. Exposure to radioactive substances and ionizing radiation—bans employment of minors where they are exposed to radioactive materials.

HO 7. Power-driven hoisting apparatus—bans operating, riding on, and assisting in the operation of most power-driven hoisting apparatus such as forklifts, nonautomatic elevators, skid-steers, skid-steer loaders, backhoes, manlifts, scissor lifts, cherry pickers, work-assist platforms, boom trucks, and cranes. Does not apply to chair-lifts at ski resorts or electric and pneumatic lifts used to raise cars in garages and gasoline service stations.

HO 8. Power-driven metal-forming, punching and shearing machines—bans the operation of certain power-driven metal-working machines but permits the use of most machine tools.*

HO 9. Mining, other than coal—bans most jobs in mining at metal mines, quarries, aggregate mines, and other mining sites including underground work in mines, work in or about open cut mines, open quarries, and sand and gravel operations.

HO 10. Power-driven meat-processing machines, slaughtering, and meat packing plants—bans the operation of power-driven meat processing machines, such as meat slicers, saws and meat choppers, wherever used (including restaurants and delicatessens). Also prohibits minors from cleaning such equipment, including the hand-washing of the disassembled machine parts. This ban also includes the use of this machinery on items other than meat, such as cheese and vegetables. HO 10 also bans most jobs in meat and poultry slaughtering, processing, rendering, and packing establishments.*

HO 11. Power-driven bakery machines—bans the operation of power-driven bakery machines such as vertical dough and batter mixers; dough rollers, rounders, dividers, and sheeters; and cookie or cracker machines. Permits 16- and 17-year-olds to operate certain lightweight, small, portable, countertop mixers and certain pizza dough rollers under certain conditions.

HO 12. Balers, compactors, and power-driven paper-products machines—bans the operation of all compactors and balers and certain power-driven paper products machines such as platen-type printing presses and envelope die cutting presses. 16- and 17-year-olds may load, but not operate or unload, certain scrap paper balers and paper box compactors under very specific guidelines.*

HO 13. Manufacturing of brick, tile, and related products—bans most jobs in the manufacture of brick, tile, and similar products.

HO 14. Power-driven circular saws, band saws, guillotine shears, chain saws, reciprocating saws, wood chippers, and abrasive cutting discs—bans the operation of, and working as a helper on, the named types of power-driven equipment, no matter what kind of items are being cut by the equipment.*

HO 15. Wrecking, demolition, and ship-breaking operations—bans most jobs in wrecking, demolition, and ship-breaking operations, but does not apply to remodel or repair work which is not extensive.

HO 16. Roofing operations and work performed on or about a roof—bans most jobs in roofing operations, including work performed on the ground and removal of the old roof, and all work on or about a roof.*

HO 17. Trenching and excavation operations—bans most jobs in trenching and excavation work, including working in a trench more than four feet deep.*

The regulations provide a limited exemption from HOs 5, 8, 10, 12, 14, 16 and 17 for apprentices and student-learners who are at least 16 years of age and enrolled in approved programs. The term "operation" as used in HOs 5, 8, 10, 11, 12 and 14 generally includes the tasks of setting up, adjusting, repairing, oiling or cleaning the equipment.

Minimum Age Standards for Employment

The FLSA and the youth employment regulations establish both hours and occupational standards for youth. Children of any age are generally permitted to work for businesses entirely owned by their parents, except those under age 16 may not be employed in mining or manufacturing and no one under 18 may be employed in any occupation the Secretary of Labor has declared to be hazardous.

18—Once a youth reaches 18 years of age, she or he is no longer subject to the Federal youth employment provisions.

16—Basic minimum age for employment. Sixteen- and seventeen-year-olds may be employed for unlimited hours in any occupation other than those declared hazardous by the Secretary of Labor.

14—Young persons 14 and 15 years of age may be employed outside school hours in a variety of nonmanufacturing and nonhazardous jobs for limited periods of time and under specified conditions.

Under 14-Children under 14 years of age may not be employed in nonagricultural occupations covered by the FLSA. Permissible employment for such children is limited to work that is exempt from the FLSA (such as delivering newspapers to the consumer and acting). Children may also perform work not covered by the FLSA such as completing minor chores around private homes or casual babysitting.

(Source: "Wage and Hour Division (WHD)," U.S. Department of Labor (DOL).)

Common Violations Regarding Youth Employment

Some of the most common violations found regarding youth employment include employing 14- and 15-year-olds outside of allowable hours; allowing youth employees to load, operate or unload a trash or cardboard compactor, allowing employees under the age of 18 to operate or to clean a meat slicer or dough mixer, or allowing employees under the age of 18 to drive on public roadways as part of their employment outside of prescribed limits.

Violators of the youth employment provisions may be subject to a civil money penalty of up to $11,000 for each minor employed in violation. Penalties for violations that cause the death or serious injury of a minor may be increased to as much as $50,000 and those penalties may be doubled (up to $100,000) when the violations are determined to be willful or repeated.

When state youth employment laws differ from the federal provisions, an employer must comply with the higher standard. Links to your state labor department can be found at www. dol.gov/whd/contacts/state_of.htm.

For additional information on the Fair Labor Standards Act (FLSA), visit the Wage and Hour Division (WHD) website (www.wagehour.dol.gov) and/or call the toll-free information and helpline, available Monday to Friday, 8 a.m. to 8 p.m. Eastern time (ET) 866-4USWAGE (866-487-9243).

Chapter 10

Other Job Opportunities for Teens

Whether you are looking for part-time work during the school year, summer jobs, or starting a full-time career. There are additional opportunities for youth ages 15–35, including students and recent graduates.

Jobs

Pathways for Students and Recent Graduates

The Pathways Program offers federal internship and employment opportunities for current students, recent graduates and those with an advanced degree. There are three different paths available:

- Who can apply: Students seeking degrees or certificates from accredited institutions (i.e., high schools; vocational and technical schools; and associate, bachelor, graduate, or professional schools) and recent graduates

- Interest areas: All

- Stipend: Salary

- Application period: Year-round

- Schedule: Year-round or summer

- Contact: National Park Service (NPS)/Office of Human Resources (OHR)

About This Chapter: This chapter includes text excerpted from "Opportunities to Get Involved," National Park Service (NPS), U.S. Department of the Interior (DOI), September 26, 2018.

Youth Conservation Corps

- Who can apply: Ages 15–18
- Schedule: summer 8–10 weeks, nonresidential (except at Yellowstone and Yosemite)
- Interest areas: conservation work projects and environmental education programs
- Application period: apply to the park that interests you or check out your state's YCC program
- Contact: NPS Youth Programs at 202-7284

Internships

Whether you're in high school or college or have recently graduated, internships are a way to gain hands-on experience while helping to protect the nation's natural and cultural heritage.

Ancestral Lands Conservation Corps

- Who can apply: Native American youth in high school or older
- Schedule: Year-round
- Interest areas: Historic preservation, traditional agriculture, interpretation, conservation, trail construction
- Stipend: Varies
- Partner: Southwest Conservation Corps (SCC)
- Contact: NPS Youth Programs at 202-513-7146

Cultural Resources Diversity Internship Program

- Who can apply: Diverse undergraduate and graduate students
- Schedule: Summer
- Interest areas: Historic preservation and cultural resources
- Stipend: $400 per week plus housing and travel stipend
- Partner: American Conservation Experience (ACE)
- Contact: NPS/Cultural Resources Office of Interpretation and Education (CROIE), Paloma Bolasny, Youth Program Coordinator, at 202-354-2174

Geoscientists-In-The-Parks Internships

- Who can apply: Undergraduate or graduate students, recent graduates

- Schedule: Primarily summer internships, with some occurring in the fall/winter or year-round

- Interest areas: Geoscience and other natural resource science fields—field- and office-based internships focus on research, inventory and monitoring, interpretation and education projects

- Stipend: $1,200 per month, plus travel allowance and park provided housing or a housing allowance

- Partner: Environmental Stewards and the Geological Society of America (GSA)

- Application periods:

  - Spring/summer internships: December 1 to January 31

  - Fall/winter internships: May 1 to June 30

- Contact: Lisa Norby, GIP Internship Coordinator, at 303-969-2318

Historically Black Colleges and Universities Internship Program

- Who can apply: Undergraduate and graduate students from Historically Black Colleges and Universities. Application periods: December 1 to February 10; apply at hbcui.gyfoundation.org

- Schedule: Summer program with a possibility to extend the internship. Program includes career workshop in Washington, D.C. in August for program participants.

- Interest areas: Historians, communication, business, archeologists, architects, curators, planners, and archivists

- Stipend: Starting from $4,000 or $4,800 for 10-week positions, plus travel and housing allowances, and could be extended through the school year. Plus travel allowance and park provided housing, offsite housing, or a housing allowance.

- Partner: The Greening Youth Foundation (GYF)

- Contact: NPS Youth Programs at 202-513-7146

Historic Preservation Training Internships

- Who can apply: Undergraduate and graduate students

- Schedule: Year-round or summer

- Interest areas: Historians, archeologists, architects, curators, planners, and archivists

- Stipend: $6,000–$18,000

- Partner: National Council for Preservation Education (NCPE)

- Contact: NPS/Cultural Resources Office of Interpretation and Education, Paloma Bolasny, Youth Program Coordinator, at 202-354-2174

Historic Sites and Structures Documentation Internships

- Who can apply: Undergraduate or graduate students

- Schedule: Summer

- Interest areas: Architecture, landscape architecture, engineering, history, on-site field work and preparation of measured and interpretive drawings and written historical reports

- Stipend: $6,000–$11,000

- Contact: NPS/Heritage Documentation Programs, contact Richard O'Connor at 202-354-2186

Latino Heritage Internship Program

- Who can apply: Undergraduate or graduate students with a focus on Latinos attending Hispanic Serving institutions

- Schedule: Summer

- Interest areas: Natural and cultural resource management, interpretation, public affairs

- Stipend: $400 a week plus travel and housing stipend

- Partners: Hispanic Access Foundation (HAF) and Environment for the Americas (EFTA)

- Contact: NPS/Cultural Resources Office of Interpretation and Education (CROIE), Paloma Bolasny, Youth Program Coordinator, at 202-354-2174

Maritime Documentation Internship

- Who can apply: Undergraduate or graduate students

- Schedule: Summer

- Interest areas: Architecture, engineering, or history, maritime preservation, on-site field work and preparation of measured and interpretive drawings and written historical reports

- Stipend: $6,000

- Partner: Council of American Maritime Museums (CAMM)

- Contact: NPS/Historic American Engineering Record (HAER), Todd Croteau, Internship Coordinator, at 202-354-2167

Mosaics in Science Diversity Internships

- Who can apply: Undergraduate or graduate students, 18–35 years old with focus on hiring students underrepresented in natural resource (STEM) fields

- Schedule: Summer; program includes career workshop in Washington, DC, in August for program participants

- Interest areas: Field- and office-based internships focused on research, inventory and monitoring, interpretation and education projects disciplines

- Stipend: $4,800, plus travel expenses and park-provided housing or a housing allowance

- Partners: Environment for the Americas and Greening Youth Foundation (GYF)

- Application period: spring/summer internships: December 1 to January 31, apply at www.mosaicsinscience.org

- Contact: Lisa Norby, Mosaics in Science Internship Coordinator, at 303-969-2318

National Park Business Plan and Consulting Internships

- Who can apply: Graduate students (MBA, MPA, MPP, environmental and/or public lands management)

- Schedule: Summer

- Interest areas: Management consulting, park management, strategic and operational planning, commercial services, public-private partnerships

- Stipend: $725 per week, plus housing and travel

- Partner: Inspiring Capital

- Contact: NPS Business Management Group

National Park Service Academy

- Who can apply: Undergraduate and graduate students ages 18–35

- Schedule: Week-long orientation during spring break and a 12-week summer internship

- Interest areas: Visitor services, education, resource management

- Stipend: Weekly living allowance plus travel and housing stipend

- Partner: Student Conservation Association (SCA)

- Contact: NPS Youth Programs at 202-513-7146

Public Land Corps

- Who can apply: Ages 16–26

- Schedule: Summer

- Interest areas: All

- Stipend: Varies

- Partner: Participants managed and recruited by nonprofit organizations (like Student Conservation Association, Corps Network, Boy Scouts and Girl Scouts, local high schools, and job training youth organizations) that receive funding from the NPS

- Contact: NPS Youth Programs at 202-513-7146

Student Conservation Association

- Who can apply: High school students and young adults

- Schedule: Year-round or summer

- Interest areas: All

- Partner: SCA places 2,600 people every year with the NPS and other federal, state, local, and private entities. Many National Park Service employees got their start with SCA!

- Contact: NPS Youth Programs at 202-513-7146

Historic American Buildings Survey (HABS)/Society of Architectural Historians (SAH) Tompkins Fellowship

- Who can apply: Graduate student in architectural history or related fields

- Schedule: Summer

- Interest area: Research

- Stipend: $12,000

- Partner: Society of Architectural Historians

- Contact: NPS/Historic American Buildings Survey, Lisa Davidson, Fellowship Coordinator, at 202-354-2179

Urban Archaeology Corps

- Who can apply: Ages 15–26

- Schedule: Year-round

- Interest area: Archeology

- Stipend: Varies

- Contact: NPS Archaeology Program, Teresa Moyer, at 202-354-2124

Volunteer

Looking to lend a hand with your youth group or family? There are many opportunities at parks and programs across the country to donate your time and services, whether it's for a few hours or year-round.

Part Two
First Steps—Résumé Preparation and Job Search

Chapter 11

Assessing Yourself and Your Future

Humans aren't really very good at assessing themselves. So, often, when we need to make decisions about our own future we have trouble. However, we're often faced with the need to make important, potentially life-altering decisions, such as what college to attend, what major to choose, and what career to pursue. And in those cases, the best way to proceed is to conduct an honest assessment of our talents, past performance, values, and interests in order to make informed choices. Fortunately, you don't have to do it alone. There are a number of avenues of assistance available, both formal and informal, to help you conduct a meaningful self-assessment.

How Assessment Can Help

Self-assessment is a guide that helps an individual make a decision. It provides insight and gives you a roadmap as you plan and think about the future.

Some benefits of assessment include:

- help identify your skills and areas of interest

- highlight your learning style and the way you do your best work

- point out areas where you need more training or experience

- help you learn about educational or occupational opportunities that will suit you best

- get you to consider new courses of study or career paths

About This Chapter: "Assessing Yourself and Your Future," © 2017 Omnigraphics.

Self-assessment can not only help identify educational programs and careers that align with your talents and interests, but can also pinpoint areas for improvement and guide you toward programs and occupations that you might want to pursue.

On the other hand, don't expect assessment to:

- guarantee that a given educational or career path will be open to you

- ensure that you'll like any given program or occupation

- predict how well you'll succeed

Getting Started

To begin a self-assessment there are a few questions you can ask yourself that might help get you the process:

What Am I Good At?

Often we think we know what we can do, but sometimes we overlook skills we've developed through the years. To help jog your memory, ask yourself such questions as:

- In which classes do I get the best grades?

- In what parts of specific classes (such as labs or team projects) do I do best?

- At what extracurricular activities do I think I excel?

- How good am I at tasks that require manual dexterity?

- How well do I envision and implement solutions to problems?

- Have I gotten good responses to oral presentations?

What Do I Enjoy?

To help determine your areas of interest, ask yourself questions such as:

- What classes do I like?

- What do I do well?

- When I'm reading or watching TV, what topics draw my attention?

- What types of things am I doing when you lose track of time?
- How do I spend my spare time?
- Among people I know, who do I think has the most interesting job?

What Is Important to Me?

In addition to areas where you excel or those you enjoy, don't forget to take into account things that you feel strongly about. Some items to consider:

- Do I feel best when I work alone or with a group?
- Do I prefer difficult challenges or more frequent accomplishments?
- How much time do I invest in physical activity?
- Am I a risk-taker, or do I prefer security?
- Does competition drive me or discourage me?
- Is it important for me to be a leader?

Assessment Tools

The above series of questions is just a way of beginning to think about the assessment process. The best way to proceed is to complete a series of questionnaires and exercises specifically developed by experts to identify skills, personality types, values, areas of interest, and other factors that go into decision-making. Some of these include:

- **Myers–Briggs Type Indicator.** This well-known 93-question test, which has been around for many years, helps identify your basic personality type, which can be useful in choosing an educational or career path.

- **Strong Interest Inventory.** Developed by a psychologist named Strong, this inventory consists of almost 300 items, to which you indicate the strength of your reaction. The results are then compared to those of people happily employed in various occupations, giving you an idea of areas to investigate further.

- **StrengthsQuest.** This 30-minute online assessment helps identify your current strengths in a variety of areas—and the personal characteristics behind them—and relates them to the development of educational and career strategies.

But these tools are just some of the more well-known tips of the iceberg. There are numerous other formal assessment tools, some of which may be more appropriate for you. A school

Today most schools have computerized assessment programs available that can help point you to information about degree programs, financial aid, and career paths. Check with your guidance counselor for details.

guidance counselor or career counselor can help you explore other means of conducting an effective self-assessment. There are also a large number of online resources available to students planning their future educational or vocational paths, many of which can be found on college and university websites. Exploring some of these may provide some extra insight and trigger some ideas.

References

1. "Assessing Yourself and Exploring Career and Educational Options," University of Minnesota Duluth (UMD), 2007.

2. "Career Choice Requires Self-Assessment," SchoolGuides.com, n.d.

3. Pelusi, Nando, Ph.D. "Assessing Yourself, Honestly," Psychology Today, June 9, 2016.

4. "Researching Occupations," College of the Rockies, n.d.

Chapter 12

Career Planning for High Schoolers

"I've always had a pretty clear idea of what I want to do," says Megan Lovely, a high school senior who hopes to become a theater director someday. She's already taking steps toward her career goal by interning with her school drama teacher, acting, and applying to colleges.

If you're still in high school, you may not be as sure of your vocation. But you can start thinking about—and planning for—your future before graduation.

"Start exploring what you want to do when you're a freshman," says Mark Danaher, a career counselor at Newington High School in Newington, Connecticut. "The high school years go very quickly."

Most people need some preparation before they are ready for the workforce, and planning should begin long before it's time to start a career. This could include taking technical courses during high school or, after graduating, attending a college or university to earn a certificate or a degree. Knowing what type of career preparation you need begins with thinking about what type of career you want.

This chapter helps high school students plan for careers. It talks about exploring your interests. It highlights the importance of internships, jobs, and other opportunities for getting experience. The chapter also describes some education or training options, both in high school and afterward, and offers some thoughts on pursuing your dream career.

About This Chapter: This chapter includes text excerpted from "Career Planning for High Schoolers," U.S. Bureau of Labor Statistics (BLS), U.S. Department of Labor (DOL), January 2015.

Explore Your Interests

High school is a great time to start thinking about careers. "All your life you've been asked what you want to do when you grow up," says Steve Schneider, a school counselor at Sheboygan South High School in Sheboygan, Wisconsin. "In high school, you start to work towards making that happen."

Many high schoolers don't yet know what they want to do. And school counselors say that's perfectly fine. In fact, students are likely to change their minds multiple times, perhaps even after they enter the workforce. And some of tomorrow's careers might not exist today.

Settling on just one occupation in high school isn't necessary. But looking into the types of careers you might like can help set you up for success. "My feeling is that high school students don't have to know the exact career they want," says Danaher, "but they should know how to explore careers and put time into investigating them and learning about their skills and interests."

Learn about Yourself

Understanding what you enjoy—and what you're good at—is the first step in exploring careers, say school counselors. "If you don't know what you want to do, the question is, 'What do you like to learn about?'" Schneider says. "If you really like science, what do you enjoy about it—the lab work, the research?"

Use the answers to those questions to identify careers that may have similar tasks. High school junior Kate Sours, for example, loves spending time with kids as a babysitter and enjoys helping people. So she focused on those two interests when she began considering potential careers.

It's important to think about what you like to do, say school counselors, because work will eventually be a big part of your life. "The whole purpose of thinking about careers is so that when you go to the workforce, you wake up in the morning and look forward to going to work," says Julie Hartline, a school counseling consultant at Cobb County public schools in Smyrna, Georgia.

Identify Possible Careers

Once you've thought about the subjects and activities you like best, the next step is to look for careers that put those interests to use. If you love sports, for example, you might consider a career as a gym teacher, recreational therapist, or coach. If you like math, a career as a cost estimator, accountant, or budget analyst might be a good fit.

But those aren't the only options for people interested in sports or math. There are hundreds of occupations, and most of them involve more than one skill area. School counselors, teachers, and parents can help point you in the direction of occupations that match your interests and skills. School counselors, for example, often have tools that they use to link interests and skills with careers. Free online resources, such as My Next Move (www.mynextmove.org), also help with career exploration.

Another approach to identifying potential career interests is to consider local employers and the types of jobs they have. There are many jobs in manufacturing and healthcare near the high school where Schneider works, for example, so he often talks to students about the range of career options in those fields—from occupations that require a six-week course after high school to those that require a bachelor's or higher degree.

Exploring careers that combine working with children and helping people led Sours to nursing. She's now considering working in a hospital's neonatal intensive care unit or pediatrics department.

Sours notes the importance of broadening, rather than narrowing, possibilities when studying careers. "Keep an open mind," she says, "because with some work, you might think, 'Oh, that's a nasty job.' But when you start exploring it, you might discover, 'This is cool. I might want to do this.'"

Do Your Research

After identifying possible occupations, you'll want to learn more about them. Resources such as Career Outlook and the Occupational Outlook Handbook can help you get started. Other sources of information include career-day programs, mentoring, and opportunities offered through your school to learn more about the world of work.

Talking directly to workers can help you get information about what they do. If you don't know workers in occupations that interest you, ask people such as parents, friends, or teachers for their contacts. Some schools have business liaisons or coordinators who help put students in touch with employers—and school counselors can assist, too. These networking efforts might pay off later, even if opportunities aren't available now.

After you've found workers who are willing to help, talk to them on the phone, by e-mail, or through online forums. Meet with them in person for informational interviews to learn more about what they do. Or ask if you can shadow them on the job to see what their daily work is like.

To find out if you'll really like an occupation, school counselors say firsthand experience is indispensable. Sours, for example, shadowed her aunt, who works in a hospital as a physical therapist. Sours liked the hospital environment so much that she attended a week-long nursing camp, where she got to see the many tasks that nurses do. "I had so much fun, and I learned so much," she says about both experiences.

Get Experience

If job shadowing gives you a taste of what an occupation is like, imagine how helpful getting experience could be. Students can begin getting career-related experiences in high school through internships, employment, and other activities. Taking part in different experiences is another step toward helping you to figure out what you like—and what you don't. These experiences may teach valuable job skills, such as the importance of arriving on time.

Put Forth Your Best You

It may seem early, but even in high school, you can start to develop habits that are sure to be appreciated by future employers. "As a student, there are things you can do to get yourself college and work ready," says career counselor Mark Danaher. For example, he says, students can develop good habits by getting to class on time, taking responsibility for their school work, and e-mailing a teacher if they're going to be absent or late.

Also, students need to remember to dress and behave appropriately whenever they might be in contact with a potential employer. "You act one way with your friends and another on the jobsite," says school counseling consultant Julie Hartline. "Mind your demeanor."

This awareness extends to online forums, too. "There are a tremendous amount of positives to social media in terms of networking," says the director of college counseling Michael Carter. "But you have to be really careful."

Employers and college admissions officers often check out applicants online and on social media sites. "They're looking into your background and want to see who you're going to be because you may represent a business or institution someday," says Carter. "Make sure that what you put out there for the world to see is how you want to be seen. Social media is a great tool, but you have to use it responsibly."

But, say school counselors, students need to remember that school takes priority over other pursuits. "It's a good idea to get experience while you're a student," says Hartline, "but not at the expense of academic success." Danaher agrees. "School should be your full-time job," he says.

Internships

Completing an internship is an excellent way to get experience. Internships are temporary, supervised assignments designed to give students or recent graduates practical job training.

Sometimes, internships or other experiential learning positions are built into educational programs, and students receive academic credit for completing them.

At Lovely's school, for example, students have the option to fulfill an internship for credit during their junior or senior year. Lovely interned during her junior year for her high school theater director. "She gave us opportunities to do everything from contacting local newspapers for ads to writing program notes to directing the middle school production," says Lovely. The experience gave Lovely a feel for a director's work—and helped to cement her career goals.

At other schools, students seek out internships on their own. Academic credit may not be awarded, but gaining hands-on experience can still be worthwhile. Check with your school counselor to see if opportunities exist at your school.

Jobs

Summer or part-time employment is another way to get experience. Paid jobs allow you to earn money, which can help you learn how to budget and save for future goals or expenses. For some students, summer is a great time to explore careers through employment. As the

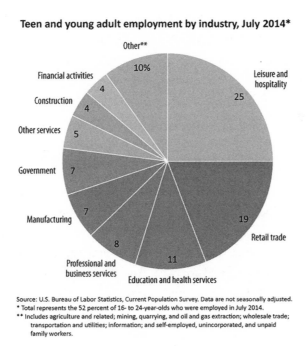

Teen and young adult employment by industry, July 2014*

Source: U.S. Bureau of Labor Statistics, Current Population Survey. Data are not seasonally adjusted.
* Total represents the 52 percent of 16- to 24-year-olds who were employed in July 2014.
** Includes agriculture and related; mining, quarrying, and oil and gas extraction; wholesale trade; transportation and utilities; information; and self-employed, unincorporated, and unpaid family workers.

Figure 12.1. Chart Showing Teen and Young Adult Employment

chart shows, young people worked in a variety of industries in July 2014, according to the U.S. Bureau of Labor Statistics (BLS).

The U.S. Department of Labor (DOL) has rules about youth employment. These rules differ depending on your age, but they often limit the types of jobs and number of hours you can work. States may have additional restrictions.

Hartline advises that students who work during the school year start with a few hours and build from there, once they find it won't interfere with their studies. "For some students, work is a motivator. For others, it's a distractor," she says.

Regardless of when or where they work, school counselors say, students who pursue employment can learn from it. "I think there's no substitute for any type of work experience," says Michael Carter, director of college counseling at St. Stephen's and St. Agnes School in Alexandria, Virginia. "Without experience, it's hard for students to appreciate what type of career they'd like to have because it's all hypothetical."

Other Activities

You can participate in other activities in high school that may spark a career interest. Examples include the yearbook committee, science club, and debate team.

By joining groups that involve community service and leadership opportunities, such as student government or honor societies, you can hone work-related skills or interests. Attending a camp in a subject area that interests you, such as engineering or writing, can help you focus on academic skills that may lead to a career.

Some student organizations aim to promote career readiness. SkillsUSA, DECA, and the Future Business Leaders of America are just a few of the national-level groups that might have student chapters at your high school.

Volunteering allows you to serve your community and bolster your experience. Religious institutions, local nonprofits, and government agencies are among the many organizations that use volunteers to fill a variety of roles. In addition to encouraging you to meet like-minded people and develop your interests, these activities also show future employers and postsecondary schools that you are motivated and engaged. And the more you shape your thoughts about a career, the better you'll know how to prepare for it.

Train for a Career

Career preparation should start in high school, but it shouldn't end with graduation. Most occupations require some type of training or education after high school. On-the-job training, apprenticeships, certificates, nondegree awards, and various levels of college degrees are typically required for entry-level jobs.

Which type of training you need depends on the career you want to pursue. Your high school may offer opportunities for getting career training or college credits before you graduate. And after graduation, your training options expand even more. The closer you get to entering the workforce, the more you'll want to narrow your choices.

In High School

Getting a solid education is an important foundation for any career. Workers in many occupations use problem-solving, communication, research, and other skills that they first learned in high school. By doing well in classes and taking part in career-training or college-preparation programs, you demonstrate that you're ready to put these skills into action.

Plan and achieve. Make sure your high school course plan prepares you for entering the next phase of training or education in your desired career. To enter an electrician apprenticeship, for example, you may need a year of high school algebra. Your school counselor can help you plan your schedule to ensure that you take the required classes.

Employers and postsecondary schools often look to your high school record to gauge how you might perform on the job or in an educational program. And finishing high school shows that you can set goals and follow through. "Starting freshman year, do the absolute best you can in your classes," says Laura Inscoe, dean of counseling and student services at Wakefield High School in Raleigh, North Carolina. "Start strong and stay strong."

But school counselors also say not to worry too much if your grades aren't as good as you'd like. "School studies open doors if you do well, but they don't shut doors if you don't," says Danaher. "You might just take a different path."

Career programs. Your high school may offer options for exploring careers while earning credit toward graduation. Some of these options also allow you to earn industry certifications, licensure, or college credit.

In her high school, for example, Sours attends a career academy for health and medical sciences. She is learning about healthcare careers and will have a chance to apply some of her skills and knowledge as she continues in the program. By graduation, she'll have earned both certifications and credits toward an applied nursing degree program at the local community college.

Career academies and other types of technical education are available in many schools to provide hands-on career training. Classes in fields such as business and finance, culinary arts, and information technology are designed to prepare you for work or postsecondary school.

College prep. If you know your goal is college, school counselors usually recommend taking the most rigorous academic classes your school offers—and those that you can successfully handle. Doing so helps bolster both your college application credentials and your readiness for college-level study.

Some college-prep programs, such as Advanced Placement and dual enrollment, may help you get a head start on earning a postsecondary degree. Taking classes in these programs may allow you to waive some college course requirements, either by achieving a high score on exams or by completing a course for both high school and college credit.

Admission to college is not based on coursework alone, however. Not all high schools offer advanced academics programs, and not all students take them. You may still have more options than you think, depending on your career goals.

After High School

About two-thirds of high-school graduates from the class of 2013 enrolled in college that fall, according to U.S. Bureau of Labor Statistics (BLS): 42 percent in baccalaureate (four-year) colleges and 24 percent in two-year schools. Of the remaining one-third of 2013 graduates, who opted not to go to college, 74 percent entered the labor force.

College-bound high school graduates may not know it, but BLS data show that wages are usually higher, and unemployment rates lower, for people who continue their education after high school.

Associate's and bachelor's degree programs range from accounting to zoology. But job training and vocational school programs may offer the type of career preparation you need for the occupation that interests you.

Job training. If you get a job or enter the military directly out of high school, you'll receive training specific to the job. Some employers may even pay for you to get related credentials, such as industry certification.

The type and length of on-the-job training you get depends on the occupation. For example, community-health workers typically need one month or less of experience on the job and informal training, in addition to a high school diploma, to become competent in the occupation.

Apprenticeships are a form of job training in which a sponsor, such as an employer, pays a trainee to learn and work in a particular occupation. Some jobs in the military include apprenticeship training, but others involve different types of hands-on learning.

Vocational school. Also known as trade or technical schools, vocational schools have programs designed to give you hands-on training in a specific field. Many of these programs lead to nondegree credentials, such as a certificate or diploma. Occupations that you can prepare for at these types of schools include automotive mechanic and emergency medical technician (EMT).

Some vocational schools specialize in a certain occupation or career field, such as truck driving, culinary arts, or cosmetology. Others provide a diverse range of programs, such as medical assisting and precision production.

Earning a certificate allows you to prepare for a career in a relatively short amount of time: Nearly all certificate programs take fewer than two years to complete. For example, you may earn a nursing assistant certificate in less than one year.

Associate's degree. Associate's degrees, which may qualify you for occupations such as dental hygienist and funeral services manager, are available through public community colleges and other two-year schools. But some four-year schools also offer associate degrees that complement or lead into their bachelor's degree programs.

Associate's degrees are available in a variety of subject areas, but most degrees awarded in the past decade have been broadly focused. According to the National Center for Education Statistics, the most popular fields of study for associate's degree recipients between 2001–2 and 2011–12 were liberal arts and sciences, general studies, and humanities.

Earning an associate's degree and then transferring to a bachelor's degree program might make sense if you're unsure of what you want to study. It also allows you to save money on tuition, because community colleges are usually less expensive than baccalaureate colleges and universities.

Bachelor's degree. If you plan to get a bachelor's degree, your school counselor can help you with the application processes for colleges and financial aid. But you should also have a plan for why you're pursuing a degree.

A good initial step is to think about what you might like to major in. If you've been considering your career interests throughout high school, declaring a major won't be difficult. "Your initial undergraduate program should be an outgrowth of your academic strengths in high school," says Carter.

Still not sure what you want to study? Look at some studies. For example, job opportunities and starting salaries vary by college major. Data may be helpful in narrowing your choices, but they shouldn't be the sole determinant of your future. "Don't let your decision be based on money alone," says Hartline. "Find something you're going to love to do."

To keep your options open as you choose a major, school counselors suggest entering a liberal arts program. Take classes in a broad range of subjects to help you figure out what you like best—and where that might lead in your future.

Be Flexible and Follow Your Dream

Everyone's career path is different, and there is no "right" way to start a career. For example, if you want to postpone your studies to discover your passion, you might decide to take a "gap year" after high school. A gap year gives you a chance to pursue meaningful volunteer, work, or travel experiences. But school counselors recommend that you have a plan to ensure that your time off is productive.

Whatever career path you choose, says Schneider, remember that you can change your mind at any time. "There's always the flexibility to shift course," he says. "A career is not a life sentence. If at some point you realize, 'I don't want to do this,' back up and ask yourself the same questions again: 'What am I good at? What do I like to do?'"

And have the confidence to work toward your ideal career, school counselors say, even if it seems out of reach. "Put a plan together and go for it," says Danaher, "even if everyone else says you're crazy, or you'll never make it. You may not make the National Basketball Association (NBA), but you might find a way to work within it doing work you really enjoy."

Chapter 13

Creating a Résumé

> You have skills that employers want. But those skills won't get you a job if no one knows you have them. Good résumés, applications, and cover letters broadcast your abilities. They tell employers how your qualifications match a job's responsibilities. If these critical preliminaries are constructed well, you have a better chance of landing interviews—and, eventually, a job.

The availability of personal computers and laser printers has raised employers' expectations of the quality of résumés and cover letters that applicants produce. E-mail and online applications help some employers sort and track hundreds of résumés. Technology has also given résumé writers greater flexibility; page limits and formatting standards are no longer as rigid as they were several years ago. "The only rule is that there are no rules," says Frank Fox, executive director of the Professional Association of Résumé Writers. "Résumés should be error free—no typos or spelling mistakes—but beyond that, use any format that conveys the information well."

However, the no-rules rule does not mean anything goes. You still have to consider what is reasonable and appropriate for the job you want. Advertisements for a single job opening can generate dozens, even hundreds, of responses. Busy reviewers often spend as little as 30 seconds deciding whether a résumé deserves consideration.

This chapter provides some guidelines for creating résumés. It describes what information your résumé should contain, how to highlight your skills for the job you want, and types of résumés.

About This Chapter: This chapter includes text excerpted from "Résumés, Applications, and Cover Letters," U.S. Bureau of Labor Statistics (BLS), U.S. Department of Labor (DOL), 2009.

Résumés: Marketing Your Skills

A résumé is a brief summary of your experience, education, and skills. It is a marketing piece, usually one or two pages long, designed to interest an employer. Good résumés match the jobseeker's abilities to the job's requirements. The best résumés highlight an applicant's strengths and accomplishments.

There are four main steps to creating a résumé: Compiling information about yourself and the occupations that interest you, choosing a résumé format, adding style, and proofreading the final document. You may also want to prepare your résumé for e-mailing and for an online application form.

Gathering and Organizing the Facts

Start working on your résumé by collecting and reviewing information about yourself: previous positions, job duties, volunteer work, skills, accomplishments, education, and activities. These are the raw materials of your résumé. This is also a good time to review your career goals and to think about which past jobs you have liked, and why. After compiling this information, research the occupations that interest you. Determine the duties they entail, credentials they require, and skills they use. Your résumé will use your autobiographical information to show that you meet a job's requirements. You will probably need to write a different résumé for each job that interests you.

Each résumé will emphasize what is relevant to one position. Remember: Even if you do not have many specialized and technical skills, most occupations also require abilities like reliability, teamwork, and communication. These are particularly important for entry-level workers.

The next step is to organize the personal information you have assembled. Most résumé writers use the following components.

Contact information. This includes your name; permanent and college campus addresses, if you are in school and your addresses differ; phone number; and e-mail address. Place your full legal name at the top of your résumé and your contact information underneath it. This information should be easy to see; reviewers who can't find your phone number can't call you for an interview. Also, make sure the outgoing message on your voicemail sounds professional. And remember to check your e-mail inbox regularly.

Qualifications summary. The qualifications summary, which evolved from the objective statement, is an overview designed to quickly answer the employer's question "Why should

I hire you?" It lists a few of your best qualifications and belongs below your contact information. A qualifications summary is optional. It can be particularly effective for applicants with extensive or varied experience because it prevents the important facts from being lost among the details.

Education. List all relevant training, certifications, and education on your résumé. Start with the most recent and work backward. For each school you have attended, list the school's name and location; diploma, certificate, or degree earned, along with year of completion; field of study; and honors received. If you have not yet completed one of your degrees, use the word "expected" before your graduation date. If you do not know when you will graduate, add "in progress" after the name of the unfinished degree. The education section is especially important for recent graduates. Include your overall grade point average, average within your major course of study, or class standing, if it helps your case. The general guideline is to include averages of 3.0 and above, but the minimum useful average is still widely debated. Graduates should also consider listing relevant courses under a separate heading. Listing four to eight courses related to a particular occupation shows a connection between education and work. College graduates need not list their high school credentials.

Experience. Résumés should include your job history: The name and location of the organizations you have worked for, years you worked there, title of your job, a few of the duties you performed, and results you achieved. Also, describe relevant volunteer activities, internships, and school projects, especially if you have little paid experience. When describing your job duties, emphasize results instead of responsibilities and performance rather than qualities. It is not enough, for example, to claim you are organized; you must use your experience to prove it.

Job descriptions often specify the scope of a position's duties—such as the number of phone lines answered, forms processed, or people supervised. If you worked on a project with other people, tell the reviewer your accomplishments came from a team effort. Also, mention any promotions or increases in responsibility you received.

Use specific accomplishments to give your experience impact. Note any improvements you made, any time or money you saved, and any problems you solved—for example, were you praised for handling difficult customers? Were you always on time or available for overtime? Did you start a new program? Mention quantifiable results you accomplished, such as a 10-percent increase in sales, a 90-percent accuracy rate, a 25-percent increase in student participation, or an "A" grade.

Activities and associations. Activities can be an excellent source of experience, especially for students in high school or college who don't have much work experience. Students can list their involvement in school or extracurricular activities as a way of showing a prospective employer their initiative.

Activities might include participation in organizations, associations, student government, clubs, or community activities, especially those related to the position you are applying for or that demonstrate hard work and leadership skills.

Special skills. If you have specific computer, foreign language, or technical skills, consider highlighting them by giving them their own category—even if they don't relate directly to the occupation you're pursuing. For jobs in information technology, for example, job seekers may list programming and computer application skills in a separate section.

But because most occupations now require computer skills, jobseekers in other fields also may list those skills separately.

Awards and honors. Include formal recognition you have received. Do not omit professional or academic awards. These are often listed with an applicant's experience or education, but some list them at the end of their résumé.

References. Usually, résumés do not include names of references, but some reviewers suggest breaking this rule if the names are recognizable in the occupation or industry. Some résumé writers end with the statement "References available upon request." Others assume reference availability is understood and use that space for more important information. Regardless of whether you mention it on the résumé, you will need to create a separate reference sheet to provide when requested and to carry with you to interviews.

A reference sheet lists the name, title, office address, and phone number of three to five people who know your abilities. Before offering them as references, of course, make sure these people have agreed to recommend you. At the top of the sheet, type your name and contact information, repeating the format you used in your résumé.

Other personal information. Your résumé should include any other information that is important to your occupation, such as a completed portfolio or a willingness to travel. Your résumé is your own, and you should customize it to fit your needs. However, some information does not belong on a résumé. Do not disclose your health, disability, marital status, age, or ethnicity. This information is illegal for most employers to request.

Filling an Application Form

Many jobs require jobseekers to complete an application instead of submitting a résumé. But an application is a résumé in disguise. Its purpose is to show your qualifications. Assembling the following information about yourself in advance will make it easier to complete applications:

- **Identification.** Be prepared to give your name, address, phone number, and Social Security number. You may also need to bring proof of identification when you pick up and drop off the application.
- **Employment history.** List the month and year you started and ended each job; your supervisor's name, address, and phone number; your job title, location, salary, and major duties; and your reason for leaving.
- **Education and certification.** Know the name and city of the school you attended and the year you received your degree and the name, level, and award and renewal dates of certification.
- **Special skills.** List any special skills you have that are closely related to the job, such as computer applications, or equipment operation.
- **References.** Provide the names, phone numbers, and addresses of three or four people who have agreed to recommend you.

When you pick up an application, don't miss an opportunity to make a good first impression. Dress as you would for the job. Politely request two copies of the form, or make your own copies of the original before you start filling it out. Read the entire application before you begin. Then, use one copy as a rough draft and the other as the final product. Write neatly with black ink.

Choosing a Format

There are three main résumé formats—chronological, functional, and combination. Each is defined by the way it organizes your experience. Choose the one that shows your experience to its best advantage.

Chronological. This résumé type is the most common. It organizes your experience around the jobs you have held. This format is an excellent choice for people with steady work histories or previous jobs that relate closely to their career objective.

To create a chronological résumé, list each position you have held, starting with the most recent and working backward. For each position, give the title of your job, the name of the organization you worked for, and the years you worked there. Next, relate the duties and accomplishments of that job. When describing jobs, use action statements, not sentences. Instead of writing "I managed a fundraising campaign," write, "Managed a fundraising campaign." Use strong verbs to begin each statement.

Be specific, but not overly detailed, in describing what you did. Employers say three to five statements are usually sufficient for each job. And no job should have more than four consecutive lines of information under it; large blocks of text are difficult to read. If you must use more space, find some way to divide the information into categories.

Your most important positions should occupy the most space on your résumé. If you've had jobs that do not relate to the position you want, consider dividing your experience into two categories: Relevant experience and other experience. Describe the relevant jobs thoroughly, and briefly mention the others. If you have had many jobs, you probably do not need to mention the oldest or least important ones. Just be careful not to create damaging gaps in your work history.

Because the chronological format emphasizes dates and job titles, it is often a poor format for career changers, people with inconsistent work histories, or new entrants to the workforce. For these applicants, the functional résumé is a better choice.

Functional. The functional résumé organizes your experience around skills rather than job titles. This format is ideal for students who have some work history, but not in positions that relate directly to the job they want. Organizing experiences around skills can connect less relevant jobs to career qualifications; a job waiting tables, for example, can be combined with other responsibilities to show organizational and customer service skills.

To create a functional résumé, identify three or four skills required for your target job. For each skill, identify three to five concrete examples to demonstrate that ability. Again, use action phrases—not complete sentences—when writing your list. Arrange your skill headings in order of importance. If you have a specific vacancy announcement, match the arrangement of your headings to that of its listed requirements. The closer the match between your skill headings and the reviewer's expectations, the more qualified you seem.

The last part of the functional résumé is a brief work history. Write only job titles, company names, and employment years. If you have gaps in your work history, you could use the cover letter to explain them, or you could fill them by adding volunteer work, community activities, or family responsibilities to your job list.

Combination. This format combines the best of the chronological format with the best of the functional format. Combination résumés are as varied as the histories they summarize. One variation begins with a chronological format but then subdivides each job description into skill categories. Another variation uses a functional format but, for each example of a skill, identifies the organization where the example occurred.

Adding Style

You will create a good impression if your résumé is attractive and easy to read. An inviting style draws attention to your qualifications. If you take pity on the reviewer's eyes, chances are better that she or he will spend more time reviewing your résumé—and will remember it better. To make your résumé easier to read and copy, print it on high-quality white or lightly colored paper. Loud, garish colors may attract attention, but they risk creating an unprofessional impression. Also, use a laser printer and keep the font size at 10 points or above. The reviewer shouldn't have to struggle to read your words.

Design. Good résumé writers use design elements strategically. Boldface, large type, capital letters, centering, or horizontal lines make headings stand out on the page. Bullets or italics can draw attention to key accomplishments. One-inch margins around the page and blank lines between sections will make all the information easier to see.

Any graphics you use should be consistent with your occupation's standards. Graphics appropriate for one occupation might be inappropriate for another. As a general rule, small design elements—such as a border or a name and address printed in letterhead style—are fine. But large, bold graphics are risky for an accountant who isn't applying for a position as a graphic artist.

To give your résumé a consistent flow, maintain the same style from beginning to end. Every section should have the same design elements. For example, if your education heading is bold and centered, every heading should be bold and centered. In the same way, choose one typeface, such as Arial or Times New Roman, and use it throughout.

When you have finished, hold your résumé at arm's length and examine it. Make sure the type is easy to read and that the material lays out evenly on the page. You may need to experiment with different styles before deciding which you like best.

Length. A long résumé is difficult for a reviewer to read and remember; and, given the volume of résumés many reviewers receive, long résumés are often ignored. Although rules about length are more flexible than they once were, general guidelines still exist. Most students and recent graduates use a one-page résumé, other workers use one or two pages, and the very experienced use two or three pages. If your résumé doesn't match this pattern, it probably contains unnecessary words or irrelevant information. Eliminate anything that does not help prove you're qualified for the job.

Proofreading

Take time to prepare the best résumé you can. You might not be the most qualified candidate for every job, but your résumé might be better than the competition. The most common mistakes are simple typographical and spelling errors. Computer spelling checkers do not catch correctly spelled words used incorrectly— "of" for "on," for example, or "their" for "there." You want your résumé to stand out, but not for the wrong reasons. Avoid mistakes by having several people proofread your résumé for you. Before you send out a résumé, review the vacancy announcement and fine-tune your résumé to meet employers' criteria. Sprinkle your résumé with language found in the position description, paying special attention to your qualifications summary if you have one.

Chapter 14

Finding a Job

Finding and getting a job can be a challenging process, but knowing more about job search methods and application techniques may increase your chances of success. CareerOneStop (www.careeronestop.org) from the U.S. Department of Labor (DOL) offers information that can help you:

- Plan your job search

- Search for a job

- Write résumés and cover letters and fill out applications

- Create a career network

- Interview for a job and negotiate your salary

The other resources are:

- State Job Banks—Search your state to locate job openings in your area.

- Occupational Outlook Handbook (www.bls.gov/ooh)—Find information on educational requirements, growth rates, median pay, and more for hundreds of career fields.

- State, Regional, and Local Resources—Locate U.S. Department of Labor (DOL) programs and services near you.

- Federal government employment—Learn how to get a job with the federal government using USAJOBS.

About This Chapter: This chapter includes text excerpted from "Find a Job," USA.gov, May 11, 2018.

Jobs for Teens and Young Adults

- Get help entering the job market. If you're 16- to 24-years old and need help finishing school, exploring career options, finding training, or searching and applying for jobs, GetMyFuture (www.careeronestop.org/GetMyFuture/default.aspx?frd=true) is for you. There's a special section on support for young people who struggle with addiction, have a criminal record, have children, need help with housing, or face other challenges.

- Learn about Job Corps (www.jobcorps.gov), a free educational and vocational training program that helps low-income people 16- to 24-years old learn a trade, earn a high school diploma or GED, and get help finding a job.

Apprenticeships

Apprenticeships combine on-the-job training and related instruction to give you skills to advance in your chosen field. Apprentice programs vary in length from one to six years. During that time, as an apprentice, you'll work and learn as an employee. When you complete a registered program, you will receive a nationally recognized certificate from the U.S. Department of Labor (DOL) as proof of your qualifications.

For more information:

- Visit the DOL's website on Registered Apprenticeships (www.dol.gov/apprenticeship)

- To locate an apprenticeship program near you, click on your state on the Search Apprenticeships Near You map of the United States (www.dol.gov/featured/apprenticeship/find-opportunities)

- If you're a woman looking for an apprenticeship in the field of construction, transportation, or protective services, check out the Women Build, Protect & Move America portal (www.dol.gov/wb/NTO). You'll find resources for local and nationwide apprenticeships as well as information about the different jobs in each field, professional trade organizations, and your rights on the job.

Self-Employment and Working from Home

You are self-employed if you operate a trade, business, or profession either by yourself or with a partner. Find out the basics of self-employment to help you succeed in the small business world:

Developing a Network

Research helps jobseekers in another important way: developing a network. Organizations tend to hire people they know or who are referred to them by someone they trust. Career experts say that organizations fill many openings through this "hidden," or unadvertised, job market. In other words, employers often fill new positions before those openings are ever publicized. A network includes family, friends, past and present employers and coworkers, association members, teachers, classmates, and others. In short, a network is everyone the candidate can communicate with. These contacts need not be close friends; they can be acquaintances, or even friends of friends. A professional network is built from these personal contacts, and the best time to start building is now. Experts suggest attending industry events, training classes, and seminars; joining a social, trade, or professional organization; and pursuing volunteer and internship positions. Even something as casual as a meeting over coffee can help a jobseeker develop connections. Focused networking gives jobseekers the opportunity to establish contacts among prospective employers to learn about work life in the organization.

(Source: "Focused Jobseeking: A Measured Approach to Looking for Work," U.S. Bureau of Labor Statistics (BLS), U.S. Department of Labor (DOL).)

- Starting and Financing a Small Business—Explore opportunities and get tips to help you succeed.

- Tax Information (www.dol.gov/general/location)—Learn about filing requirements for the self-employed, reporting responsibilities, and more.

- Health Insurance—Explore coverage options for the self-employed.

- Social Security—Information for the self-employed covers how to report your earnings when you file your taxes.

Work from Home

Are you thinking about basing your business out of your home? The U.S. Small Business Administration (SBA) offers a guide for home-based businesses. This includes the licenses and permits you need to run a home-based business.

Home Office Deduction

If you use a portion of your home for business, you may be able to take a home office tax deduction.

Work-at-Home Scams

Learn what to watch out for to avoid work-at-home scams. In one common scam, you may be tricked into paying to start your own Internet business. These scammers will keep asking you to send money for more services related to this fake business opportunity. To file a complaint about a scam, contact the Federal Trade Commission (FTC).

Federal Government Telework Guidelines

If you're a federal employee looking for information on teleworking, visit www.telework.gov.

Note: The federal government never charges a fee for information about, or applications for, government jobs. You can search and apply for federal government jobs for free at USA-JOBS (www.usajobs.gov).

Federal Employment Assistance for People with Disabilities

If you have a disability and you're looking for work, these resources can help:

- The Ticket to Work (choosework.ssa.gov/about/index.html) program helps 18-to-64-year-old Social Security disability recipients develop job skills that can lead to a higher standard of living. The program is supportive, free, and voluntary.

- The AbilityOne.gov (www.abilityone.gov) program provides employment opportunities with nonprofit agencies and community rehabilitation programs across the country for people who are blind or who have other significant disabilities.

- Learn how to find and apply for federal jobs open to people with disabilities through standard methods and through the Schedule A program. Find out about special federal hiring opportunities for young people and veterans.

Chapter 15

Networking for Teens

Networking is a fancy term for getting to know people and for cultivating productive relationships. Networking is an important professional skill that can help people be successful in their field of work. It is never too early to start networking. As a teen, the earlier you learn the art of networking, the greater your career success rate will be.

Importance of Teen Networking

Networking can help teens to:

- get to know fellow teens

- develop social skills

- get recommendations for college admissions and scholarships

- connect with professionals

- find opportunities to volunteer or work as an intern

- find part-time jobs

- find potential employers and clients

- choose the right career path

- earn extra bucks while studying

About This Chapter: "Networking for Teens," © 2019 Omnigraphics.

Tips for Teen Networking

Here are few tips and suggestions that can help teens build a strong network.

Get Guidance from Your Parents

Your parents may have years of experience in networking. So it is always a good idea to take their guidance. Also, you can ask your parents to provide contacts with their friends and peers.

Be Nice

- Pleasant and positive personas are two key factors of networking.

- Smile

- Be polite

- Listen more than you talk

- Make proper eye contact when someone is talking to you

- Be helpful to others

These behaviors help ensure that you are seen as a likable person and will help you build healthy relationships.

Be Open to New People

Some teens may feel a bit nervous when meeting new people. If you are such a person, start your initial networking with people with whom you are already acquainted, such as your peers, teachers, and neighbors. Gradually, you will gain the confidence needed to meet and connect with new people. At that point, try to get out of your comfort zone and widen your social circle.

Be Yourself

Networking is not an opportunity to sell yourself, but rather a platform to be yourself. Therefore, do not hide your personality, feelings, or interests while networking. Let the people with whom you meet know who you really are. Always try to be authentic and keep the relationship as casual and professional as possible.

Join Clubs and Organizations

Schools or colleges offer many clubs and organizations in which teens can participate. You can join any club or organization that suits your interest. This will provide an opportunity for you to mingle with like-minded peers. There may be chances for you to meet professionals in the particular field of work. You may also take part in various community activities outside the school or college, which can help you expand your network.

Use Social Media Efficiently

Social media is an invaluable tool to build your network. Numerous social media websites let you stay connected with anyone or anything—friends, family, neighbors, schools, colleges, classmates, teachers, mentors, companies, employers, and coworkers.

Although social media is beneficial in many ways, it has its downsides, too. Here are few tips for safe social networking.

- Do not reveal your login credentials (username and password) to anyone.

- Take care of your privacy. Review your privacy settings regularly.

- Connect only with people you know or trust.

- Think twice about what you write in an open forum. Avoid posting something that you would not want your teachers or employers to see.

References

1. Cairns, Hilary. "How to Network in High School and College," College Raptor, March 16, 2017.

2. "6 Networking Tips for Teens," Leading Learners, July 10, 2015.

3. "Learning How to Network in High School," eCampusTours, July 31, 2014.

4. Butts, Thalia. "Five Networking Tips for Teens," Vox, June 26, 2015.

5. "Social Networking Advice for Teenagers," Webwise, March 30, 2006.

Chapter 16

Apprenticeship: Earn While You Learn

"I like that I can have a full-time job and pay my mortgage while going to school," says chef's apprentice Brian Schmitt of Davenport, Iowa. "And I like that my job is directly applicable to the work that I want to do."

Many people work and learn at the same time. But in addition to getting a paycheck, apprentices like Schmitt are also getting a career boost: their on-the-job experience and technical instruction are part of a formal program to help them master an occupation.

Formal apprenticeship programs connect job seekers who want to learn new skills with employers who want to train workers in jobs that use those skills. Most programs last about four years, although some take as little as one year and others as long as six years. At the end of a registered apprenticeship program, apprentices get a nationally recognized certificate of completion as proof of their skills. But it's not always easy to find apprenticeship programs. It helps to know where to look—and what to look for.

This chapter is an overview of registered apprenticeships. The first section explains what apprenticeship programs are, some of the occupations they prepare you for, and what advantages they offer. The second section describes how to find, choose, and apply for an apprenticeship. The third section helps you plan for success.

About Apprenticeships

Whether you're new to the labor force, changing careers, or just looking to expand your skills, there might be an apprenticeship that appeals to you. People start apprenticeships

About This Chapter: This chapter includes text excerpted from "Apprenticeship: Earn While You Learn," U.S. Bureau of Labor Statistics (BLS), U.S. Department of Labor (DOL), 2013.

at almost any age, but many apprenticeship sponsors require participants to be at least 18. Although many apprentices have a high-school diploma or equivalent, others have more or less education than that. And about seven percent of active registered apprentices nationwide in 2012 were veterans, according to the U.S. Department of Labor (DOL).

Most formal apprenticeship programs are registered with the DOL. These programs prepare workers for occupations in industries such as construction, manufacturing, and healthcare. The opportunity to earn money, train for an occupation, and build a career foundation are just some of the benefits.

Registered Apprenticeship Programs

Registered apprenticeships must meet certain guidelines set by the DOL. People who complete these programs receive a nationally recognized certificate of completion, either from the DOL or from an approved state agency.

According to DOL, there were more than 358,000 registered apprentices in more than 21,000 apprenticeship programs in 2012. The actual number of apprenticeships may be higher, however, because DOL and state apprenticeship agencies do not oversee all programs.

Apprenticeship programs are sponsored by individual employers, employer associations, and labor unions. Sponsors pay wages, which often start out at about half those of a fully qualified worker. Wages increase as registered apprentices advance in the occupation.

For most programs, apprentices must complete 2,000 hours of on-the-job training and at least 144 hours of related technical instruction each year. Apprentices usually work full-time, under the direction of experienced workers, to meet training requirements.

Many apprentices receive their technical instruction by attending classes at an apprenticeship training center, technical school, or community college. Apprentices may go to class one or two days a week, either before or after work, or go to school full-time for several weeks each year. Frequently, sponsors pay for this technical instruction.

Apprenticeable Occupations

In 2012, DOL counted more than 250 occupations with registered apprentices. Apprenticeship isn't the only way to prepare for many of these occupations, but it's often a popular way. According to the U.S. Bureau of Labor Statistics (BLS), apprenticeship is a typical entry path for 15 occupations:

- Boilermakers

- Brickmasons and blockmasons

- Carpenters

- Electricians

- Elevator installers and repairers

- Funeral directors

- Glaziers

- Mechanical insulation workers

- Plumbers, pipefitters, and steamfitters

- Real estate appraisers and assessors

- Reinforcing iron and rebar workers

- Sheet metal workers

- Stonemasons

- Structural iron and steel workers

- Terrazzo workers and finishers

Table 16.1 shows the 10 occupations with the largest number of registered apprentices in 2012, according to DOL. All of these occupations are in construction, but occupations in other career areas also have apprenticeships.

Descriptions of some apprenticeship career areas are listed below, along with examples of occupations categorized in each area and the typical length of an apprenticeship program for each. For apprenticeships that do not match a title in the Standard Occupational Classification (SOC) manual, a SOC title is given in parentheses. Career areas and occupations are arranged roughly in order of the number of registered apprentices in 2012.

Construction. Construction workers build and repair homes, office buildings, and other structures. Common construction apprenticeships include:

- Electricians, four years

- Carpenters, four years

- Plumbers, three or four years

Table 16.1. Most Popular Apprenticeship Occupations and Median Hourly Wage of All Workers in the Occupation, 2012

Occupation	Active Apprentices, Fiscal Year 2012	Median Hourly Wage, May 2012
Electrician	36,742	$23.96
Carpenter	15,479	$19.2
Plumber	13,201	$23.62[1]
Pipefitter	8,586	$23.62[1]
Construction craft laborer	7,947	$14.42[2]
Sheet metal worker	7,714	$20.81
Roofer	5,479	$16.97
Structural steel/ironworker	5,041	$22.18
Painter	3,560	$16.92[3]
Pipefitter (sprinkler fitter)	3,266	$23.62[1]

1. *Data are for plumbers, pipefitters, and steamfitters.*

2. *Data are for construction laborers.*

3. *Data are for construction and maintenance painters.*

Note: *Data for active apprentices are from the Registered Apprenticeship Partners Information Management Data System (RAPIDS). RAPIDS is used by 33 states: 25 Office of Apprenticeship states and 8 of the 25 State Apprenticeship Agency states.*

(Sources: U.S. Department of Labor (DOL) Office of Apprenticeship (active apprentices data), U.S. Bureau of Labor Statistics (BLS) Occupational Employment Statistics (OES) program (wage data).)

- Construction craft laborers, two years

- Pipefitters, four or five years

Installation, maintenance, and repair. Workers in this group install and fix goods and equipment. Apprenticeable occupations in this group include:

- Millwrights, three or four years

- Line repairers and maintainers (Line installers and repairers), three or four years

- Heating, air conditioning, and refrigeration mechanics and installers, three years

- Telecommunications equipment installers and repairers, except line installers, three or four years

- Automobile mechanics (Automotive service technicians and mechanics), four years

Production. These workers operate machines and equipment to manufacture goods. Occupations with apprentices include:

- Machinists, three or four years

- Machine operators (Multiple machine tool setters, operators, and tenders, metal and plastic), one year

- Tool and die makers, four years

- Welders, three years

- Cabinetmakers, four years

Food, personal care, or child care. Workers in this group make food or provide personal care or services to the public. Apprenticeable occupations include:

- Cooks, two or three years

- Bakers, three years

- Childcare development specialists, two years

- Childcare workers, two years

- Barbers, one year

- Animal trainers, two years

Protective services. By providing a range of services in their communities, these workers help to keep people safe. Occupations with apprentices include:

- Correctional officers, one year

- Wildland firefighter specialists, two years

- Forest firefighters, two years

- Firefighters, three years

- Police officers, two years

- Paramedics, two years

Healthcare. Workers in this group help to administer care in hospitals, doctor's offices, nursing facilities, and other settings. Healthcare occupations that offer apprenticeships include:

- Pharmacy support staff (pharmacy technicians), one year

- Nursing assistants, one year

- Long-term care nurse managers (medical and health services managers), one year

- Dental assistants, one year

- Home health aides, one year

Architecture, engineering, or computers. These workers use specialized knowledge to design or work with concepts, systems, or structures. Occupations with apprentices include:

- Mine inspectors (Mining and geological engineers, including mining safety engineers), four years

- Electromechanical technicians, three years

- Computer programmers, two years

- Utilities instrument technicians

- Electronics engineering technicians, four years

- Computer operators, three years

Other. People apprentice in a wide range of other occupations. These include:

- Heavy truck drivers, one year

- Administrative services managers, two years

- Landscape technicians (Landscaping and groundskeeping workers), two years

By offering pathways to career-ready skills, a paycheck, and debt-free college credit, registered apprenticeship is the gold standard of work-based learning.

This program brings many high-school students a future they never imagined. Bobby didn't think he had many options after graduating from high school in rural Kentucky. Apprenticeship changed his life forever. During Bobby's junior year of high school, he entered an apprenticeship program in advanced manufacturing with an employer in his hometown. After graduating, Bobby earned 30 college credits paid by the employer and completed over 1,700 hours of on-the-job training. Now, he works full-time for the same company and is set to earn more money than his parents ever dreamed of for their family.

Employers see apprenticeship as a powerful tool for finding and developing talent. Parents and students see the value in a structured, earn-and-learn postsecondary pathway. Academic leaders see apprenticeship as a clear strategy for ensuring their high-school and college graduates have the skills and competencies they need for tomorrow's jobs.

(Source: "Apprenticeship Works for High School," U.S. Department of Education (ED).)

- Decorators (Merchandise displayers and window trimmers), four years

- Tree trimmers, two years

Advantages of an Apprenticeship

Apprenticeship programs have many advantages, including a paycheck, hands-on training, technical instruction—which is often free—and a solid start to a career.

A paycheck. Apprentices start earning money right away, which is a big draw for many who choose this type of career preparation. In addition to wages, some apprentices are eligible for health insurance or other employee benefits.

Apprentices usually make at least minimum wage. As apprentices' skills progress, their wages typically increase. "You're going to start off pretty low on the salary scale because you're preparing for a trade that takes a long time to learn," says Drew Haigh, a moldmaker apprentice in San Dimas, California. "You'll make your money over time."

According to the DOL, the average wage for a journey-level, or fully qualified, worker who completed an apprenticeship in 2012 was $24.77 an hour, or $51,522 a year. And a 2012 DOL-sponsored report by Mathematica Policy Research found that people who completed their apprenticeships have higher average lifetime earnings than those who did not.

But even before they earn journey-level wages, some apprentices say that their starting wage is an improvement over what they had been making. For example, Tyrell Ellis earns about $17 an hour in his first year as a sheet-metal worker apprentice in Mattapan, Massachusetts. "Before the apprenticeship I was making $10 an hour, working all kinds of hours," says Ellis. "I would have to work nonstop every day to make what I make now."

Hands-on training. While on the job, apprentices learn practical skills from experienced workers. Having worked under many mentors has helped Dan Glass to develop a wide range of skills. "You learn something different from everyone," says Glass, a third-year outside lineman (power-line installer and repairer) apprentice in Delta Junction, Alaska.

By the end of their apprenticeship, people usually have had experience with all of the major aspects of their occupation. "It's an effective way to learn," says Schmitt. He adds that because apprentices get their skills on the job, they don't face the same learning curve that many inexperienced workers do when they begin a new job.

Technical instruction. Apprentices receive related technical instruction that they use on the job. "When you go to work the next day, you get to apply what you've learned," says

Monique Gerard, who recently finished a steamfitter apprenticeship in Peoria, Illinois. "You really get to hone your skills."

Apprentices' technical instruction is usually provided by people who work in the industry, and their sponsor frequently pays. Completed classes may count toward certification or licensure requirements, which help boost apprentices' credentials and are sometimes necessary to work in an occupation. Some apprentices earn college credits or an associate or bachelor degree during their program.

And apprentices often appreciate how much they gain from the instruction. "I've learned so much in my class this past year that it's really amazing," says Bob Solden, in his first year of a CNC (computer numerically controlled) machinist apprenticeship in Petaluma, California. "I feel like I'm gaining so much knowledge."

Build a career foundation. At the end of their programs, apprentices earn a certificate of completion, issued by the DOL or a state apprenticeship agency. This certificate is recognized by employers around the country. Because apprentices' credentials are widely accepted, people who have finished an apprenticeship program frequently have increased occupational mobility. "It puts you in a position where you can go anywhere in the United States and get a job in a short amount of time at a decent wage, rather than having to start out at the entry level," says Schmitt. During the course of an apprenticeship program, apprentices are encouraged to make contacts in their industry. This networking may help them get a job when they reach journey-level status. Some apprentices finish the program and then start a career with the same employer who sponsored them.

Getting an Apprenticeship

Getting an apprenticeship is similar to getting a job: you need to find a program, apply for an opening, and qualify for selection.

Finding Apprenticeships

Apprenticeships involve commitment, so you'll need to find and choose a program that's right for you.

Search for programs. You can look for apprenticeship openings in a variety of ways. State apprenticeship agencies are often a good resource and usually, keep lists of apprenticeships. Another way to identify apprenticeship programs is to visit an American Job Center (AJC).

You might also search for apprenticeships advertised in a newspaper or online. Or you can contact a local union or other apprenticeship sponsors directly to ask about opportunities. The DOL's Office of Apprenticeship website provides contact information for all of the sponsors in the registered apprenticeship database, searchable by state and county.

In addition, community colleges and other schools sometimes post openings for available apprenticeships, which may be offered as part of an educational program. Some workers approach their employer about creating an apprenticeship position in a job they already have.

Special programs. Some programs are designed for specific groups. For example, school-to-apprenticeship programs allow high schoolers in some states to get started in an apprenticeship while they are students.

Apprenticeships for active-duty service members provide training in some military occupations. And some correctional institutions offer programs for inmates.

Preapprenticeship programs are another option. These programs help people qualify and prepare for apprenticeships. Participants might learn about career options and what an apprenticeship involves, for example, while they develop occupational skills.

Choosing a program. Apprenticeships vary in their schedules, pay, costs, technical instruction, and other details. Costs, for example, might include application fees, union dues, school tuition, books, and tools or other equipment, such as safety boots or uniforms.

Before you choose a program, it is important to learn about the occupation you're interested in. Talk to people in the occupation or tour a jobsite to get a better sense of the work culture and tasks.

Gerard didn't really know what steamfitters did until she asked someone about the basics of the work. After learning more about it, she decided to apply—and is glad she did. "I've never been happier in any job in my life," Gerard says. "The skilled trades are fantastic to get into. I am doing something productive and important."

Application and Selection

To get an apprenticeship, you must first apply for one. Apprentices are typically chosen through a competitive process, which often involves interviews, rankings, and other factors.

Applying. Apprenticeship requirements vary by sponsor and program. For many programs, you must be at least 18 years old and have a high-school diploma or equivalent.

You might also need to have completed certain classes in school or to pass an aptitude test in subjects such as math, physics, and reading comprehension. Related work experience is sometimes necessary. And some programs require drug tests or a physical exam to verify that you are able to do key tasks in the occupation.

When you apply for an apprenticeship program, you may need to pay a fee of about $20 to $45 and submit other material. This supplemental material might include written recommendations, school transcripts, and proof of identification, such as a birth certificate or driver's license.

Interviews. Applicants who meet the initial requirements usually have one or more interviews with their prospective sponsor. Interviewers want to know more about your qualifications, that you'll be reliable, and whether you are really interested in doing the work. Prepare for an apprenticeship interview as you would for a job interview: dress nicely, think about how you will answer common interview questions, and be ready to discuss your work-related skills and interests. In addition, sponsors usually want to know that you understand the work involved in the occupation you will train for. "Before they invested in me, they wanted to make sure I was completely devoted to it," says Haigh. "You have to be really committed to want to do a 4-year apprenticeship."

Rankings. Qualified apprenticeship applicants are often ranked on factors such as aptitude test results, interview performance, education, and work experience. As sponsors need apprentices, the most competitive applicants—those with the highest rankings—are chosen first. Applicants with lower rankings might need to wait until there's another opening.

The wait may last several weeks to several years. Gerard, for example, had to wait for six months before being contacted about an opening. Sometimes, people apply for an apprenticeship more than once.

Networking. For apprenticeship applicants—and other—jobseekers, networking can be beneficial. It allows you to meet people in the occupations you might be apprenticing for and helps you to learn more about a program. Applicants might also gain a better sense of what to expect in an apprenticeship. In addition, your networking contacts may recommend you to sponsors. "Definitely make connections, because that's a big part of the application and selection process," says Shamir Turner, a sheet-metal worker apprentice from Somerville, Massachusetts. "I'm not sure I would have gotten into my apprenticeship program if I hadn't known someone who could vouch for me."

Plan for Success

Those who are in or have completed apprenticeships have a few pointers to help prospective apprentices succeed. For example, Schmitt says that apprentices should remember that they are entry-level workers. "Set your expectations realistically," he says. "Be willing to pay your dues for a few years, and don't get discouraged if you're not running the show." Ellis agrees. "Expect to be the lowest one on the totem pole and to do whatever is asked of you, even if it's just getting coffee," he says. Others who've succeeded encourage apprentices to take advantage of any additional training or certification programs offered to them. Apprentices should also try to learn as much as they can from their mentors about different aspects of the work. "What you get out of it," says Schmitt, "is what you put into it."

Chapter 17

Internships: Previewing a Profession

An ounce of experience can be worth a ton of research—especially when it comes to exploring careers. Internships are one of the best ways to get that experience and test a career choice. And later, when it's time to get a job, internships attract employers. Internships provide short-term, practical experience for students, recent graduates, and people changing careers. Most internships are designed for college students, but many are open to high schoolers; others welcome career changers seeking exposure to a new field. Internship positions are available in a number of disciplines. They can be arranged through your school or the organization for which you'll work. And they often provide either pay or academic credit—sometimes, both. Regardless of how it is coordinated, completing an internship increases your chances of getting

Nearly all young people—98.6 percent—hold at least one job between the ages of 18 and 25. The average young person holds 6.3 jobs between 18 and 25. Some work part-time or summers only, while others see full-time permanent employment as their path to economic independence. Employment can be beneficial for youth by teaching responsibility, organization, and time management and helping to establish good work habits, experience, and financial stability. There are many advantages to working during high school, especially for low-income youth, including higher employment rates and wages in later teen years and lower probabilities of dropping out of high school. Knowing how to find and keep a job is not only critical for admission to the adult world but also is an important survival skill for which there is little in the way of formal, structured preparation.

(Source: "Employment," (Youth.gov).)

About This Chapter: This chapter includes text excerpted from "Internships: Previewing a Profession," U.S. Bureau of Labor Statistics (BLS), U.S. Department of Labor (DOL), June 23, 2006.

a job that you'll enjoy. Not only do you discover your job likes and dislikes, but you enter the job market with experience that is related to your career goals. This chapter is geared toward college students. It discusses the who, where, which, and how of pursuing an internship.

Who Should Pursue an Internship?

Almost anyone—both students and nonstudents who have yet to settle into a career—can benefit from doing an internship, no matter what their motivations. A liberal arts major, for example, may have a less obvious career path than, say, a nursing student. But even well-directed students can benefit from the practical experience that an internship provides. After all, a hospital emergency room, a pediatrician's office, and a nursing home each provide different work environments for nurses.

College students often take part in a summer internship after their junior year. Other students might work as interns during the school year, receiving academic credit toward their degree. Some students participate in more than one internship over the course of their academic careers. Part of an internship's value comes from the opportunity for experiential learning. Whether students have some, little, or no idea about the kind of work that they want to do, they can get firsthand knowledge about a particular type of work or work environment.

Where Are Internships Located?

Internships may be located anywhere in the world. It's probably easier for students to arrange something closer to their homes or schools than to set up something halfway around the world. But with a little effort, an internship can be created just about any place.

There are several ways to locate available internship opportunities. Public libraries, career centers, and offices of school counselors usually have resources that contain hundreds, even thousands, of national listings. These internships include positions with fashion designers, publishing companies, biotechnology research firms, software developers, and federal and state government agencies, to name a few examples. Job fairs can also be a source of information about internship opportunities, as can the Internet. For example, the U.S. government has a list of available internships online.

In addition, colleges and universities usually maintain local listings of employers who hire interns. Career counselors and academic advisors may be aware of possibilities, and professors may know what types of internships students in a particular field of study have had in the past. Programs that offer academic credit typically have an internship coordinator who oversees placement and monitors interns' progress. Some companies have formal internship programs. Others accept informal arrangements. Directly contacting companies, or visiting the career section of their websites, is usually the best way to learn whether they offer internships. Students might also be able to propose and set up their own internships.

Which Internships Are Best?

The best internships allow students to learn by doing, helping them to focus their career goals. Not surprisingly, most students choose an internship that is related to their major or to their career objectives. But many students aren't sure what they want to major in, let alone what they want to do for a career. And the differences between one internship and another can be hard to discern, particularly for students who are new to the working world. Making several important decisions can help students choose the best internship for them.

Perhaps most important, and most difficult, for some students is to decide which fields or occupations they are interested in. Career counselors, academic advisors, and vocational guidance publications, including the Occupational Outlook Handbook (OOH), can aid in the process. A related decision that students must make is which industry to work in. Occupations, and their related internships, differ from one industry to the next: An internship for a would-be management analyst would be much different in a bank, for example, than in a non-profit organization. Internship duties often vary, but any position can be worthwhile. Whether interns do odd jobs around the office or do challenging work that is related to their fields of study, they get a feel for workplace culture and make contacts that may be valuable for career networking.

How Do I Apply for an Internship?

Start early when applying for internships. Deadlines for turning in application materials vary, but many summer internships require that applications be submitted by February or March. Career counselors often say that Thanksgiving break is a good time to start gathering materials and researching opportunities for a summer internship. Other experts suggest starting the process a few semesters before the desired internship period.

Applying for an internship might seem overwhelming, especially for those who have never written a résumé or cover letter. But preparing these documents when applying for an internship means not having to start from scratch when applying for a job.

In addition to requiring a résumé and cover letter, internship sponsors might request other items, such as a completed application, transcripts, coursework samples, and references. Applying for several internships increases the chances for success. Because high-profile employers are likely to get many applications, students who use personal or school contacts are most likely to stand out. Reviewing application materials for accuracy and completeness before submitting them is a must. The most careful students have someone else read over their application as well. Materials should be sent on time, with a follow-up telephone call confirming that the application was received.

Some internship sponsors might require candidates to appear for an interview. To prepare for such a meeting, students should read up on employment interviewing, participate in mock interviews, and attend interviewing workshops offered at their school. And students who follow up with a thank you note after the interview make a good impression.

Career counselors, books, and other resources can be helpful in the application and interviewing process.

Still Not Convinced?

Students who still aren't sure of an internship's value should consider this: Job seekers who have completed an internship have an edge in the job market. According to a survey by the National Association of Colleges and Employers (NACE), employers reported that, on average, more than three out of five college hires had internship experience. Moreover, many employers hire directly from their internship programs. The association's survey also reported that, on average, more than half of all students were offered a full-time job after completing their internship. Internships aren't the only path to postcollege success, of course. But the process of researching, finding (or creating), and applying for an internship may be as valuable as the benefits gained from the internship itself. The entire experience is likely to make your job search easier—after all, you'll have previewed the steps.

Chapter 18

Job Scams

What Is a Job Scam?

Dishonest people are sometimes called scammers. They might promise to help you find a job. The scammers promise to help you if you pay them. But after the scammers take your money, you get nothing. This is a job scam.

How Do I Know a Job Is a Scam?

Most fake job offers have things in common. A job scam:

- Promises you a job
- Guarantees that you will make money
- Often says you can work at home
- Might offer government jobs no one knows about

Scammers advertise fake jobs:

- In the newspaper
- Online
- On signs, posters, and flyers

About This Chapter: Text beginning with the heading "What Is a Job Scam?" is excerpted from "Job Scams," Consumer.gov, Federal Trade Commission (FTC), September 28, 2012; Text beginning with the heading "Signs of a Job Scam" is excerpted from "Job Scams," Federal Trade Commission (FTC), October 2013.

How Do Job Scams Work?

You might see an ad on a poster, online, or in the newspaper. The ad promises that you will get a job. The ad might guarantee that you will make a certain amount of money. You might respond to the website or phone number in the ad. You will hear more promises. And then someone will ask you to pay:

- To get the job
- For more job listings
- For supplies to start a business at home
- For a certification that is supposed to get you a job

If you pay, you will not get the job they promised. Instead, you might get:

- A list of jobs that is old
- Job search advice you could get for free
- A certificate that will not help you get a job
- Nothing at all

You will not get your money back, even if they promised you would.

How Can I Tell What Is Real and What Is a Scam?

Here are some ways to spot a job scam. Scammers:

- Promise to get you a job
- Ask you to pay before they help you
- Promise you a government job
- Promise you can make lots of money working from home

If someone really could help you, they would not promise these things. No one can promise that you will get a job.

What If I Already Sent Money to Someone Who Promised Me a Job?

You probably will not get your money back. But you can help other people not get scammed.

If you sent money and got no help, report it to the Federal Trade Commission (FTC).

- Call the FTC at 877-382-4357

- Report them online at: ftc.gov/complaint

The FTC uses complaints to build cases against scammers. Any information you can provide helps investigators.

How Do I Spot a Job Scam?

Scammers might promise you a job, lots of money, or work you can do at home. But they make you pay them before they help you. If you pay them, you will lose your money and will not get a job.

Look for these signs of a scam. Scammers might:

- Promise you a job

- Promise you a government job

- Offer you the secret to getting a job

- Promise that you will make lots of money by working at home

- Offer you a certificate to improve your chances of getting a job

Scammers always will ask you to pay first. That is the biggest sign of any scam. Never pay in advance. Someone might say you cannot lose. It is not true. You will lose money.

How Can I Avoid a Job Scam?

- Never deal with anyone who promises you a job. No one can promise you a job.

- Do not pay in advance for information about a job. Even if there is a money-back guarantee.

- Do not deal with anyone who says you have to act fast.

- Ignore promises to make thousands of dollars working in your own home. Those promises are lies.

Signs of a Job Scam

Scammers advertise jobs where legitimate employers do—online, in newspapers, and even on TV and radio. Here's how to tell whether a job lead may be a scam:

You Need to Pay to Get the Job

They may say they've got a job waiting, or guarantee to place you in a job, if you just pay a fee for certification, training materials, or their expenses placing you with a company. But after you pay, the job doesn't materialize. Employers and employment firms shouldn't ask you to pay for the promise of a job.

You Need to Supply Your Credit Card or Bank Account Information

Don't give out your credit card or bank account information over the phone to a company unless you're familiar with them and have agreed to pay for something. Anyone who has your account information can use it.

The Ad Is for "Previously Undisclosed" Federal Government Jobs

Information about available federal jobs is free. And all federal positions are announced to the public on usajobs.gov. Don't believe anyone who promises you a federal or postal job.

Job Placement Services

Many job placement services are legitimate. But others lie about what they'll do for you, promote outdated or fake job openings, or charge up-front fees for services that may not lead to a job. In fact, they might not even return your calls once you pay.

Before you enlist a company's help:

Check with the Hiring Company

If a company or organization is mentioned in an ad or interview, contact that company to find out if the company really is hiring through the service.

Get Details—in Writing

What's the cost, what will you get, and who pays—you or the company that hires you? What happens if the service doesn't find a job for you or any real leads? If they're reluctant to answer your questions, or give confusing answers, you should be reluctant to work with them.

Get a copy of the contract with the placement firm, and read it carefully. A legitimate company will give you time to read the contract and decide, not pressure you into signing then and there. Make sure any promises—including refund promises—are in writing. Some listing services and "consultants" write ads to sound like jobs, but that's just a marketing trick: They're really selling general information about getting a job—information you can find for free on your own.

Know Whether It's Job Placement or Job Counseling

Executive or career counseling services help people with career directions and decisions. They may offer services like skills identification and self-evaluation, résumé preparation, letter writing, interview techniques, and general information about companies or organizations in a particular location or job field.

But job placement isn't guaranteed. Fees can be as high as thousands of dollars, and you often have to pay first.

The National Career Development Association (NCDA) offers some tips on finding and choosing a career counselor, and explains the different types of counselors active in the field.

Check for Complaints

Your local consumer protection agency, state Attorney General's Office, and the Better Business Bureau can tell you whether any complaints have been filed about a company. Just keep in mind that a lack of complaints doesn't mean the business is on the up-and-up. You may want to do an Internet search with the name of the company and words like "review," "scam," or "complaint." Look through several pages of search results. And check out articles about the company in newspapers, magazines, or online as well.

Where to Look for Jobs

You've read the many résumé and interview tips from respected sources available for free online, and scoured online job boards and newspaper classifieds. Some other places to look for leads in your job search include:

CareerOneStop

Sponsored by the U.S. Department of Labor (DOL), CareerOneStop lists hundreds of thousands of jobs. It also links to employment and training programs in each state, including programs for people with disabilities, minorities, older workers, veterans, welfare recipients, and young people. For federal jobs, all open federal positions are announced to the public on usajobs.gov.

State and County Offices

Your state's Department of Labor may have job listings or be able to point you to local job offices that offer counseling and referrals. Local and county human resources offices provide some placement assistance, too. They can give you the names of other groups that may be helpful, such as labor unions or federally funded vocational programs.

College Career Service Offices

Whether it's a four-year university or a community college, see what help yours can offer. If you're not a current or former student, some still may let you look at their job listings.

Your Library

Ask if they can point you to information on writing a résumé, interviewing, or compiling a list of companies and organizations to contact about job openings.

Report a Job Scam

If you've been targeted by a job scam, file a complaint with the FTC. For problems with an employment-service firm, contact the appropriate state licensing board (if these firms must be licensed in your state), your state Attorney General, and your local consumer protection agency.

Chapter 19

Types of Job Scams

Criminals don't like getting caught. So, when they want to send and receive stolen money, they get someone else to do the dirty work. Some scammers develop online relationships and ask their new sweetheart or friend to accept a deposit and transfer funds for them. Other cons recruit victims with job ads that seem like they're for legit jobs, but they're not. Law enforcement calls the victims 'money mules.' If you get involved with one of these schemes, you could lose money and personal information, and you could get into legal trouble.

Scammers post ads for imaginary job openings for payment-processing agents, finance support clerks, mystery shoppers, interns, money transfer agents, or administrative assistants. They search job sites, online classifieds, and social media to hunt for potential money mules. For example, if you post your résumé on a job site, they might send you an e-mail saying, "We saw your résumé online and want to hire you." The ads often say:

- The company is outside the United States

- All work is done online

- You'll get great pay for little work

If you respond, the scammer may interview you or send an online application. He does that to collect your personal information and make the job offer seem legitimate. At some point,

About This Chapter: Text in this chapter begins with excerpts from "Scammers Say 'Help Wanted,'" Federal Trade Commission (FTC), June 14, 2016; Text beginning with the heading "Business Opportunity" is excerpted from "Business Opportunity," Federal Trade Commission (FTC), December 11, 2012; Text under the heading "False Promises from a Work-At-Home Scam" is excerpted from "False Promises from a Work-at-Home Scam," Federal Trade Commission (FTC), August 17, 2017; Text under the heading "Envelope-Stuffing Schemes" is excerpted from "Envelope-Stuffing Schemes," Federal Trade Commission (FTC), February 2010.

the scammer will ask for your bank account number, or tell you to open a new account, and then send you instructions about transferring money.

If you think you're involved with a money transfer scam:

- Stop transferring money

- Close your bank account

- Notify your bank and the wire transfer service about the scam

- Report it to the Federal Trade Commission (FTC)

If you're looking for work, check out the FTC's tips about jobs and making money and warning signs of a job scam.

Business Opportunity

Looking for a job or to earn extra income? Ever thought about starting your own business? Buying into a business opportunity that makes big claims about what you can earn might sound like the answer. But don't sign up just yet.

Even legitimate business opportunities involve risk. For example, if you're considering buying a franchise, you'll want to find out more about how to shop for a franchise opportunity, the obligations of a franchise owner, and questions to ask before you invest.

Starting a Business

Before you sink money into a business opportunity, it's a good idea do some research and get specific information from the promoter.

Thinking about Buying a Franchise?

Buying a franchise is a major financial investment and a serious personal commitment. Understanding your abilities and goals is one step toward deciding whether a franchise is right for you.

Bogus Business Opportunities

Want to buy a business? Here's how the business opportunity rule can help you evaluate the opportunity—and the seller.

Starting an Internet Business

Thinking about an Internet startup? The promise of big bucks and terrific working conditions can be tempting, but consider these factors before you hand over any money.

Multi-Level Marketing

There are multilevel marketing plans—and then there are pyramid schemes. Before signing on the dotted line, get more information.

Work-at-Home Offers

Many work-at-home opportunities are promoted by scam artists. These can cost you more than you can earn.

Work-at-Home Businesses

Many work-at-home opportunities are promoted by scam artists. If you pay in, it's likely that you will spend more than you can earn.

At-Home Medical Billing Businesses

Many medical billing business opportunities are worthless. Their promoters lie about their earnings potential and fail to provide key information.

Envelope-Stuffing Schemes

Offers that promise quick and easy income from stuffing envelopes at home virtually never pay off.

False Promises from a Work-at-Home Scam

It's hard to pass up a job opportunity that promises a large income and the flexibility of working entirely from home. Especially when the opportunity appears at the top of your online search results and includes video testimonials of success stories, making it seem legitimate. The problem is, most of these job opportunities are scams and won't deliver on their promises.

The FTC announced that a federal court put a temporary stop to a work-at-home scam that failed to live up to its promises. According to the FTC, Work At Home (WAH) EDU made false claims that people could earn "hundreds of dollars, per hour from home, without any special skills or experience" by paying for a $97 work-at-home program. Once people paid, they were told that for $194.95 more, they could buy the advanced program and earn a whopping six figures a month. Unfortunately, none of it was true.

If you're looking to work from home, here are some questions to ask to help you determine if a program is legitimate:

- What tasks will I have to perform? Are any other steps involved?

- What is the total cost of this work-at-home program? What will I get for my money?

- Will I be paid a salary or commission?

- Who will pay me? When will I get my first paycheck?

- What is the basis for your claims about my likely earnings? What documents can you show me to prove your claims are true before I give you any money?

Before you hand over any money, also make sure you know what information you're entitled to under the FTC's Business Opportunity Rule. Doing an online search of the company's name with the words "complaint," "reviews," or "scam" also can be a good way to hear what others have to say. Scammers know that finding a job can be tough. To trick people looking for honest work, scammers advertise where real employers and job placement firms do. They also make upbeat promises about your chances of employment, and virtually all of them ask you to pay them for their services before you get a job. But the promise of a job isn't the same thing as a job. If you have to pay for the promise, it's likely a scam.

Envelope-Stuffing Schemes

$550–$3,000 weekly. $2 for each circular you mail...

Free Postage... Free Supplies... No Advertising!

Paychecks mailed to you every week!

Advance paycheck forms included in your package!!

Sound familiar? Ads for envelope-stuffing "opportunities" can be anywhere—from your mailbox to your inbox, in the newspaper or on an online search. Promoters usually advertise that for a "small" fee, they'll tell you how to earn big money stuffing envelopes at home. They may say you will earn money for each envelope stuffed, making it possible for you to earn hundreds—or even thousands—of dollars each week.

But when it comes to offers promising quick and easy income stuffing envelopes at home, be skeptical—and check it out.

The ads may sound appealing, especially if you're looking for a home-based business. But according to the Federal Trade Commission (FTC), the nation's consumer protection agency, ads like these don't tell the whole story—namely, that the promoters aren't really offering a job.

Here's what happens: once you send your money, you're likely to get a letter telling you to get other people, even your friends and relatives, to buy the same envelope-stuffing "opportunity" or another product. The only way you can earn money is if people respond to your solicitations the same way you responded. The promoters rarely pay anyone.

Promises of big earnings through an envelope-stuffing scheme are false. But if you are tempted to send any money or sign up to receive more information, ask the promoter:

- Who will pay me?

- Where is your business located?

- How long have you been in business?

- How and when will I get my first paycheck?

- Will I be paid a salary or will my pay be based on commission?

- What will I have to do?

- What is the total cost of the envelope-stuffing program?

- What will I get for my money?

- Will I have to pay for supplies, ads, or postage?

The answers to these questions may help you determine whether an envelope-stuffing opportunity is appropriate for your circumstances.

It also may help to check out the company with your local consumer protection agency, state Attorney General, and the Better Business Bureau (BBB) in your community and the community where the company is located, which you can find at bbb.org. You can find out whether they've received complaints about the promotion that interests you, but remember—just because there aren't complaints doesn't mean the promotion is legitimate. Unscrupulous promoters may settle complaints, change their names or move to avoid getting caught. In addition, consider other people's experience by entering the company or promoter's name with the word "complaints" into a search engine. Read what others have to say. After all, you are making a decision that involves spending your money.

If you've spent money and time on a work-at-home program and now believe it may be a scam, contact the company and ask for a refund. Let company representatives know that you plan to notify officials about your experience. If you can't resolve the dispute with the company, file a complaint with the following organizations:

- The Federal Trade Commission. The FTC works for the consumer to prevent fraud and deception. Visit ftc.gov/complaint or call 877-FTC-HELP (877-382-4357).

- Your local postal inspector. The U.S. Postal Inspection Service (USPIS) investigates fraudulent mail practices. Visit postalinspectors.uspis.gov.

- The Attorney General's office in your state or the state where the company is located. Find yours at naag.org; the office will be able to tell you whether you're protected by any state law that may regulate work-at-home programs.

- Your local consumer protection offices

- Your local Better Business Bureau (BBB), which you can find at bbb.org

- The advertising manager of the publication that ran the ad. The manager may be interested to learn about the problems you've had with the company.

Part Three
On the Job

Chapter 20

The Rules of the Game: Preparing Youth for the World of Work

Dressed in matching navy blue T-shirts, members of the HIRE Ground day labor crew show up for work at 7:45 a.m. sharp. A normal day for crew members might include sweeping the facilities of San Francisco's Larkin Street Youth Services (LSYS), which runs the HIRE Ground program, painting a local hotel, or watering plants and cleaning storefronts for local businesses—all under the watchful eye of an adult supervisor.

Crew members not only get paid ($6.25 an hour, or $7.25 an hour with a high-school diploma or GED), they also learn "what it's like to be at work," says Andrew Niklaus, director of education and employment services at Larkin Street, a Family and Youth Services Bureau (FYSB) grantee agency, where communicating with supervisors and peers, interacting with the public, and working independently at times all fit into the job description.

The day labor experience, part of Larkin's multifaceted HIRE UP youth employment program, helps runaway and homeless youth and other at-risk young people take an important step, one that precedes job readiness class, technical and vocational training, or getting a traditional job.

"Someone who has just exited the street, more likely than not, isn't going to be ready to hold a job," Niklaus explains.

Niklaus isn't just talking about a lack of training or education. He and other youth service professionals and youth employment advocates say that young people in general, and especially youth in at-risk situations, often lack the fundamental skills and attitudes necessary

About This Chapter: This chapter includes text excerpted from "The Rules of the Game: Preparing Youth for the World of Work," Administration for Children and Families (ACF), U.S. Department of Health and Human Services (HHS), August 11, 2006.

for entry-level employment. Before entering the workforce, youth employment advocates say, young people need to learn about the importance of things longtime workers take for granted, like showing up for work on time, dressing appropriately, managing stress, resolving conflicts with bosses and coworkers, communicating with others, and working as part of a team.

Young people need to learn these so-called soft skills, or nontechnical skills, before they show up for their first jobs, because many employers don't want to have to teach new workers skills they consider basic. U.S. Secretary of Labor Elaine L. Chao reflected on this issue at the White House Conference on Helping America's Youth in October 2005. "Many employers tell the Labor Department that they can teach workers the technical skills for just about any job," she said. "What they need are workers who are ready to learn. Workers who can show up on time, get along with others, complete assignments, and take direction."

Cindy Perry, director of special projects for the San Diego Workforce Partnership (SDWP), has heard the same comment from employers. "Preferably, these were the skills your parents were teaching you," she says.

The disconnect between the basic skills employers expect and the deficiencies they detect in entry-level workers stems in part from the changing nature of work, says Sondra Stein, project manager for the Equipped for the Future (EFF) Work Readiness Credential Project, a joint endeavor of the federal government's National Institute for Literacy (NIFL), the U.S. Chamber of Commerce (USCC), five states, the District of Columbia (DC), and major industry groups.

For instance, she says, in the past, entry-level workers in manufacturing jobs worked primarily alone, all day long. "You don't work on your own anymore in the workplace," she says, and that leads to a slew of consequences for job seekers. "In every industry, workers have to make more decisions, work with more people, communicate more."

Given that reality, young people with unstable family backgrounds who don't learn important interpersonal, decision making, and communications skill at home or in their communities are at a disadvantage in today's labor market, Stein says.

In addition, compared to their peers with stable home lives and residences, runaway and homeless youth are "less likely to get connected to any kind of (early) work experience" where they could learn workplace norms and expectations, says Kate O'Sullivan, director of quality initiatives at the National Youth Employment Coalition (NYEC) in Washington, DC.

That's where HIRE Ground, the U.S. Department of Labor's (DOL) Job Corps (a residential training program for at-risk young people ages 16–24), and other job readiness programs come in, helping young people to gain the nontechnical skills and the workplace savvy they need to succeed on the job. "What's really important for (at-risk youth) is to make it explicit," Stein says, "because they don't have expectations. They've never had it modeled."

That modeling may come via a simulated work environment or a program like HIRE Ground. Many transitional living and youth employment programs, including Larkin Street, also have developed "job readiness" curricula that cover a range of topics such as conflict resolution, communication skills, self-exploration, dress and hygiene, résumé building, and interviewing.

In addition to teaching the "soft skills," many successful work readiness programs emphasize "biculturalism," Stein says, contrasting the culture of the street and the culture of mainstream America and making clear when different behaviors are appropriate.

Programs also need to show an appreciation of the culture that young people come from, says Terry Simmons, program administrator and career coach at Career Builders, a state workforce development intermediary in Baton Rouge, Louisiana, and a partner in the FYSB-funded Louisiana Positive Youth Development (PYD) Collaboration Demonstration Project.

"A huge part of getting these kids to conform is confirming that their culture is legitimate," Simmons says.

He recommends teaching young people to adapt to diverse environments by offering them a dual message: that hip-hop and other aspects of youth culture are valid and significant, but at the same time, "if they go in with gold teeth and tattoos, it's going to be hard to get a mainstream job."

Tips on Preparing Young People for the World of Work

- Youth who've lived on the streets for a long time may not consider hygiene important, and they may never have owned an alarm clock.

- Introduce young people to workplace expectations and norms through a sponsored work program such as a supervised day labor program or through a simulated work environment in which they can practice work readiness skills.

- If you plan to use a job readiness curriculum, choose one that takes into account the special needs of youth and the realities of adolescent development.

- Guide youth in assessing their skills using a tool such as the Skills Profiler developed by O*Net, a program of the U.S. Department of Labor (DOL).

- Help young people decide whether to obtain a job readiness credential. Credentials that confirm a worker's basic job skills are offered by some state and local workforce initiatives.

- Connect job readiness to life skills training. Many skills valuable for entry-level workers are taught in transitional living and life skills curricula. Tools such as the Ansell Casey Life Skills Assessment (ACLSA) or the Daniel Memorial Institute's (DMI) Assessments for Life Skills can help you determine the particular skills each young person needs to learn.

- Model workplace norms in your job readiness program or class, for instance by asking youth to attend from 9 to 5, providing stipends, creating a dress code, and requiring that youth behave as they would be expected to at a workplace.

- Teach young people about participation and collaboration in the workplace by asking them to create a mission statement and rules for the class.

- Use role playing to help young people learn how to act in specific workplace situations, such as a job interview, a dispute with a coworker or supervisor, or a racist incident.

- Introduce young people to working professionals, either in one-on-one meetings or by arranging for youth to "shadow" someone during a regular workday, so they can observe how people act, dress, and talk at work.

Chapter 21

What New Workers in Entry-Level Jobs Need to Be Able to Do

A new credential developed through a partnership of the federal government, five states, the District of Columbia, the U.S. Chamber of Commerce (USCC), and major industry groups, will allow workforce programs to measure how well they prepare young people for entry-level jobs. Though some states and localities have work readiness certificate programs, no national credential has existed until now.

Based on the Equipped for the Future work readiness standards developed by the federal government's National Institute for Literacy (NIFL), the assessment tool that leads to the national credential was field-tested across the country in early 2006. Field-test sites included two Family and Youth Services Bureau (FYSB) Runaway and Homeless Youth Program (RHY) grantees in Washington, DC, Covenant House and Latin American Youth Center (LAYC). The exam is slated to debut in June 2006.

Funding from the National Institute for Literacy, which is administered by the U.S. Secretaries of Education, Labor, and Health and Human Services, helped to support the first phase of the credential's development.

According to the assessment, new workers in entry-level jobs need to be able to do the following:

Communication Skills

- Speak so others can understand

About This Chapter: This chapter includes text excerpted from "The Rules of the Game: Preparing Youth for the World of Work," Administration for Children and Families (ACF), U.S. Department of Health and Human Services (HHS), August 11, 2006.

- Listen actively

- Read with understanding

Observe Critically

- Interpersonal skills

- Cooperate with others

- Resolve conflict and negotiate

Decision Making Skills

- Use math to solve problems and communicate

- Solve problems and make decisions

Lifelong Learning Skills

- Take responsibility for learning

- Use information and communications technology

The laws enforced by the United States Equal Employment Opportunity Commission's (EEOC) protect you from employment discrimination when it involves:

- Unfair treatment because of your race, color, religion, sex (including pregnancy, gender identity, and sexual orientation), national origin, disability, age (age 40 or older), or genetic information

- Harassment by managers, coworkers, or others in your workplace, because of your race, color, religion, sex (including pregnancy, gender identity, and sexual orientation), national origin, disability, age (age 40 or older), or genetic information

- Denial of a reasonable workplace change that you need because of your religious beliefs or disability

- Improper questions about or disclosure of your genetic information or medical information

- Retaliation because you complained about job discrimination or assisted with a job discrimination proceeding, such as an investigation or lawsuit

---

Chapter 22

Workplace Skills

Twenty-five percent of the global workforce is comprised of young people. Transitioning from your studies to work can be a challenge, however, and teens have to make major decisions based on how they want to progress in their career. After they have decided to start their career with a particular organization, one of the first steps they need to take is to learn the skills required in the workplace. Developing these skills helps ensure a smooth transition and helps new employees to develop core and employable skills that lead to workplace success.

Many employers require specialized skills for a specific job. However, any job also needs a range of other professional workplace skills. This chapter focuses on the general employable skills needed for teens to compete in the work environment. Some of the basic skills include communication, self-management, planning and organizing, teamwork, interpersonal effectiveness, learning skills, strong work ethics, analytical and problem-solving skills, and technology skills.

> What are your current skills, abilities, and talents? If you struggle to answer this, as many people do, ask three significant people in your life what they think are your skills and talents. You may be surprised.
>
> *(Source: "Mastering Soft Skills for Workplace Success," U.S. Department of Labor (DOL).)*

Communication

Effective communication is necessary and vital for workplace success. On-the-job communication includes listening, speaking, and writing skills. Successful employees should be able

---

About This Chapter: "Workplace Skills," © 2019 Omnigraphics.

to understand and interpret what others say, and express their thoughts clearly to their fellow workers. Writing skills are equally important, as most jobs require correspondence. An effective communicator always has an advantage over others.

Self-Management

Self-management means completing work assignments without direct oversight every single time a task is assigned to you, meeting assigned deadlines, delegating work as necessary to complete deadlines, and resolving issues that could impede your progress. Employers expect responsible behavior from their employees and expect them to complete all tasks in a timely manner.

To improve your self-management skills:

- Complete an internship
- Join a volunteer organization
- Ask for new responsibilities

Planning and Organizing

The ability to effectively plan and organize your work is essential for success in your work career. As you transition from your studies to work, you will discover that you will need to forego certain activities and become disciplined about managing your work. Planning ahead for work is always beneficial; and employers always prefer someone who can plan well ahead of a deadline and execute the work in a diligent and timely manner. Planning and organizing involves knowing what is required to get a job done, how to do the job, and when to do the job.

To improve your planning and organizing skills:

- Create a timetable and stick to it
- Travel alone
- Manage time commitments around your studies, work, and family
- Help with family chores
- Organize an event

Teamwork

Teamwork is essential in any work environment, as most jobs require people to work together to accomplish a specific task. Many teens' teamwork skills are honed from being a part of team projects in college, playing team sports, or taking part in other extracurricular activities. The ability to work well with others is an important skill employers look for when recruiting.

Interpersonal Effectiveness

Interpersonal effectiveness is required for success in the workplace. Positive relationships with fellow workers ensure a smooth workflow within an organization. Skills such as effective communication and teamwork form the structure for displaying interpersonal effectiveness.

Learning Skills

Learning opportunities will present themselves to take place almost every day in a workplace setting, and you will be required to update your skills constantly. This means that work environments are natural environments in which you can improve your adaptability skills and ability to learn and grow.

To improve your learning skills:

- Start a new course or hobby
- Do some research on the required topics

Strong Work Ethics and Values

In this day and age, scams and dishonest methods of earning money are on the rise, and employers are looking for ethical people who can work honestly. Self-confidence, a positive attitude, dependability, and honesty are the qualities most valued by today's employers.

Analytical and Problem-Solving Skills

Solving problems is a skill every successful employee should possess. Teens should be able to apply their reasoning, creativity, and out-of-the-box thinking on the job. When a difficult situation arises, employees with analytical and problem-solving skills are able to deal with the situation more efficiently.

To improve your analytical and problem-solving skills:

- Take initiative when a crisis arises
- Learn from experienced people how they have dealt with problems
- Research about solutions for particular problems

Technology Skills

The ability to use technology is a must for today's workforce since most workplaces are computerized. The basic technology skills that workers need include being able to use a computer, send and receive e-mails, and create text documents and spreadsheets. Specific job-related technology skills may also include the ability to use programming languages, video-editing software, handle a cash register, or use social media.

While some skills, such as leadership and taking initiative, may be developed over several years on the job, the skills outlined above serve as a base for any job. Employers seek people who have already mastered these skills and can learn more as they move forward.

References

1. "8 Job Skills You Should Have," Youth Central, February 20, 2018.

2. Chinn, Diane. "The Definition of Workplace Skills," bizfluent, September 26, 2017.

3. "Youth Employability," Skills for Employment, October 17, 2013.

4. "Top 10 Employability Skills," Opportunity Job Network, May 30, 2010.

Chapter 23

Workplace Ethics

Workplace ethics are the moral principles that govern the behavior of individuals within the workplace. Every person has some inherited ethical behaviors that are learned from family, friends, and society. In addition, the organizations may specify a set of basic rules and guidelines for their employees based on their work culture. These rules and guidelines usually address topics such as the language of communication, work hours, dress codes, and so on, and may vary from organization to organization. Teens who are entering a professional work environment should possess these basic ethical behaviors in order to be successful in their work lives.

Fundamental Workplace Ethics

Some fundamental workplace ethics that every teen should learn and possess follow:

- **Punctuality.** Always arrive at work on time. Arriving late will not only affect your productivity but also leave the impression that you are not committed to your job.

- **Attire.** Wear a uniform if your job or organization demands it. Otherwise, wear a professional outfit. Your attire is an important factor that creates an impression about your character and professionalism.

- **Time management.** Prioritize your tasks properly and try to deliver projects before their deadlines. Never delay unless there is a justifiable reason. If you are unable to complete a task within the stipulated time, be honest in explaining the situation to your manager. Avoiding unnecessary distractions such as television, social media, phone calls, and so on during office hours can help you manage your time efficiently.

About This Chapter: "Workplace Ethics," © 2019 Omnigraphics.

- **Adaptability.** Organizations always strive to improve their processes in order to achieve better results; therefore, employees should be ready to adapt to improvements and changes. When a change occurs, consider it an opportunity to improve yourself and move ahead.

- **Team player.** Developing a good rapport with your employer, supervisors, coworkers, customers, and clients is important to being a team player. Do not complain, gossip, or talk negatively about others in your workplace. Share your ideas and resources with your peers. Secrecy will result in counterproductivity. It is also essential that you don't share confidential information with anyone other than the people who are authorized to know it.

- **Positive attitude.** Be a self-motivated go-getter. Take initiatives and try to learn things by yourself. Improve your performance and productivity through continuous learning.

- **No blame games!** Do not blame others for your mistakes. Take responsibility for your own words and deeds.

A list of work ethics for an employee might include:

- To show up on time
- To tend to company business for the whole time while at work
- To treat the company's resources, equipment, and products with care
- To give respect to the company; that means honesty and integrity

(Source: "Mastering Soft Skills for Workplace Success," U.S. Department of Labor (DOL).)

How Parents Can Help

As the first teachers of their children, parents play a vital role in emphasizing and inculcating strong ethical behaviors in their teenagers. Here are a few things that parents should and should not do when their teenagers enter into the world of work.

- Help your children to manage their time by setting alarms and assisting them with transportation.

- Talk to your children regularly about their jobs and how well they are performing.

- Do not talk poorly about your children's employers or coworkers—and do not allow your children to do so.

- Do not encourage your children to bring home office supplies from their workplace.

- Do not visit your children's workplace often. It may sometimes embarrass them.

- Do not argue with your children's supervisors.

- Encourage your children when they encounter challenging tasks, but do not interfere with the dynamics of their work. Let them face and handle difficult situations on their own.

Benefits of Workplace Ethics

If employees in an organization have ethical behaviors, then:

- there will be a healthy relationship between employees and employer

- the work environment will be trouble-free and more productive

- team coordination among the employees will improve

- the productivity and brand value of the organization will increase

- decision-making and the implementation of advanced technologies will be easier

- workplace harassment and legal issues will be minimized

References

1. Anastasia. "Work Ethic Definition and Elements of a Strong Work Ethic," Cleverism, March 19, 2016.

2. Amico, Sam. "Workplace Ethics and Behavior," Chron, June 30, 2018.

3. Loretto, Penny. "The Top 10 Work Values Employers Look For," TechnoSmarts, April 24th, 2015.

4. Reddy, Chitra. "Ethics in the Workplace: Top 10 Benefits and Importance," Wise Step, May 8, 2017.

5. McQuerrey, Lisa. "Teen Summer Jobs," Chron, August 7, 2018.

Chapter 24

Workplace Safety

Millions of teens in the United States work. Surveys indicate that 80 percent of teens have worked by the time they finish high school. While work provides numerous benefits for young people, it can also be dangerous. Every year, approximately 53,000 youth are injured on the job seriously enough to seek emergency room treatment. In fact, teens are injured at a higher rate than adult workers.

As new workers, adolescents are likely to be inexperienced and unfamiliar with many of the tasks required of them. Yet despite teen workers' high job injury rates, safety at work is usually one of the last things they worry about. Many of the teens' most positive traits—energy, enthusiasm, and a need for increased challenge and responsibility—can result in their taking on tasks they are not prepared to do safely. They may also be reluctant to ask questions or make demands on their employers.

Health and safety education is an important component of injury prevention for working teens. While workplace-specific training is most critical, young people also need the opportunity to learn and practice general health and safety skills that they will carry with them from job to job. Teens should be able to recognize hazards in any workplace. They should understand how hazards can be controlled, what to do in an emergency, what rights they have on the job, and how to speak up effectively when problems arise at work.

School and community-based programs that place youth in jobs offer an important venue for teaching these skills. One national program that recognizes the importance of including

About This Chapter: Text in this chapter begins with excerpts from "Talking Safety: Teaching Young Workers about Job Safety and Health," Centers for Disease Control and Prevention (CDC), 2010; Text beginning with the heading "Safe Work for Young Workers" is excerpted from "Safe Work for Young Workers," Occupational Safety and Health Administration (OSHA), May 10, 2012.

these skills as part of the educational experience is the Career Cluster Initiative, developed by the U.S. Department of Education (ED) Office of Vocational and Adult Education (OVAE) and implemented in a number of states. OVAE identified 16 career clusters that include the major job opportunities in today's workforce. Examples of clusters are finance, architecture and construction, and health science. Each cluster has a curriculum framework and a set of core knowledge and skills students should master, which includes workplace health and safety.

Three U.S. Department of Labor (DOL) agencies have responsibility for the administration and enforcement of the laws enacted to protect the safety and health of workers in America.

- **Occupational Safety and Health Administration: (OSHA)**
  - OSHA administers the Occupational Safety and Health (OSH) Act.
  - Safety and health conditions in most private industries are regulated by OSHA or OSHA-approved state plans.
  - Nearly every employee in the nation comes under OSHA's jurisdiction with some exceptions such as miners, some transportation workers, many public employees, and the self-employed.
  - Employers subject to the OSH Act also have a general duty to provide work and a workplace free from recognized, serious hazards.
  - OSHA also administers the Whistleblower Protection program, ensuring an employer cannot retaliate by taking "adverse action" against workers who report injuries, safety concerns, or other protected activity.

- **Mine Safety and Health Administration (MSHA)**
  - DOL's MSHA has responsibility for administration and enforcement of the Mine Safety and Health Act of 1977, which protects the safety and health of workers employed in the nation's mines.
  - The Act applies to all mining and mineral processing operations in the United States, regardless of size, number of employees, or method of extraction.

- **The Fair Labor Standards Act (FLSA)**
  - FLSA contains rules concerning the employment of young workers, those under the age of 18, and is administered and enforced by DOL's Wage and Hour Division. Intended to protect the health and well-being of youth in America, the FLSA contains minimum age restrictions for employment, restrictions on the times of day youth may work, and the jobs they may perform.

- **Other resources**
  - Office of Workers' Compensation Programs—Administers four major disability compensation programs which provide wage replacement benefits, medical treatment,

vocational rehabilitation and other benefits to certain workers or their dependents who experience work-related injury or occupational disease. You can also read more at the workers' compensation topic page.

- Office of the Ombudsman for the Energy Employees Occupational Illness Compensation Program (EEOMBD) and the SHARE initiative also play a role in the administration of DOL workplace safety and health programs.

(Source: "Workplace Safety and Health," U.S. Department of Labor (DOL).)

Safe Work for Young Workers

Safe work is rewarding work. Your employer has the responsibility to provide a safe workplace. Employers must follow all Occupational Safety and Health Administration (OSHA) safety and health standards to prevent you from being injured or becoming ill on the job. If you are under age 18, there may be limits on the hours you work, the jobs you do and the equipment you use.

You Have Rights at Work

You have the right to:

- Work in a safe place

- Receive safety and health training in a language that you understand

- Ask questions if you don't understand instructions or if something seems unsafe

- Use and be trained on required safety gear, such as hard hats, goggles, and earplugs

- Exercise your workplace safety rights without retaliation or discrimination

- File a confidential complaint with OSHA if you believe there is a serious hazard or that your employer is not following OSHA standards

Your Employer Has Responsibilities

Your employer must:

- Provide a workplace free from serious recognized hazards and follow all OSHA safety and health standards

- Provide training about workplace hazards and required safety gear*
- Tell you where to get answers to your safety or health questions
- Tell you what to do if you get hurt on the job

Employers must pay for most types of safety gear.

Ways to Stay Safe on the Job

To help protect yourself, you can:

- Report unsafe conditions to a shift/team leader or supervisor
- Wear any safety gear required to do your job
- Follow the safety rules
- Ask questions
- Ask for help if needed

Hazards

Young workers get injured or sick on the job for many reasons, including:

- Unsafe equipment
- Inadequate safety training
- Inadequate supervision
- Dangerous work that is illegal or inappropriate for youth under 18
- Pressure to work faster
- Stressful conditions

Workplace hazards associated with specific jobs are another major cause of injuries and illnesses. Employers must work to reduce or minimize hazards in the workplace and train employees how to work safely on the job.

Workplace Hazards
Retail/Grocery Stores/Convenience Stores

- Equipment and machinery

- Heavy lifting
- Violent crime
- Repetitive hand motion
- Slippery floors

Food Service/Fast Food

- Sharp objects
- Hot cooking equipment
- Slippery floors
- Electricity
- Heavy lifting
- Violent crime

Janitorial/Cleanup/Maintenance

- Hazardous chemicals
- Slippery floors
- Heavy lifting
- Blood on discarded needles
- Electricity
- Vehicles

Office/Clerical

- Repetitive hand motion (computer work)
- Back and neck strain
- Stress

Outdoor Work

- Exposure to the sun
- Heat

- Landscaping
- Pesticides and chemicals
- Machinery and vehicles
- Electricity
- Heavy lifting
- Noise

Construction

- Falls
- Machines and tools
- Hazardous materials
- Confined space
- Electricity
- Struck-by
- Vehicle back-over
- Noise

Industry

- Moving equipment
- Hot equipment
- Hazardous chemicals
- Electricity
- Heat
- Noise

Agriculture

Child labor laws apply to agricultural workers under 16 years of age.

- Machinery

144

- Struck-by

- Falls

- Electricity

- Confined space

- Hazardous chemicals

- Organic dust (e.g., grain)

- Heat

Chapter 25

Workers' Rights

Worker Protection Is the Law of the Land

You have the right to a safe workplace. The Occupational Safety and Health Act of 1970 (OSH Act) was passed to prevent workers from being killed or otherwise harmed at work. The law requires employers to provide their employees with working conditions that are free of known dangers. The OSH Act created the Occupational Safety and Health Administration (OSHA), which sets and enforces protective workplace safety and health standards. OSHA also provides information, training, and assistance to employers and workers.

Workers' Rights under the OSH Act

The OSH Act gives workers the right to safe and healthful working conditions. It is the duty of employers to provide workplaces that are free of known dangers that could harm their employees. This law also gives workers important rights to participate in activities to ensure their protection from job hazards. This chapter explains workers' rights to:

- File a confidential complaint with OSHA to have their workplace inspected

- Receive information and training about hazards, methods to prevent harm, and the OSHA standards that apply to their workplace. The training must be done in a language and vocabulary workers can understand.

- Review records of work-related injuries and illnesses that occur in their workplace

About This Chapter: This chapter includes text excerpted from "Workers' Rights," Occupational Safety and Health Administration (OSHA), October 15, 2011.

- Receive copies of the results from tests and monitoring done to find and measure hazards in the workplace

- Get copies of their workplace medical records

- Participate in an OSHA inspection and speak in private with the inspector

- File a complaint with OSHA if they have been retaliated against by their employer as the result of requesting an inspection or using any of their other rights under the OSH Act

- File a complaint if punished or retaliated against for acting as a "whistleblower" under the additional 21 federal statutes for which OSHA has jurisdiction

A job must be safe or it cannot be called a good job. OSHA strives to make sure that every worker in the nation goes home unharmed at the end of the workday, the most important right of all.

Who Does OSHA Cover?
Private Sector Workers

Most employees in the nation come under OSHA's jurisdiction. OSHA covers most private sector employers and employees in all 50 states, the District of Columbia, and other U.S. jurisdictions either directly through federal OSHA or through an OSHA approved state plan. State-run health and safety plans must be at least as effective as the federal OSHA program. To find the contact information for the OSHA Federal or State Program office nearest you, call 800-321-OSHA (800-321-6742) or go to www.osha.gov.

State and Local Government Workers

Employees who work for state and local governments are not covered by federal OSHA, but have OSH Act protections if they work in those states that have an OSHA-approved state plan. The following 22 states or territories have OSHA-approved programs:

- Alaska
- Arizona
- California
- Hawaii
- Indiana

- Iowa
- Kentucky
- Maryland
- Michigan
- Minnesota
- Nevada
- New Mexico
- North Carolina
- Oregon
- South Carolina
- Tennessee
- Utah
- Vermont
- Virginia
- Washington
- Wyoming
- Puerto Rico

Five additional states and one U.S. territory have OSHA-approved plans that cover public sector workers only:

- Connecticut
- Illinois
- Maine
- New Jersey
- New York
- Virgin Islands

Private sector workers in these five states and the Virgin Islands are covered by federal OSHA.

Federal Government Workers

Federal agencies must have a safety and health program that meets the same standards as private employers. Although OSHA does not fine federal agencies, it does monitor federal agencies and responds to workers' complaints. The United States Postal Service (USPS) is covered by OSHA.

Not Covered under the OSH Act

- Self-employed

- Immediate family members of farm employers

- Workplace hazards regulated by another federal agency (for example, the Mine Safety and Health Administration (MSHA), the U.S. Department of Energy (DOE), or U.S. Coast Guard (USCG)).

Worker Rights in State-Plan States

States that assume responsibility for their own occupational safety and health programs must have provisions at least as effective as Federal OSHA's, including the protection of worker rights.

Any interested person or group, including employees, with a complaint concerning the operation or administration of a state program may submit a complaint to the appropriate Federal OSHA regional administrator. This is called a Complaint About State Program Administration (CASPA). The complainant's name will be kept confidential. The OSHA regional administrator will investigate all such complaints, and where complaints are found to be valid, require appropriate corrective action on the part of the state.

Right to a Safe and Healthful Workplace
Employers' "General Duty"

Employers have the responsibility to provide a safe and healthful workplace that is free from serious recognized hazards. This is commonly known as the General Duty Clause of the OSH Act.

OSHA Standards: Protection on the Job

OSHA standards are rules that describe the methods that employers must use to protect their employees from hazards. There are four groups of OSHA standards: General Industry,

Construction, Maritime, and Agriculture. (General Industry is the set that applies to the largest number of workers and worksites). These standards are designed to protect workers from a wide range of hazards. These standards also limit the amount of hazardous chemicals, substances, or noise that workers can be exposed to; require the use of certain safe work practices and equipment; and require employers to monitor certain hazards and keep records of workplace injuries and illnesses.

Examples of OSHA standards include requirements to:

- Provide fall protection, such as a safety harness and lifeline

- Prevent trenching cave-ins

- Ensure the safety of workers who enter confined spaces such as manholes or grain bins

- Prevent exposure to high levels of noise that can damage hearing

- Put guards on machines

- Prevent exposure to harmful levels of substances like asbestos and lead

- Provide workers with respirators and other needed safety equipment (in almost all cases, free of charge)

- Provide healthcare workers with needles and sharp instruments that have built-in safety features to prevent skin punctures or cuts that could cause exposure to infectious diseases

- Train workers using a language and vocabulary they understand about hazards and how to protect themselves

Employers must also comply with the General Duty Clause of the OSH Act. This clause requires employers to keep their workplaces free of serious recognized hazards and is generally cited when no specific OSHA standard applies to the hazard.

Right to Be Provided Protective Equipment Free of Charge

In some situations, it is not possible to completely eliminate a hazard or reduce exposures to a safe level, so respirators, goggles, earplugs, gloves, or other types of personal protective equipment are often used by themselves or in addition to other hazard control measures. Employers must provide the most protective equipment free of charge. Employers are responsible for knowing when protective equipment is needed.

Right to Information

OSHA gives workers and their representatives the right to see information that employers collect on hazards in the workplace. Workers have the right to know what hazards are present in the workplace and how to protect themselves. Many OSHA standards require various methods that employers must use to inform their employees, such as warning signs, color-coding, signals, and training. Workers must receive their normal rate of pay to attend training that is required by OSHA standards and rules. The training must be in a language and vocabulary that workers can understand.

Right to Know about Chemical Hazards

The Hazard Communication Standard (HCS), known as the "right-to-know" standard, requires employers to inform and train workers about hazardous chemicals and substances in the workplace. Employers must:

- Provide workers with effective information and training on hazardous chemicals in their work area;

- This training must be in a language and vocabulary that workers can understand;

- Keep a current list of hazardous chemicals that are in the workplace;

- Make sure that hazardous chemical containers are properly labeled with the identity of the hazardous chemical and appropriate hazard warnings; and

- Have and make available to workers and their representatives Safety Data Sheets (SDSs) (formerly known as Material Safety Data Sheets or MSDSs) for each substance that provides detailed information about chemical hazards, their effects, how to prevent exposure, and emergency treatment if an exposure occurs.

Right to Know about Laws and Your Rights

Employers must display the official OSHA Poster, *Job Safety and Health: It's the Law*, in a place where workers will see it. It can be downloaded from the OSHA website, www.osha.gov. Preprinted copies can also be obtained from OSHA.

Right to Get Copies of Workplace Injury and Illness Records

OSHA's Recordkeeping Rule requires employers in higher-hazard industries with more than ten employees to keep accurate and complete records of work-related injuries and illnesses.

(Certain low-hazard workplaces such as offices are not required to keep such records). Employers must record any serious work-related injury or illness on the OSHA Form 300. A serious injury or illness is one that required medical treatment other than first aid, restricted work or days away from work. (Details of each incident are entered on a separate form, the OSHA Form 301). This OSHA Form 300 becomes an ongoing log of all recordable incidents. Each year from February 1 through April 30, employers must post a summary of the injury and illness log from the previous year (OSHA Form 300A) in a place where workers can see it. Workers and their representatives have the right to receive copies of the full OSHA Form 300 log. Following a request, employers must make copies available at the end of the next business day.

These injury and illness logs are important because they provide a comprehensive guide to possible hazards in the workplace that may need correcting. The logs should be used to focus on areas with high injury and illness rates, and to find and fix hazards in order to prevent future occurrences.

Right to Exposure Data

Many OSHA standards require employers to run tests of the workplace environment to find out if their workers are being exposed to harmful levels of hazardous substances such as lead or asbestos, or high levels of noise or radiation. These types of tests are called exposure monitoring. OSHA gives workers the right to get the results of these tests.

Right to Your Medical Records

Some OSHA standards require medical tests to find out if a worker's health has been affected because of exposures at work. For example, employers must test for hearing loss in workers exposed to excessive noise or for decreased lung function in workers exposed to asbestos. Workers have a right to their medical records. Workers' representatives also have a right to review these records but they must first get written permission from the worker to gain access to their medical information.

OSHA Worksite Investigations

OSHA conducts on-site inspections of worksites to enforce the OSHA law that protects workers and their rights. Inspections are initiated without advance notice, conducted using on-site or telephone and facsimile investigations, and performed by highly trained compliance officers. Worksite inspections are conducted based on the following priorities:

- Imminent danger

- A fatality or hospitalizations

- Worker complaints and referrals

- Targeted inspections—particular hazards, high injury rates

- Follow-up inspections

Inspections are conducted without employers knowing when or where they will occur. The employer is not informed in advance that there will be an inspection, regardless of whether it is in response to a complaint or is a programmed inspection.

Right to File a Complaint with OSHA to Request an On-Site OSHA Inspection

On-site inspections can be triggered by a worker complaint of a potential workplace hazard or violation. If your workplace has unsafe or unhealthful working conditions, you may want to file a complaint. Often the best and fastest way to get a hazard corrected is to notify your supervisor or employer. Current workers or their representatives may file a written complaint and ask OSHA to inspect their workplace if they believe there is a serious hazard or that their employer is not following OSHA standards or rules. Workers and their representatives have the right to ask for an inspection without OSHA telling their employer who filed the complaint. It is a violation of the OSH Act for an employer to fire, demote, transfer or retaliate in any way against a worker for filing a complaint or using other OSHA rights.

A complaint can be filed in a number of ways:

1. Mail or submit the OSHA Complaint Form—Download the OSHA complaint form from the website (or request a copy from your local OSHA regional or area office), complete it and then fax or mail it back to your nearest OSHA regional or area office. Written complaints that report a serious hazard and are signed by a current worker or representative and submitted to the closest OSHA area office are given priority and are more likely to result in onsite OSHA inspections. A worker or their representative can request (on the form) that OSHA not let their employer know who filed the complaint. Please include your name, address and telephone number so OSHA can contact you to follow up. This information is confidential.

2. Online—Go to the online Complaint Form on the OSHA website, at www.osha.gov/pls/osha7/eComplaintForm.html. Complaints that are sent in online will most likely be investigated using OSHA's phone/fax system whereby the employer is contacted by phone or fax (not an actual inspection) about the hazard. A written complaint that

reports a serious hazard and is signed by a current worker(s) or their representative and mailed or otherwise submitted to an OSHA area or regional office is more likely to result in an on-site OSHA inspection. Complaints received online from workers in OSHA-approved state plan states will be forwarded to the appropriate state plan for response.

3. Telephone—Call your local OSHA regional or area office at 800-321-OSHA (800-321-6742). OSHA staff can discuss your complaint and respond to any questions you have. If there is an emergency or the hazard is immediately life-threatening, call your local OSHA regional or area office.

Who Else Can File a Complaint?

Employee representatives, for the purposes of filing a complaint, are defined as any of the following:

- An authorized representative of the employee bargaining unit, such as a certified or recognized labor organization.

- An attorney acting for an employee.

- Any other person acting in a bona fide representative capacity, including, but not limited to, members of the clergy, social workers, spouses, and other family members, healthcare providers and government officials or nonprofit groups and organizations acting upon specific complaints or injuries from individuals who are employees. In general, the affected employee should have requested, or at least approved, the filing of the complaint on his or her behalf.

- In addition, anyone who knows about a workplace safety or health hazard may report unsafe conditions to OSHA, and OSHA will investigate the concerns reported.

Rights of Workers during an Inspection

During an inspection, workers or their representatives have the following rights:

- Have a representative of employees, such as the safety steward of a labor organization, go along on the inspection;

- Talk privately with the inspector; and

- Take part in meetings with the inspector before and after the inspection.

155

When there is no authorized employee representative, the OSHA inspector must talk confidentially with a reasonable number of workers during the inspection. Workers are encouraged to:

- Point out hazards

- Describe injuries or illnesses that resulted from these hazards

- Discuss past worker complaints about hazards

- Inform the inspector of working conditions that are not normal during the inspection

Following the Inspection

At the end of the inspection, the OSHA inspector will meet with the employer and the employee representatives in a closing conference to discuss any violations found and possible methods by which any hazards found will be abated. If it is not practical to hold a joint conference, the compliance officer will hold separate conferences.

When the OSHA area director determines that there has been a violation of OSHA standards, regulations, or other requirements, the area director issues a citation and notification of proposed penalty to an employer. A citation includes a description of the violation and the date by when the corrective actions must be taken. Depending on the situation, OSHA can classify a violation as serious, willful, or repeat. The employer can also be cited for failing to correct a violation for which it has already been cited. Employers must post a copy of a citation in the workplace where employees will see it.

Workers' Rights Following Issuance of Citations

Workers and employers can contest citations once they are issued to the employer. Workers may only contest the amount of time the employer is given to correct the hazard. Workers or their representatives must file a notice of contest with the OSHA area office within 15 days of the issuance of a citation.

Employers have the right to challenge whether there is a violation, how the violation is classified, the amount of any penalty, what the employer must do to correct the violation and how long they have to fix it. Workers or their representatives may participate in this appeals process by electing "party status." This is done by filing a written notice with the Occupational Safety and Health Review Commission (OSHRC). The OSHRC hears appeals of OSHA citations. They are an independent agency separate from the U.S. Department of Labor (DOL).

For more information, write to:

U.S. Occupational Safety and Health (OSHA)
Review Commission
1120 20th St. N.W. Ninth Fl.
Washington, DC 20036
Phone: 202-606-5400
Fax: 202-606-5050
Website: www.oshrc.gov

Right to Information If No Inspection Is Conducted or No Citation Issued

The OSHA area director evaluates complaints from employees or their representatives according to the procedures defined in the OSHA Field Operations Manual. If the area director decides not to inspect the workplace, she or he will send a letter to the complainant explaining the decision and the reasons for it. OSHA will inform complainants that they have the right to request a review of the decision by the OSHA regional administrator. Similarly, in the event that OSHA decides not to issue a citation after an inspection, employees have a right to further clarification from the area director and an informal review by the regional administrator.

Right to Use Your Rights: Protection against Retaliation Whistleblower Protection

The OSH Act prohibits employers from retaliating against their employees for using their rights under the OSH Act. These rights include filing an OSHA complaint, participating in an inspection or talking to the inspector, seeking access to employee exposure and injury records, raising a safety or health issue with the employer, or any other workers' rights described above.

Protection from retaliation means that an employer cannot punish workers by taking "adverse action," such as:

- Firing or laying off
- Blacklisting
- Demoting
- Denying overtime or promotion

- Disciplining

- Denying benefits

- Failing to hire or rehire

- Intimidation

- Making threats

- Reassignment affecting prospects for promotion

- Reducing pay or hours

You can file a complaint alleging retaliation with OSHA if your employer has punished you for using any employee rights established under the OSH Act. If you have been retaliated against for using your rights, you must file a complaint with OSHA within 30 calendar days from the date the retaliatory decision has been both made and communicated to you (the worker). Contact your local OSHA office by calling, within 30 days of the alleged retaliation, 800-321-OSHA (800-321-6742), or send a letter to your closest regional or area office. No form is required. In states with approved state plans, employees may file a complaint with both the State and Federal OSHA.

Following a complaint, OSHA will contact the complainant and conduct an interview to determine whether an investigation is necessary.

If the evidence shows that the employee has been retaliated against for exercising safety and health rights, OSHA will ask the employer to restore that worker's job, earnings, and benefits. If the employer refuses, OSHA may take the employer to court. In such cases, a U.S. Department of Labor (DOL) attorney will represent the employee to obtain this relief.

If There Is a Dangerous Situation at Work

If you believe working conditions are unsafe or unhealthful, it's recommended that you bring the conditions to your employer's attention, if possible. You may file a complaint with OSHA concerning a hazardous working condition at any time. However, you should not leave the worksite merely because you have filed a complaint. If the condition clearly presents a risk of death or serious physical harm, there is not sufficient time for OSHA to inspect, and, where possible, you have brought the condition to the attention of your employer, you may have a legal right to refuse to work in a situation in which you would be exposed to the hazard. If a worker, with no reasonable alternative, refuses in good faith to expose himself or herself to a dangerous condition, she or he would be protected from subsequent retaliation. The condition must be of such a nature that a reasonable person would conclude that there is a real danger of death or serious harm and that there is not enough time to contact OSHA and for OSHA to inspect. Where possible, the employee must have also sought from his employer, and been unable to obtain, a correction of the condition.

Chapter 26

Workplace Stress

The last months of the year are when we all may feel a little more stress due to the demands of the holidays. Unfortunately, stress at work can be a year-round issue further exacerbated during these months.

Work organization and job stress are topics of growing concern in the occupational safety and health field and at National Institute for Occupational Safety and Health (NIOSH). The expressions "work organization" or "organization of work" refer to the nature of the work process (the way jobs are designed and performed) and to the organizational practices (e.g., management and production methods and accompanying human resource policies) that influence the design of jobs.

Job stress results when there is a poor match between job demands and the capabilities, resources, or needs of workers. Stress-related disorders encompass a broad array of conditions, including psychological disorders (e.g., depression, anxiety, posttraumatic stress disorder (PTSD)) and other types of emotional strain (e.g., dissatisfaction, fatigue, tension), maladaptive behaviors (e.g., aggression, substance abuse), and cognitive impairment (e.g., concentration and memory problems). In turn, these conditions may lead to poor work performance or even injury. Job stress is also associated with various biological reactions that may lead ultimately to compromised health, such as cardiovascular disease (CVD).

Stress is a prevalent and costly problem in today's workplace. About one-third of workers report high levels of stress, and high levels of stress are associated with substantial increases in

About This Chapter: Text in this chapter begins with excerpts from "Workplace Stress," Centers for Disease Control and Prevention (CDC), November 23, 2016; Text beginning with the heading "What's the Problem?" is excerpted from "Stress at Work," Centers for Disease Control and Prevention (CDC), September 15, 2017.

health service utilization (HSU). Additionally, periods of disability due to job stress tend to be much longer than disability periods for other occupational injuries and illnesses. Evidence also suggests that stress is the major cause of turnover in organizations.

Attention to stress at work has intensified in the wake of sweeping changes in the organization of work. Organizational downsizing and restructuring, dependence on temporary and contractor-supplied labor, and adoption of lean production practices are examples of trends that may adversely influence aspects of job design (e.g., work schedules, workload demands, job security) that are associated with the risk of job stress.

There is also growing appreciation that work organization can have broader implications for the safety and health of workers—not just for stress-related outcomes. For example, long hours of work may increase exposures to chemical and physical hazards in the workplace, or night shifts may expose workers to a heightened risk of violence.

The good news is that there are steps organizations can take to reduce job stress. As a general rule, actions to reduce job stress should give top priority to organizational change to improve working conditions. But even the most conscientious efforts to improve working conditions are unlikely to eliminate stress completely for all workers. For this reason, a combination of organizational change and stress management is often the most useful approach for preventing stress at work. The best design for a stress prevention program will be influenced by several factors—the size and complexity of the organization, available resources, and especially the unique types of stress problems faced by the organization.

Case Example

Theresa is a contract worker in the customer service department of a large company. She is always on the phone because the computer continuously routes calls to her; she never has a moment to herself. She even needs to schedule her bathroom breaks. All day long she listens to complaints from unhappy customers. She tries to be helpful but she can't promise anything without getting her boss's approval. She often feels caught between what the customer wants and company policy. To make matters worse, Theresa's mother's health is deteriorating and she can't even take time off to look after her. Theresa also has health problems of her own, and attributes migraine headaches and high blood pressure to stress at work. Because she is a contract worker, Theresa doesn't have benefits, and has to work a second stressful job to get health insurance. She finally sees her doctor, who recommends she take an extended leave because she is at risk for a possible heart attack, but Theresa doesn't have enough sick leave and can't afford to have her income reduced.

What's the Problem?

The ways that work processes are structured and managed, called "work organization," can directly heighten or alleviate workers' on-the-job stress. Studies suggest that work organization also may have a broad influence on worker safety and health, and may contribute to occupational injury, work-related musculoskeletal disorders (MSDs), cardiovascular disease, and even may intensify other occupational health concerns (such as complaints about indoor air quality (IAQ)).

Who's at Risk?

One-fourth to one-third of U.S. workers report high levels of stress at work. Americans spend eight percent more time on the job than they did 20 years ago (47 hours per week on average), and 13 percent also work a second job. Two-fifths (40%) of workers say that their jobs are very stressful, and more than one-fourth (26%) say they are "often burned out or stressed" by their work.

Not all stress is bad. But chronic (ongoing) stress can lead to health problems. Preventing and managing chronic stress can lower your risk for serious conditions like heart disease, obesity, high blood pressure, and depression.

You can prevent or reduce stress by:

- Planning ahead
- Deciding which tasks need to be done first
- Preparing for stressful events

Some stress is hard to avoid. You can find ways to manage stress by:

- Noticing when you feel stressed
- Taking time to relax
- Getting active and eating healthy
- Talking to friends and family

(Source: "Manage Stress," Office of Disease Prevention and Health Promotion (ODPHP), U.S. Department of Health and Human Services (HHS).)

Can It Be Prevented?

Yes. As widespread corporate and government restructuring continues to have an effect on workers in today's rapidly changing economy, it is important to recognize that stress does not have to be 'just part of the job.' Work stress can be prevented through changes in the work organization and the use of stress management, with an emphasis on work organization changes as a primary step.

The Bottom Line

Work-related stress is a real problem that can negatively impact health and safety. Identifying stressful aspects of work can help in devising strategies for reducing or eliminating workplace stress. Some strategies include:

- Clearly defining worker roles and responsibilities

- Improving communication

- Making sure workers participate in decisions about their jobs

Chapter 27

Work–Life Balance

Work–life balance is a familiar concept in the adult world, but is rarely associated with teens. Teens also experience tremendous pressure and must juggle various activities—such as sports, their studies, extracurricular activities, and part-time jobs—however. Although teens spend the majority of their time studying, their part-time jobs can be quite demanding. And, since most teens are working for the first time, it may take them a while to gain a solid understanding of the world of work. Managing all of these activities at the same time can be overwhelming and stressful for teenagers, but establishing work–life balance can enable teens to socialize, focus on their studies, participate in a sport, pursue a hobby, and work a part-time job without getting overworked. This chapter explores the ways in which teens can have a good work–life balance.

How Do I Balance a Job and School?

For some students, working while in college is a necessity; for others, it is a way to build a résumé or earn extra money for luxuries. Whatever the reason, it's important to know the pros and cons of working while you're attending school.

If you have a job, determine how many hours a week you'll be able to work and still be able to stay on track with school demands. For example, if you want to earn more money and potentially reduce your need for student loans (or reduce the amount that you borrow), then you could consider working more hours. Managing a schedule with limited free time is an excellent way to prepare for your future. But remember, you may also need to take fewer classes to accommodate your work schedule. Keep in mind that part-time enrollment will delay your graduation, postpone your ability to earn a higher income, and possibly impact your eligibility for some federal aid. Tuition and fees may also be higher for part-time enrollment.

About This Chapter: "Work–Life Balance," © 2019 Omnigraphics.

You may opt to work fewer hours and maximize the benefit of your student loans by taking a heavier class load instead of the minimum requirements. By taking extra classes, you may be able to graduate earlier. Alternatively, you may find that taking classes during the summer leaves you better able to balance work and school during the academic year and still stay on track to graduate on time. Keep in mind that the longer it takes to complete your program of study, the more you will pay in total.

(Source: "Budgeting," Federal Student Aid, U.S. Department of Education (ED).)

Ways of Achieving Good Work–Life Balance
Realistic Goal Setting

Goal setting is important for anyone who wants to manage her or his resources wisely and be successful. When teens set goals early stages in life, they are better equipped to meet life's challenges and plan for their future. Goal setting enables them to gain insight into where they are headed. Some teens tend to overthink, however, and may plan too many things at the same time—a recipe for failure. This could result in activities becoming taxing and life feeling hectic, which in turn can make them lose interest in achieving some goals. Setting practical goals that can be achieved in a week, two weeks, and a month will help teens keep momentum while not making them too weary or overwhelmed.

Choosing the Right Career

Choosing our career is one of the most important decisions we make, and college-bound teenagers may find this decision particularly difficult when they are asked to decide before they even begin college. The courses available to teens, the scope of available subject matter, a teen's particular interests, available job opportunities, and many other factors help determine a teen's career choice. However, if a wrong field is chosen without taking into consideration their talents, the areas in which they are gifted, and their interests, then a lot of time and energy can be wasted in unproductive work and they may still struggle to find fulfillment in their career. Finding a career that genuinely interests a teen and suits her or him is tremendously beneficial, however, and will enable the teen to develop a life they can balance with engaging extracurricular activities.

Acknowledging Feelings

When teens are actively involved in many activities, their lives can feel really busy, and too much involvement can lead to stress and a sense of being overwhelmed. Acknowledging our feelings around such particular activities is a vital step in maintaining our work–life balance. If an activity feels overwhelming and no longer holds your interest, then dropping out of the activity would be beneficial, while continuing to pursue it could cause more harm than good.

Relaxation Time

Any learning activity requires lot of attention and focus, and it can drain our energy. Hence, teens who are involved in various learning activities should take the time to just relax and rest. During our teen years, we are generally very active and do not think that downtime is needed, but taking breaks and relaxing can do a world of good for a teen. When rest and relaxation become a part of our daily, weekly, and monthly routine, we achieve work–life balance.

Some relaxation activities include:

- Reading any interesting book
- Riding a bike
- Visiting a friend
- Taking a walk, etc.

Part-Time Jobs

Part-time jobs can take a toll on teenager, and employers may demand more hours of work. Statistics prove that teens who work part-time earn lower grades. A part-time job, however, teaches financial responsibility, provides experience and exposure, and enables teens to develop a deeper sense of self-worth. Balancing both work and studies is the challenge. Managing time and being resourceful is the key to work–life balance.

References

1. "Life Balance," Sutter Health Palo Alto Medical Foundation, February 5, 2005.

2. Marcus, Lilit. "Work-Life Balance Matters, Even (and Especially!) for Your First Job," April 30, 2014.

3. "The Great Teen Balancing Act: Sleep, Sport, Social Life, Study and, Part Time Jobs," Developing Minds, March 26, 2013.

4. "Work–Life Balance for Teens," Maine Teen Camp, January 23, 2011.

Part Four
Managing Your Earnings

Chapter 28

MyMoney Five

Making the most of your money starts with five building blocks for managing and growing your money—The MyMoney Five. Keep these five principles in mind as you make day-to-day decisions and plan your financial goals.

The Five Principles

- **Earn**—Make the most of what you earn by understanding your pay and benefits.

- **Save and invest**—It's never too early to start saving for future goals such as a house or retirement, even by saving small amounts.

- **Protect**—Take precautions about your financial situation, accumulate emergency savings, and have the right insurance.

- **Spend**—Be sure you are getting a good value, especially with big purchases, by shopping around and comparing prices and products.

- **Borrow**—Borrowing money can enable some essential purchases and builds credit, but interest costs can be expenses. And, if you borrow too much, you will have a large debt to repay.

Earn

The Earn principle is about more than the amount you are paid through work. This principle is about knowing the fine print and details about your paycheck, including deductions

About This Chapter: This chapter includes text excerpted from "My Money Five," MyMoney.gov, Financial Literacy and Education Commission (FLEC), May 31, 2013.

and withholdings. To put it another way: In order to make the most of what you earn, it helps to understand your pay and benefits.

Actions You Can Take

- Learn about the details of your paycheck, including any deductions.

- Review the taxes that are withheld, including Social Security and Medicare taxes.

- Explore and sign up for workplace benefits.

- Invest in your future—with education and training.

Hints and Tips

- Remember, your employer has to subtract certain taxes and other items from your wages every pay period. Your take-home pay (net income) is what you receive after any taxes and deductions are subtracted.

- Usually, your deductions and withholdings include federal, state and city income taxes, Social Security and Medicare taxes, your contributions for retirement savings, and payments for health insurance provided as part of your job.

- Be sure you take advantage of all the credits and deductions that help lower your taxes.

- It's a good idea to sign up if your employer offers a retirement savings program. If so, you can arrange to have retirement savings automatically moved from your paycheck to a retirement account. Many employers will match part of every dollar you save this way, and you will benefit from it when you retire.

Save and Invest

Saving is a key principle. People who make a habit of saving regularly, even saving small amounts, are well on their way to success. It's important to open a bank or credit union account so it will be simple and easy for you to save regularly. Then, use your savings to plan for life events and to be ready for unplanned or emergency needs.

Actions You Can Take

- Open and keep an account at a bank or credit union that meets your needs.

- Start saving, form a savings habit, and pay yourself first!

- Track your savings and investments, and monitor what you own.

- Plan for short- and long-term goals.

- Build up emergency savings for unexpected events.

- Consult with a qualified professional on investments, and other key financial matters.

- Save for retirement, children's education, and other major items.

Hints and Tips

- An easy way to save is to pay yourself first. This means that, each pay period, before you are tempted to spend money, commit to putting some in a savings account. See if you can arrange with your bank to automatically transfer a certain amount from your paycheck or your checking account to savings every month.

- People who keep track of their savings often end up saving more, because they have it on their minds. New phone apps are available to help people pass up purchases they don't really need—you might want to try one!

- If you are making investments, it's good to consult with a qualified professional about your plans. Before you purchase investments, be sure to build an emergency savings fund to cover your needs for at least three months. Keep the savings in an insured bank or credit union account that you can access if you need it.

- Many professionals call themselves "financial planners." Before you hire one, ask for a description of the services offered. A good place to check the credentials of an investment advisor is your state's consumer protection office, the state's Attorney General's office, or the issuing agency for any professional licenses or certifications.

Protect

The Protect principle means taking precautions about your financial situation. It stresses the importance of accumulating savings in case of an emergency, and buying insurance. Be vigilant about identity theft, and keep aware of your credit record and credit score.

Actions You Can Take

- Keep your financial records in order.

- Watch out for fraud and scams, and protect your identity.

- Choose insurance to meet your needs, including healthcare insurance.

Hints and Tips

- A good system for keeping personal money records will include copies of important documents like your will, property ownership documents, information about savings and insurance, and other important documents. Your will should include an overview of what happens to property after a major life event occurs.

- Assume that any offer that "sounds too good to be true"—especially one from a stranger or an unfamiliar company—is probably a fraud.

- Look at your bank statements and bills as soon as they arrive and report any discrepancy or anything suspicious, such as an unauthorized withdrawal or charge.

- Be wary of request to "update" or "confirm" personal information, especially your Social Security number (SSN), bank account numbers, credit card numbers, personal identification numbers, your date of birth, or your mother's maiden name in response to an unsolicited call, letter, or e-mail.

Spend

The fundamental concept of the Spend principle is to make a budget or a plan for using your money wisely. It's helpful to set short- and long-term financial goals and manage your money to meet them.

Actions You Can Take

- Live within your means.

- Be a smart shopper, and compare prices and quality.

- Track your spending habits and develop a budget or spending plan.

- Plan for short- and long-term financial goals.

Hints and Tips

- A good way to take control of your spending is to set the maximum amounts you plan to spend each week or each month. Once you've set the maximum, stick with your plan.

- It's helpful to track your spending over a few weeks or months to get a handle on how you are using your dollars and cents. Look into using online systems or phone apps for keeping track of your spending—you will be amazed at what you'll learn about your habits!

- Be careful not to let a sale or discount coupon persuade you to purchase something you don't really need and that isn't in your spending plan.

- When planning a big purchase, take time to comparison shop and check prices at a few different stores, by phone or online.

Borrow

Sometimes it's necessary to borrow for major purchases, such as an education, a car, a house, or maybe even to meet unexpected expenses. Your ability to get a loan generally depends on your credit history, and that depends largely on your track record of repaying what you've borrowed in the past and paying your bills on time. This is why it is crucial to keep your credit history strong.

Actions You Can Take

- Track your borrowing habits.

- Pay your bills on time.

- When you need to borrow, be sure to plan, understand, and shop around for a loan with a low annual percentage rate (APR).

- Learn about credit and how to use it effectively.

- Pay attention to your credit history, as reflected by your credit score and on your credit report.

Hints and Tips

- Borrowing money is a way to purchase something now and pay for it over time. But you usually pay "interest" when you borrow money. The longer you take to pay back the money you borrowed, the more you will pay in interest.

- It pays to shop around to get the best deal on a loan. Compare loan terms from several lenders, and it's okay to negotiate the terms.

- When repaying a loan, it may be better to pay more than the minimum amount due each month. This allows you to pay less in interest over the life of the loan.

- One of your most important aids when shopping for a loan is the APR—the Annual Percentage Rate. This is the total cost, including interest charges and fees, described as a yearly rate.

- Paying your bills on time will help increase your credit score. Even if you fell into trouble with borrowing in the past, you can get on solid footing and rebuild your credit history by making regular payments as agreed.

- You are entitled to a free copy of your credit report every 12 months from each of the three nationwide credit bureaus. Go to www.AnnualCreditReport.com or call toll free 877-322-8228 to order the free reports. Beware of imposter sites.

Chapter 29

Youth Financial Knowledge and Capability

Teaching financial capability is important because youth are increasingly facing higher levels of debt:

- The average debt of students when they graduated from college rose from $18,550 (in 2004) to $28,950 (in 2014), an increase of 56 percent.

- From 2004–2009, the median credit card debt among college students increased 74 percent.

Unfortunately, many youths have not received either formal or informal guidance on financial matters. So, they may not be ready to make sound financial choices:

- A survey of 15-year-olds in the United States found that 18 percent of respondents did not learn fundamental financial skills that are often applied in everyday situations, such as building a simple budget, comparison shopping, and understanding an invoice.

- A report on the results of a financial literacy exam found that high school seniors scored on average 48 percent correct, showing a strong need for more comprehensive financial education for youth in high school.

- According to the 2008 wave of the National Longitudinal Survey of Youth (NLSY), only 27 percent of youth knew what inflation was and could do simple interest rate calculations.

About This Chapter: Text in this chapter begins with excerpts from "Facts about Youth Financial Knowledge and Capability," Youth.gov, April 28, 2016; Text beginning with the heading "Four Strategies to Help Youth Achieve Financial Capability" is excerpted from "Four Strategies to Help Youth Achieve Financial Capability," Consumer Financial Protection Bureau (CFPB), September 7, 2016.

Financial illiteracy is more common among low-income individuals because they typically do not have wide access to accurate financial information. With such illiteracy, youth in low-income households can fall victim later as adults to scams, high-interest rate loans, and increasing debt. Training low-income individuals in financial management can be an effective way to improve their knowledge in five areas:

- Predatory lending practices

- Public and work-related benefits

- Banking practices

- Savings and investing strategies

- Credit use and interest rates

Young people often learn about money informally through socialization, such as observing and listening to their caregivers, influential adults, and peers. Youth are not consistently introduced to more formal instruction on money matters—for example, through a classroom curriculum or other training on saving, spending, allowances, and the importance of focusing on short-term goals (i.e., purchasing an item, saving money, paying off a debt) to be able to get to long-term financial goals (i.e., saving for college, buying a house).

Distinguishing what youth do not understand about financial topics is important. It is also beneficial to understand the specific concerns that youth have when it comes to money.

A survey of a diverse group of youth and adults regarding what they wanted to learn about finance, found that concerns among youth differed within youth groups depending on their background. The survey also found a disconnect between what adults thought youth should learn and what youth prioritized, for example:

- Pregnant or parenting teens and teens in the juvenile justice system or on probation were most concerned about learning how to save money for a home; whereas migrant teens and teens in school were most interested in learning how to save money for college.

- Almost 70 percent of adults in the survey felt that teens should learn about how to complete and file a tax return form, but only 39 percent of the teens were interested in learning about this topic.

  - However, more than half of the teens in the juvenile justice system or on probation and almost half of the migrant teens showed an interest in learning how to complete and file a tax return.

- Although a majority of teens wanted to learn about money, more than half wanted to learn in an easy way. This could include strategies that are convenient, utilize technology, and are not time-consuming for youth.

Financial capability is "the capacity, based on knowledge, skills and access, to manage financial resources effectively." Many Americans, including a large number of young people, currently experience low levels of financial capability, suffer from high levels of economic vulnerability, and encounter barriers to building economic stability. Developing financial skills is important for all young people, especially for disadvantaged youth who may have limited resources and access to financial education and services. One promising opportunity to provide information about financial capability arises when young people are participating in youth employment programs.

Developing financial skills is important to all young people. It is especially important to disadvantaged youth who may have limited resources and access to financial education and services. High school students are not very literate when it comes to financial matters.

Momentum has grown in recent years to improve youth financial literacy. Research has shown that in states where financial education is a high school graduation requirement, youth are more likely to create and adhere to a budget and less likely to engage in risky credit behaviors. Yet while financial literacy is important, financial literacy initiatives should also include opportunities for youth to build the skills they need to manage their finances; programs should provide a stronger focus on expanding access to financial services that youth can use to successfully apply their financial knowledge. Financial capability initiatives take financial education to the next level, and encourage young people to transform knowledge into behavior by coupling learning with access to financial products and services.

(Source: "Building Financial Capability in Youth Employment Programs," Administration for Children and Families (ACF), U.S. Department of Health and Human Services (HHS).)

Four Strategies to Help Youth Achieve Financial Capability

How young people can acquire the three "building blocks" of financial capability to help them effectively navigate the financial marketplace as adults.

Educators, policymakers, parents, and caregivers all have important roles to play. The report lays out four key strategies for implementing these developmental building blocks.

The building blocks are:

1. Executive function

2. Financial habits and norms

3. Financial knowledge and decision-making skills

These building blocks include critical attributes and abilities, which begin to develop in early childhood and continue throughout the teenage years and adolescence. Educators, policymakers, parents, and caregivers all have important roles to play. The chapter lays out four key strategies for implementing these developmental building blocks.

Introducing the Building Blocks

Table 29.1 describes the building blocks for financial capability, what they support in adulthood, and examples of how they apply to financial decisions that many adults face.

Table 29.1. Building Blocks for Financial Capability

	1. Executive Function	2. Financial Habits and Norms	3. Financial Knowledge and Decision-Making Skills
What it is	Self-control, working memory, problem-solving	Healthy money habits, norms, rules of thumb	Factual knowledge, research and analysis skills
What it supports in adulthood	Future orientation, perseverance, planning and goal setting, general cognitive flexibility	Decision shortcuts for navigating day-to-day financial life and effective routine money management	Deliberate financial decision-making strategies, like financial planning, research, and intentional decisions
Examples of financial application in adulthood	Saving, setting financial goals, developing and executing budgets	Having a system to pay bills on time	Effective comparison shopping

The three building blocks typically emerge over three developmental stages: early childhood (ages 3–5), middle childhood (ages 6–12), and the teen years and young adulthood (ages 13–21).

During early childhood, executive function is the most important building block for a child to develop because it supports future orientation, perseverance, and planning abilities. Children rely on these abilities when setting financial goals and developing and executing budgets when they're older.

During middle childhood, children begin to develop financial habits and norms, which they typically acquire through observation of their parents and peers. At this stage, children begin to gain a sense of what is normal or appropriate regarding spending, saving, and other financial matters. Financial habits and norms shape the decision shortcuts that they will go on to use with routine financial choices.

During adolescence, teens begin to have more direct experiences with the financial world (for example, working at a first job or buying a car) and, therefore, improve their financial knowledge and decision-making skills. During this developmental stage, financial education experiences or programs should help teens improve their financial knowledge as well as research and analysis skills.

Strategies

To help program leaders, financial educators, policymakers, and other stakeholders apply the financial capability developmental model in their work, the following set of strategies help youth develop financial capability:

1. For Young Children, Focus on Developing Executive Function

People use executive function skills to set goals, plan, save for the future, and stick to a budget. Developing executive function (the first building block) is especially important during the early years because it lays a critical foundation for further growth of mental abilities, skills, and attitudes. Everyone, including parents and educators, can help create environments that nurture the development of a child's executive function. As an example, a study shows preschool children who viewed a video of Cookie Monster resisting his favorite treat were able to wait four minutes longer for a snack than children who did not.

2. Help Parents and Caregivers Actively Shape Their Child's Financial Socialization

Financial socialization is an ongoing process by which children and youth develop the attitudes, habits, and norms that guide financial behavior. Children absorb these habits and norms (the second building block) by watching their peers and adults. Parents and caregivers play a central role in supporting their child's financial socialization, because they can demonstrate healthy financial values and behaviors and talk about everyday financial decisions. Encourage financial education programs and initiatives to help parents and caregivers take a more active role in their children's financial socialization.

3. Provide Children and Youth with Opportunities to Learn from Experience

Learning from direct, hands-on experience helps support financial capability, because it allows young people to acquire and practice financial decision-making skills and habits. Incorporating activities that build financial decision-making skills (the third building block) can help children and young adults build confidence in their ability to successfully complete financial tasks in the real world. Research indicates that effective experiential financial learning opportunities:

- Support independent decision-making by providing guidance and opportunities for reflection

- Take advantage of teachable moments—opportunities to explain new information, values, norms, behaviors, or skills

- Provide opportunities for repeated practice

- Incorporate planning and goal setting

4. Teach Financial Research Skills

According to research, it's important to know how to do purposeful financial investigations and analyze options, and then know how to follow through on financial decisions. Most major financial decisions that adults make (like paying for college, owning a home, and planning for retirement) require them to gather information through research, use the information to consider trade-offs, and act on that information in a way that serves their life goals. Helping young people build financial research skills means:

- Equipping them with the knowledge and skills they need to find and evaluate relevant financial information

- Helping them develop mental "guideposts" so they can recognize situations in which they should seek out additional information (for example, case studies can encourage teenagers to check their budget and comparison shop before purchasing an expensive item)

Chapter 30

Youth Tax Education

Why Pay Taxes?

The government provides public goods and services for the community as a whole. To pay its bills, the government needs revenue, or a source of income. The money that the federal government uses to pay its bills comes mostly from taxes. Taxes shift resources from private individuals and businesses to the government.

How Taxes Evolve

Taxes have been a part of American history since our earliest days. In fact, taxes are one of the reasons the colonists fought for independence from Great Britain in the first place. When our Constitution was being written, the authors knew that our young country would need taxes for items such as roads and defense. They put provisions in the Constitution that spelled out exactly how the formal tax legislation process would work. A proposed tax law, called a bill, follows specific steps through both houses of Congress.

The informal tax legislation process is the way you as a citizen can affect legislation by making your views known to legislators. You can take part in the informal tax legislation process by joining lobbying groups, attending town meetings, circulating and signing petitions, and voting for candidates sympathetic to your views. You can also write, call, or e-mail members of Congress.

The Taxpayer's Responsibilities

The U.S. income tax system is based on the idea of voluntary compliance; it is the taxpayer's responsibility to report all income. Tax evasion is illegal. Some people try to evade paying taxes by failing to report all or some of their income.

About This Chapter: Text in this chapter begins with excerpts from "IRS Offers Tips for Teenage Taxpayers with Summer Jobs," Internal Revenue Service (IRS), July 5, 2017; Text beginning with the heading "Tax Benefits for Education" is excerpted from "Tax Benefits for Education: Information Center," Internal Revenue Service (IRS), March 6, 2018.

Money-making activities that aren't reported to the government are part of an underground economy. If taxpayers fail to pay what officials say they owe, the IRS can collect back taxes and assess a penalty.

Tax avoidance is perfectly legal. The IRS allows taxpayers to claim certain deductions, credits, and adjustments to income. For instance, some homeowners can claim a deduction for interest they pay on a home mortgage. Many people pay more federal income tax than necessary because they misunderstand tax laws and fail to keep good records.

The Taxpayer's Rights

Taxpayers have a definite responsibility to file an accurate and timely tax return, but they also have certain rights. The fundamental right is that of confidentiality. All taxpayers have the right to privacy of their tax information. Only authorized tax personnel can examine, or audit, a tax return. Even law enforcement agencies have no right to examine a suspect's tax returns. In addition, taxpayers have the right to appeal any IRS-proposed adjustments to a tax return. The taxpayer can contest the IRS determination of tax liability in a court or by asking the IRS Appeals Office to review the case.

(Source: "The Whys of Taxes," Internal Revenue Service (IRS).)

Students and teenagers often get summer jobs. This is a great way to earn extra spending money or to save for later. The Internal Revenue Service (IRS) offers a few tax tips for taxpayers with a summer job:

1. **Withholding and estimated tax.** Students and teenage employees normally have taxes withheld from their paychecks by the employer. Some workers are considered self-employed and may be responsible for paying taxes directly to the IRS. One way to do that is by making estimated tax payments during the year.

2. **New employees.** When a person gets a new job, they need to fill out a Form W-4, Employee's Withholding Allowance Certificate. Employers use this form to calculate how much federal income tax to withhold from the employee's pay. The IRS Withholding Calculator tool on IRS.gov can help a taxpayer fill out the form.

3. **Self-employment.** A taxpayer may engage in types of work that may be considered self-employment. Money earned from self-employment is taxable. Self-employment work can be jobs like babysitting or lawn care. Keep good records on money received and expenses paid related to the work. IRS rules may allow some, if not all, costs associated with self-employment to be deducted. A tax deduction generally reduces the taxes you pay.

4. **Tip income.** Employees should report tip income. Keep a daily log to accurately report tips. Report tips of $20 or more received in cash in any single month to the employer.

5. **Payroll taxes.** Taxpayers may earn too little from their summer jobs to owe income tax. Employers usually must withhold Social Security and Medicare taxes from their pay. If a taxpayer is self-employed, then Social Security and Medicare taxes may still be due and are generally paid by the taxpayer, in a timely manner.

6. **Newspaper carriers.** Special rules apply to a newspaper carrier or distributor. If a person meets certain conditions, then they are self-employed. If the taxpayer does not meet those conditions, and are under age 18, they may be exempt from Social Security and Medicare taxes.

7. **Reserve Officers' Training Corps (ROTC) pay.** If a taxpayer is in an ROTC program, active duty pay, such as pay for summer advanced camp, is taxable. Other allowances the taxpayer may receive may not be taxable.

8. **Use IRS Free File.** Taxpayers can prepare and e-file their federal income tax return for free using IRS Free File. Free File is available only on IRS.gov. Some taxpayers may not earn enough money to have to file a federal tax return, by law, but may want to if taxes were withheld. For example, a taxpayer may want to file a tax return because they would be eligible for a tax refund or a refundable credit. IRS Free File can help with these issues.

Avoid scams. The IRS will never initiate contact using social media or text message. First contact generally comes in the mail. Those wondering if they owe money to the IRS can view their tax account information on IRS.gov to find out.

Tax Benefits for Education

Tax credits, deductions, and savings plans can help taxpayers with their expenses for higher education.

- A tax credit reduces the amount of income tax you may have to pay.

- A deduction reduces the amount of your income that is subject to tax, thus generally reducing the amount of tax you may have to pay.

- Certain savings plans allow the accumulated earnings to grow tax-free until money is taken out (known as a distribution), or allow the distribution to be tax-free, or both.

- An exclusion from income means that you won't have to pay income tax on the benefit you're receiving, but you also won't be able to use that same tax-free benefit for a deduction or credit.

Credits

An education credit helps with the cost of higher education by reducing the amount of tax owed on your tax return. If the credit reduces your tax to less than zero, you may get a refund. There are two education credits available: the American opportunity tax credit (AOTC) and the lifetime learning credit (LLC).

Who Can Claim an Education Credit?

There are additional rules for each credit, but you must meet all three of the following for either credit:

1. You, your dependent or a third party pays qualified education expenses for higher education.

2. An eligible student must be enrolled at an eligible educational institution.

3. The eligible student is yourself, your spouse or a dependent you list on your tax return.

If you're eligible to claim the lifetime learning credit and are also eligible to claim the American opportunity credit for the same student in the same year, you can choose to claim either credit, but not both. You can't claim the AOTC if you were a nonresident alien for any part of the tax year unless you elect to be treated as a resident alien for federal tax purposes.

The law requires that both you and your qualifying student have a valid Social Security number or Individual Taxpayer Identification Number (ITIN), issued before the due date for your tax return, in order to claim the AOTC.

To claim the AOTC or LLC, use Form 8863, Education Credits (American Opportunity and Lifetime Learning Credits). Additionally, if you claim the AOTC, the law requires you to include the school's Employer Identification Number (EIN) on this form.

Deductions
Tuition and Fees Deduction

The Bipartisan Budget Act (BBA), enacted on February 9, 2018, renewed the tuition and fees deduction for tax year 2017. If you already filed your 2017 federal tax return and find you can claim the deduction, you can do so by filing an amended return on Form 1040X. Amended returns cannot be filed electronically and can take up to 16 weeks to process. The Tuition and Fees Deduction was extended for tax years 2015 and 2016 earlier.

You may be able to deduct qualified education expenses paid during the year for yourself, your spouse or your dependent. You cannot claim this deduction if your filing status is married filing separately or if another person can claim an exemption for you as a dependent on his or her tax return. The qualified expenses must be for higher education.

The Tuition and Fees Deduction can reduce the amount of your income subject to tax by up to $4,000. This deduction, reported on Form 8917, Tuition and Fees Deduction, is taken as an adjustment to income. This means you can claim this deduction even if you do not itemize deductions on Schedule A (Form 1040). This deduction may be beneficial to you if, for example, you don't qualify for the American opportunity or lifetime learning credits.

You may be able to take one of the education credits for your education expenses instead of a tuition and fees deduction. You can choose the one that will give you the lower tax. You cannot claim the tuition and fees deduction as well as an education credit for the same expense.

Student Loan Interest Deduction

Generally, personal interest you pay, other than certain mortgage interest, is not deductible on your tax return. However, if your modified adjusted gross income (MAGI) is less than $80,000 ($160,000 if filing a joint return), there is a special deduction allowed for paying interest on a student loan (also known as an education loan) used for higher education. Student loan interest is interest you paid during the year on a qualified student loan. It includes both required and voluntary interest payments.

For most taxpayers, MAGI is the adjusted gross income as figured on their federal income tax return before subtracting any deduction for student loan interest. This deduction can reduce the amount of your income subject to tax by up to $2,500.

The student loan interest deduction is taken as an adjustment to income. This means you can claim this deduction even if you do not itemize deductions on Form 1040's Schedule A.

Qualified Student Loan

This is a loan you took out solely to pay qualified education expenses (defined later) that were:

For you, your spouse, or a person who was your dependent when you took out the loan. Paid or incurred within a reasonable period of time before or after you took out the loan. For education provided during an academic period for an eligible student.

Loans from the following sources are not qualified student loans:

- A related person

- A qualified employer plan

Qualified Education Expenses

For purposes of the student loan interest deduction, these expenses are the total costs of attending an eligible educational institution, including graduate school. They include amounts paid for the following items:

- Tuition and fees

- Room and board

- Books, supplies, and equipment

- Other necessary expenses (such as transportation).

The cost of room and board qualifies only to the extent that it is not more than the greater of:

- The allowance for room and board, as determined by the eligible educational institution, that was included in the cost of attendance (for federal financial aid purposes) for a particular academic period and living arrangement of the student, or

- The actual amount charged if the student is residing in housing owned or operated by the eligible educational institution

Business Deduction for Work-Related Education

If you are an employee and can itemize your deductions, you may be able to claim a deduction for the expenses you pay for your work-related education. Your deduction will be the amount by which your qualifying work-related education expenses plus other job and certain miscellaneous expenses is greater than two percent of your adjusted gross income. An itemized deduction may reduce the amount of your income subject to tax.

If you are self-employed, you deduct your expenses for qualifying work-related education directly from your self-employment income. This reduces the amount of your income subject to both income tax and self-employment tax.

Your work-related education expenses may also qualify you for other tax benefits, such as the American opportunity credit, tuition, and fees deduction and the lifetime learning credit.

You may qualify for these other benefits even if you do not meet the requirements listed above. You cannot claim this deduction as well as the tuition and fees deduction for the same expense, nor can you claim this deduction as well as an education credit for the same expense.

To claim a business deduction for work-related education, you must:

- Be working

- Itemize your deductions on Schedule A (Form 1040 or 1040NR) if you are an employee

- File Schedule C (Form 1040), Schedule C-EZ (Form 1040), or Schedule F (Form 1040) if you are self-employed

- Have expenses for education that meet the requirements discussed under Qualifying Work-Related Education, below

Qualifying Work-Related Education

You can deduct the costs of qualifying work-related education as business expenses. This is education that meets at least one of the following two tests:

- The education is required by your employer or the law to keep your present salary, status, or job. The required education must serve a bona fide business purpose of your employer.

- The education maintains or improves skills needed in your present work.

However, even if the education meets one or both of the above tests, it is not qualifying work-related education if it:

- Is needed to meet the minimum educational requirements of your present trade or business, or

- Is part of a program of study that will qualify you for a new trade or business

You can deduct the costs of qualifying work-related education as a business expense even if the education could lead to a degree.

Education Required by Employer or by Law

Education you need to meet the minimum educational requirements for your present trade or business is not qualifying work-related education. Once you have met the minimum educational requirements for your job, your employer or the law may require you to get more education. This additional education is qualifying work-related education if all three of the following requirements are met.

- It is required for you to keep your present salary, status or job

- The requirement serves a business purpose of your employer

- The education is not part of a program that will qualify you for a new trade or business.

When you get more education than your employer or the law requires, the additional education can be qualifying work-related education only if it maintains or improves skills required in your present work.

Education to Maintain or Improve Skills

If your education is not required by your employer or the law, it can be qualifying work-related education only if it maintains or improves skills needed in your present work. This could include refresher courses, courses on current developments and academic or vocational courses.

Savings Plans
Qualified Tuition Programs (QTP) (529 Plans)

States may establish and maintain programs that allow you to either prepay or contribute to an account for paying a student's qualified education expenses at a postsecondary institution. Eligible educational institutions may establish and maintain programs that allow you to prepay a student's qualified education expenses. If you prepay tuition, the student (designated beneficiary) will be entitled to a waiver or a payment of qualified education expenses. You can't deduct either payments or contributions to a QTP. For information on a specific QTP, you will need to contact the state agency or eligible educational institution that established and maintains it.

No tax is due on a distribution from a QTP unless the amount distributed is greater than the beneficiary's adjusted qualified education expenses. Qualified expenses include required tuition and fees, books, supplies and equipment including computer or peripheral equipment, computer software and internet access and related services if used primarily by the student enrolled at an eligible education institution. Someone who is at least a half-time student, room and board may also qualify.

Coverdell Education Savings Account (ESA)

A Coverdell ESA can be used to pay either qualified higher education expenses or qualified elementary and secondary education expenses. Income limits apply to contributors, and the total contributions for the beneficiary of this account cannot be more than $2,000 in any year, no matter how many accounts have been established. A beneficiary is someone who is under age 18 or is a special needs beneficiary.

Contributions to a Coverdell ESA are not deductible, but amounts deposited in the account grow tax-free until distributed. The beneficiary will not owe tax on the distributions if they are less than a beneficiary's qualified education expenses at an eligible institution. This benefit applies to qualified higher education expenses as well as to qualified elementary and secondary education expenses.

Here are some things to remember about distributions from Coverdell accounts:

- Distributions are tax-free as long as they are used for qualified education expenses, such as tuition and fees, required books, supplies and equipment, and qualified expenses for room and board

- There is no tax on distributions if they are for enrollment or attendance at an eligible educational institution. This includes any public, private, or religious school that provides elementary or secondary education as determined under state law. Virtually all accredited public, nonprofit, and proprietary (privately owned profit-making) postsecondary institutions are eligible.

- Education tax credits can be claimed in the same year the beneficiary takes a tax-free distribution from a Coverdell ESA, as long as the same expenses are not used for both benefits.

- If the distribution exceeds qualified education expenses, a portion will be taxable to the beneficiary and will usually be subject to an additional 10 percent tax. Exceptions to the additional 10 percent tax include the death or disability of the beneficiary or if the beneficiary receives a qualified scholarship.

Scholarships and Fellowships

A scholarship is generally an amount paid or allowed to, or for the benefit of, a student at an educational institution to aid in the pursuit of studies. The student may be either an undergraduate or a graduate. A fellowship is generally an amount paid for the benefit of an individual to aid in the pursuit of study or research, whether the amount is tax-free or taxable depends on the expense paid with the amount and whether you are a degree candidate.

A scholarship or fellowship is tax-free only if you meet the following conditions:

- You are a candidate for a degree at an eligible educational institution.

- You use the scholarship or fellowship to pay qualified education expenses.

Qualified Education Expenses

For purposes of tax-free scholarships and fellowships, these are expenses for:

- Tuition and fees required to enroll at or attend an eligible educational institution

- Course-related expenses, such as fees, books, supplies, and equipment that are required for the courses at the eligible educational institution. These items must be required of all students in your course of instruction

However, in order for these to be qualified education expenses, the terms of the scholarship or fellowship cannot require that it be used for other purposes, such as room and board, or specify that it cannot be used for tuition or course-related expenses.

Expenses That Don't Qualify

Qualified education expenses do not include the cost of:

- Room and board

- Travel

- Research

- Clerical help

- Equipment and other expenses that are not required for enrollment in or attendance at an eligible educational institution

This is true even if the fee must be paid to the institution as a condition of enrollment or attendance. Scholarship or fellowship amounts used to pay these costs are taxable.

Exclusions from Income

You may exclude certain educational assistance benefits from your income. That means that you won't have to pay any tax on them. However, it also means that you can't use any of the tax-free education expenses as the basis for any other deduction or credit, including the lifetime learning credit.

Employer-Provided Educational Assistance

If you receive educational assistance benefits from your employer under an educational assistance program, you can exclude up to $5,250 of those benefits each year. This means your employer should not include the benefits with your wages, tips, and other compensation shown in box one of your Form W-2.

Educational Assistance Program

To qualify as an educational assistance program, the plan must be written and must meet tax-free other requirements. Your employer can tell you whether there is a qualified program where you work.

Educational Assistance Benefits

Tax-free educational assistance benefits include payments for tuition, fees, and similar expenses, books, supplies, and equipment. The payments may be for either undergraduate- or graduate-level courses. The payments do not have to be for work-related courses. Educational assistance benefits do not include payments for the following items:

- Meals, lodging, or transportation

- Tools or supplies (other than textbooks) that you can keep after completing the course of instruction

- Courses involving sports, games, or hobbies unless they:

  - Have a reasonable relationship to the business of your employer, or

  - Are required as part of a degree program.

Benefits over $5,250

If your employer pays more than $5,250 for educational benefits for you during the year, you must generally pay tax on the amount over $5,250. Your employer should include in your wages (Form W-2, box one) the amount that you must include in income.

Working Condition Fringe Benefit

However, if the benefits over $5,250 also qualify as a working condition fringe benefit, your employer does not have to include them in your wages. A working condition fringe benefit is a benefit which, had you paid for it, you could deduct as an employee business expense.

Educator Expense Deduction

Educators can deduct up to $250 ($500 if married filing jointly and both spouses are eligible educators, but not more than $250 each) of unreimbursed business expenses. The educator expense deduction, claimed on either Form 1040 Line 23 or Form 1040A Line 16, is available even if an educator doesn't itemize their deductions. To do so, the taxpayer must be a K–12 instructor, counselor, principal, or aide for at least 900 hours a school year in a school that provides elementary or secondary education as determined under state law.

Those who qualify can deduct costs like books, supplies, computer equipment and software, classroom equipment and supplementary materials used in the classroom. Expenses for participation in professional development courses are also deductible. Athletic supplies qualify if used for courses in health or physical education.

Chapter 31

Budgeting

While you're in college or career school, you'll need to learn how to manage your finances, plan for changes, and prepare for the unexpected. Budgeting will help you build decision-making skills and reach your financial and academic goals.

Why Should I Create a Budget?

A budget is a guide that keeps you on the path to reach your financial goals. Budgeting keeps your finances under control, shows when you need to make adjustments to your spending, and helps you decide where your money goes instead of wondering where it all went.

Budgeting helps you answer these important questions:

- Where does all my money go?

- Is there a way to spend less?

- How will I handle unexpected expenses like replacing a broken cell phone or repairing my car?

- How can putting money into savings help me with some of my bigger financial goals?

Budgeting Helps You Achieve Academic and Financial Goals

Writing down your goals is the first step in creating a plan to make them realities. A budget will also help you prepare for unexpected expenses and obstacles. Budgeting involves

About This Chapter: This chapter includes text excerpted from "Budgeting," Federal Student Aid, U.S. Department of Education (ED), April 10, 2014.

challenging decision-making, but setting goals will make the tough choices a little easier. As you create a budget, you'll want to set short-, medium-, and long-term goals and track your progress toward achieving them.

Short-Term Goals

Short-term goals might be within the next couple of months. Consider your needs, wants, and priorities. A short-term goal may be as simple as buying your textbooks (so that you don't have to use a credit card), a weekend road trip with friends, or your next cell phone bill.

Medium-Term Goals

Medium-term goals involve thinking a bit farther into the future, perhaps the next one to three years. These goals could include buying a new laptop computer, saving $1,000 for an emergency fund, completing your program of study, or saving $5,000 for a down payment on a car.

Long-Term Goals

What do you want to do beyond three years and into the future? Long-term goals could include paying off your student loans after graduation, saving toward a down payment on a house, or saving for retirement.

Budgeting Makes It Easier to Plan, Save, and Control Your Expenses

When you set up your budget, you'll be able to see whether your expenses exceed your income and, if so, where you can identify expenses that can be reduced. Once you're paying attention to your income and spending, you can make informed decisions that will help you meet your financial goals.

Plus, if you have problems keeping your spending under control, a budget will help you manage your spending. Following a budget can help you free up money for the things that really matter to you.

Budgeting Can Help You Avoid Debt and Improve Your Credit

When you stick to a budget, you avoid spending more than you earn and you can avoid or reduce your credit card debt. If you have received student loans to help with the cost of college or career school, then a budget will help you make the most of the money you've borrowed and can help you determine how long it will take to repay your debt and how much it will cost. If you do borrow, being able to pay what you owe on time each month will have a positive impact on your creditworthiness and your financial future.

How Do I Create a Budget?

Creating a budget is pretty straightforward and starts with this simple equation: What you earn (your income) minus what you spend (your expenses).

The steps involved in creating a budget include:

- Determining your time frame and setting goals

- Finding a budgeting tool that works for you

- Identifying your income and expenses

- Subtracting your expenses from your income to see if you have money left over or if you have a shortfall

- Making any needed adjustments

Budgeting is not just a one-time event. You'll need to track your spending over time and update your budget as needed.

What Should I Know about Budgeting after I Leave School?

Your expenses will change after you leave school. For example, if you recently graduated, you usually won't be required to begin paying off your student loans for six months, but when that payment is added to your monthly expenses, it will have a big impact on your budget. When you leave school, you'll want to update your budget to include student loan payments, as well as your new income and living costs. Leaving school can be an exciting (and stressful) time, but you don't want to stop tracking and managing your finances.

As you move through changes in your life, you'll need to constantly reevaluate your income and expenses. Your goals will change as well. You may want to buy a car, get married, have children, continue your education, or start a business, and all these activities affect your budget in some way. Think of your budget as a living document. You have the power to revise it at any time to keep track of your finances and reach your goals.

Creating Your Budget

Creating a budget may sound complicated, but all you need to do to get started is set aside some time and get organized—the benefits will make the effort worthwhile. The following steps will help you set up your budget and manage your finances by helping you track your income and expenses.

1. Determine a Time Span for Your Budget

You can create your budget for a month, academic year, or calendar year. If you are currently attending college or career school, you may want to consider creating a monthly budget for an academic term, such as your fall semester. Keep in mind that your income may vary from month to month, and not all of your expenses will be the same each month. Larger expenses (such as car insurance and books) and seasonal expenses (such as a trip home during the holidays or a higher electricity bill in summer when the air conditioning is on) need to be incorporated into your budget.

2. Choose a Tool to Help You Manage Your Budget

To create a budget, you'll want to use a tool for tracking your income and expenses. You can use pen and paper, a simple automated spreadsheet, or a budgeting app. Many banks offer budgeting tools, so see what works best for you.

The Financial Awareness Counseling Tool (FACT) (studentloans.gov/myDirectLoan/financialAwarenessCounselingLanding.action) is a free interactive tool that can help you manage your finances. FACT covers topics ranging from managing your budget to avoiding default. Plus, you can access your loan information and receive personalized feedback to help you better understand your financial obligations.

3. Review Your Monthly Income

First, estimate how much money you will have coming in each month. Here are some tips for assessing your income:

- Your income may come from sources such as your pay from work, financial contributions from family members, or financial aid (scholarships, grants, work-study, and loans).

- If you're working while in school, review your records to determine how much your take-home pay is each month. If you earn most of your money over the summer, you may want to estimate your yearly income and then divide it by 12.

- Include income from any financial aid credit balance refunds—money that may be left over for other expenses after your financial aid is applied toward tuition and fees.

Table 31.1. Monthly Income Tracking Example

Income Source	Monthly Income
Income from work	$1,200
Tax refund ($360 total divided by 12)	$30
Estimated financial aid credit balance refund ($2,100 total divided by 12)*	$175
Monthly support from parents and/or family member	$250
Other income	—
Total Monthly Income	**$1,655**

***Note:** If you are getting ready to attend school, you'll want to estimate your federal aid credit balance by taking your estimated financial aid and subtracting your expected tuition and fees. If you have not yet received an aid offer from your school, you can use FAFSA4caster to get an early estimate of your eligibility for federal student aid.*

4. Identify and Categorize Your Expenses

To estimate your monthly expenses, you'll want to start by recording everything you spend money on in a month. This may be a bit time-consuming but will definitely be worthwhile in helping you understand where your money is going and how to better manage it. After that, gather your bank records and credit card statements that will show you other expenditures that may be automatically paid.

If you are currently attending college or career school or getting ready to go, you'll also need to estimate your college costs. In addition to tuition and fees (unless covered by financial aid), you'll want to make sure to include books and supplies, equipment and room materials, and travel expenses.

If you are still researching your school options, keep in mind that college and career school costs can vary significantly from school to school. Once you've identified your expenses, you should group them into two categories—fixed expenses and variable expenses.

- Fixed expenses stay about the same each month and include items such as rent or mortgage payments, car payments, and insurance. These obligations are generally nonnegotiable until you realize that you are spending too much money on rent and take steps to find a cheaper place! When creating a monthly budget, divide the amount due by the number of months the bill covers. For example, take your yearly $1,200 insurance bill that's paid in two $600 installments six months apart, and divide it by 12 to know you need to set aside $100 per month.

- Variable expenses are those that are flexible or controllable and can vary from month to month. Examples of variable expenses include groceries, clothing, eating out, and entertainment. You'll want to examine these expenses to make sure they stay under control and don't bust your budget at the end of the month.

Table 31.2. Monthly Expenses Tracking Example

Fixed Expenses	Projected Cost
Rent or dorm fee	$500
Books	$70
Electricity	$35
Gas and water	$22
Cable and Internet	$50
Car insurance ($600 divided by 12 months)	$50
Parking fee ($84 divided by 12)	$7
Car maintenance and repairs ($480 divided by 12 months)	$40
Cell phone (basic charges)	$60
Car loan payment	$125
Money set aside for savings	$50
Total Fixed Expenses	**$1,009**

Variable Expenses	Projected Cost
Groceries	$250
Dining out	$50
Entertainment (example: concerts)	$50
Music downloads	$20
Movies (theater and downloads)	$48
Medical (including prescriptions)	$40
Hair and nails	$40
Clothing	$50
Laundry and dry cleaning	$10
Health club	$40
Credit card monthly payment	$25
Public transportation	$25
Gas for car	$60
Total Variable Expenses	**$708**
Total Expenses	**$1,717**

5. Save for Emergencies

Include "Savings" as a fixed expense in your monthly budget. Pay yourself first every month! Your savings can be used as an emergency fund to help you deal with unexpected expenses. The ideal amount of an emergency fund typically covers three to six months of your expenses.

6. Balance Your Budget

Now that you've identified your sources of income and expenses, you'll want to compare the two to balance your budget. To do so, you simply subtract your expenses from your income.

Table 31.3. Balance Your Budget

Total Monthly Income	$1,655
Minus Total Expenses	$1,717
(= + / - Difference)	-$62

If you have a positive balance, then your income is greater than your expenses. In other words, you're earning more money than you're spending. If you have a positive balance, you shouldn't start looking at new ways to spend your money. Instead, focus on putting the extra money toward your savings to cover your emergency fund or to support future goals such as buying a car. Also, if you have a positive balance but you've borrowed student loan funds, pay back some of your loans and consider borrowing less in the future.

If you have a negative balance, then you are spending more money than you have. You'll want to balance your budget and make sure your expenses don't exceed your income. Balancing your budget may include monitoring your variable expenses, reducing your expenses, and/or finding ways to increase your income. Spending less can be a lot easier than earning more. Consider eating out less frequently and making your own lunch. Rent books rather than buying them, or buy books to download to your computer. Use a shopping list when grocery shopping, and buy only what you need. Ask yourself before buying anything, "Do I really need this?"

7. Maintain and Update Your Budget

Now that you've created your budget, you'll want to make sure it remains a living document and you update it over time. Here are some smart practices to keep in mind:

- **Review your budget on a monthly basis.** Regular review and maintenance of your budget will keep you on top of things and may help you avoid being blindsided by something unexpected.

- **Forgive yourself for small spending mistakes and get back on track.** Most people overspend because they buy things on impulse. The next time you're tempted to make an impulse buy, ask yourself the following questions:
  - What do I need this for?
  - Can I afford this item?
  - If I buy this item now, will I still be happy that I bought it a month from now?
  - Do I need to save this money for a financial goal?
  - Will this item go on sale? Should I wait to buy it?
  - Does it matter if I buy brand-name or can I get by with generic?

If you take a moment to think about what you're buying, you're more likely to make a choice that fits your budgeting goals.

Budgeting Tips

As you create and maintain your budget, you'll want to keep some important tips and suggestions in mind.

Get Started

Here are some important points to keep in mind as you build your budget and identify what goes into your income and expenses.

- **Overestimate your expenses.** It's better to overestimate your expenses and then underspend and end up with a surplus.
- **Underestimate your income.** It's better to end up with an unexpected cash surplus rather than a budget shortfall.
- **Involve your family in the budget planning process.** Determine how much income will be available from family sources such as parents or your spouse. Discuss how financial decisions will be made.
- **Prepare for the unexpected by setting saving goals to build your emergency fund.** Budgeting will help you cover unusual expenses and plan for changes that may happen while you're in school.
  - Planning to move off campus? Short-term budgeting goals for the year can include saving for the rent deposit and furniture for your new apartment.

- Starting an internship next semester? Adjust your budget to save for buying new clothes to wear to work and paying increased transportation costs.

- Finishing school in the next year? Budget to include job search expenses such as résumé preparation, travel to interviews and job fairs, and professional exam fees. Also, you may need to think about how you will manage your money between leaving school and finding a job—this is a time when an emergency fund can really help out.

Differentiate between Needs and Wants

One benefit of budgeting is that it helps you determine if you have the resources to spend on items that you want versus those you need.

- Start by making a list of things you'd like to save up for.

- Identify whether each item on the list is something you absolutely need or is really a want.

- If you decide you want something, ask yourself if you will still be happy you bought the item in a month.

- Next, prioritize each item on the list.

- Once you have set your priorities, you can then determine whether you should incorporate each item into your budget.

Table 31.4. Needs and Wants

First Step My Needs and Wants	Second Step Need or Want?	Third Step Priority Importance? 1=must have 2=really want 3=would be nice
Save for a vacation	Want	3
Buy a new computer	Want	2
Go to college	Need	1
Buy a better car	Want	2
Save for an emergency fund	Need	1
Save money for a down payment on a house	Need	3
Pay off credit cards	Need	1

> ## Pay Yourself First!
> Include "Savings" as a recurring expense item in your monthly budget. Small amounts that you put away each month do add up.

Manage Your Budget

Keeping track of all of your spending may seem like a lot of work. But if you're organized, keep good records, and use some of the following tips, you'll find it's easier than you may think. And, don't be too hard on yourself if you slip up.

- **Record your actual expenses.** Have you noticed how fast your cash disappears? To get a handle on where your cash is going, carry a small notebook or use a phone app to record even the smallest expenditures such as coffee, movie tickets, snacks, and parking. Some expenses that are often ignored include music downloads, charges for extra cell phone usage, and entertainment expenses. Search for an online tool to assist you—many are free!

- **Organize your records.** Decide what system you're going to use to track and organize your financial information. There are mobile apps and computer-based programs that work well, but you can also track your spending using a pencil and paper. Be sure to be consistent and organized, and designate a space to store all your financial information. Good record-keeping saves money and time!

- **Create a routine.** Manage your money on a regular basis, and record your expenses and income regularly. If you find that you can't record your expenses every day, then record them weekly. If you wait longer than two weeks to record information, you may forget some transactions and be overwhelmed by the amount of information you need to enter.

- **Include a category in your budget called "Unusual."** There will be some expenses every month that won't fall neatly into one category or that you couldn't have planned for. An "Unusual" category will help you budget for these occasional expenses.

- **Review your spending for little items that add up to big monthly expenditures.** The daily cup of coffee and soda at a vending machine will add up. Consider packing your lunch rather than eating out every day. Spending $10 a day eating out during the week translates to $50 a week and $200 a month. A $5 packed lunch translates into a savings of $1,200 a year. Save even more by looking for ways to manage and reduce your transportation and entertainment expenses.

- **Make your financial aid credit balance refund last. If your school applies your financial aid to your tuition and fees and there's money left over, the school will refund that money to you so you can use it for other education-related expenses** (textbooks, transportation, food, etc.). Remember that your financial aid is supposed to help you cover your cost of attendance for the whole semester or term, so be sure to make that refund stretch over time rather than spending it all as soon as you get it.

- **Comparison shop.** Comparison shopping is simply using common sense to compare products in an attempt to get the best prices and best value. This means doing a little research before running out to buy something, especially when it comes to more expensive items. Make the most of tools like phone apps for comparing prices and value.

- **Use credit cards wisely.** Think very carefully before you decide to get your first credit card. Is a credit card really necessary, or would another payment option work just as well? If you receive a credit card offer in the mail, don't feel obligated to accept it. Limit the number of cards you get.

- **Don't spend more on your credit card than you can afford to pay in full on a monthly basis.** Responsible use of credit cards can be a shopping convenience and help you establish a solid credit rating and avoid financial problems. Consider signing up for electronic payment reminders, balance notices, and billing statement notifications from your credit card provider.

Expect the Unexpected

Your emergency fund should be used for expenses that fall outside the categories of annual and periodic bills. Unexpected expenses are the result of life events such as job loss, illness, or car repairs. Redefine your notion of "unexpected" bills to encompass these unforeseen events rather than more common but infrequent expenses. The good news is that if you do not use your emergency fund, you will have savings—which should always be a priority when managing your finances. And, if you have to use your emergency fund, you may avoid unnecessary borrowing.

Chapter 32

Electronic Banking

For many people, electronic banking means 24-hour access to cash through an automated teller machine (ATM) or direct deposit of paychecks into checking or savings accounts. But electronic banking involves many different types of transactions, rights, responsibilities—and sometimes, fees. Do your research. You may find some electronic banking services more practical for your lifestyle than others.

Electronic Fund Transfers (EFTs)

Electronic banking, also known as electronic fund transfer (EFT), uses computer and electronic technology in place of checks and other paper transactions. EFTs are initiated through devices like cards or codes that let you, or those you authorize, access your account. Many financial institutions use an automated teller machine (ATM) or debit cards and personal identification numbers (PINs) for this purpose. Some use other types of debit cards that require your signature or a scan. For example, some use radio-frequency identification (RFID) or other forms of "contactless" technology that scan your information without direct contact with you. The federal Electronic Fund Transfer Act (EFT Act) covers some electronic consumer transactions.

Here are some common EFT services:

ATMs are electronic terminals that let you bank almost virtually any time. To withdraw cash, make deposits, or transfer funds between accounts, you generally insert an ATM card and enter your PIN. Some financial institutions and ATM owners charge a fee, particularly if you don't have accounts with them or if your transactions take place at remote locations.

About This Chapter: This chapter includes text excerpted from "Electronic Banking," Federal Trade Commission (FTC), August 2012.

Generally, ATMs must tell you they charge a fee and the amount on or at the terminal screen before you complete the transaction. Check with your institution and at ATMs you use for more information about these fees.

Direct deposit lets you authorize specific deposits—like paychecks, Social Security checks, and other benefits—to your account on a regular basis. You also may preauthorize direct withdrawals so that recurring bills—like insurance premiums, mortgages, utility bills, and gym memberships—are paid automatically. Be cautious before you preauthorize recurring withdrawals to pay companies you aren't familiar with; funds from your bank account could be withdrawn improperly. Monitor your bank account to make sure direct recurring payments take place and are for the right amount.

Pay-by-phone systems let you call your financial institution with instructions to pay certain bills or to transfer funds between accounts. You must have an agreement with your institution to make these transfers.

Personal computer banking lets you handle many banking transactions using your personal computer. For example, you may use your computer to request transfers between accounts and pay bills electronically.

Debit card purchase or payment transactions let you make purchases or payments with a debit card, which also may be your ATM card. Transactions can take place in person, online, or by phone. The process is similar to using a credit card, with some important exceptions: a debit card purchase or payment transfers money quickly from your bank account to the company's account, so you have to have sufficient funds in your account to cover your purchase. This means you need to keep accurate records of the dates and amounts of your debit card purchases, payments, and ATM withdrawals. Be sure you know the store or business before you provide your debit card information to avoid the possible loss of funds through fraud. Your liability for unauthorized use, and your rights for dealing with errors, may be different for a debit card than a credit card.

Electronic check conversion converts a paper check into an electronic payment in a store or when a company gets your check in the mail.

When you give your check to a cashier in a store, the check is run through an electronic system that captures your banking information and the amount of the check. You sign a receipt and you get a copy for your records. When your check is given back to you, it should be voided or marked by the merchant so that it can't be used again. The merchant electronically sends information from the check (but not the check itself) to your bank or other financial institution, and the funds are transferred into the merchant's account.

When you mail a check for payment to a merchant or other company, they may electronically send information from your check (but not the check itself) through the system; the funds are transferred from your account into their account. For a mailed check, you still should get notice from a company that expects to send your check information through the system electronically. For example, the company might include the notice on your monthly statement. The notice also should state if the company will electronically collect a fee from your account—like a "bounced check" fee—if you don't have enough money to cover the transaction.

Be careful with online and telephone transactions that may involve the use of your bank account information, rather than a check. A legitimate merchant that lets you use your bank account information to make a purchase or pay on an account should post information about the process on its website or explain the process on the phone. The merchant also should ask for your permission to electronically debit your bank account for the item you're buying or paying on. However, because online and telephone electronic debits don't occur face-to-face, be cautious about sharing your bank account information. Don't give out this information when you have no experience with the business, when you didn't initiate the call, or when the business seems reluctant to discuss the process with you. Check your bank account regularly to be sure that the right amounts were transferred.

Not all electronic fund transfers are covered by the EFT Act. For example, some financial institutions and merchants issue cards with cash value stored electronically on the card itself. Examples include prepaid phone cards, mass transit passes, general purpose reloadable cards, and some gift cards. These "stored-value" cards, as well as transactions using them, may not be covered by the EFT Act, or they may be subject to different rules under the EFT Act. This means you may not be covered for the loss or misuse of the card. Ask your financial institution or merchant about any protections offered for these cards.

When it comes to reimbursing a friend for lunch, most people use cash or write checks. But an increasing number of others instead turn to their computer or smartphone to make a person-to-person or "P2P" payment.

P2P payments can be convenient, but there are potential costs and risks, in areas such as the privacy of your personal information. *FDIC Consumer News* first introduced readers to P2P payments in 2011, and now they are offering their latest suggestions.

How a P2P service works: Banks and other companies offer different P2P payment services. Most share certain features: You establish an online account and designate one or more payment sources (such as your checking account, credit card or prepaid card) that you'll use to pay people. To send money to someone, you'll provide the recipient's information — in many cases, his or her e-mail address. To get money from someone, you may need to provide your bank account information or other details to the sender's P2P service provider.

Fees: There are numerous possibilities. Is there a fee to sign up? A fee to send money? A fee to receive money? Is there a single, fixed transaction fee for a service or is it calculated as a percentage of the transaction amount?

"Shop around to find a service with costs that seem reasonable," Khalil recommended. "And if you are the recipient and the fee to receive money seems high, don't be shy about telling the sender you would prefer to be paid another way."

Privacy: Be aware of the service's privacy practices and how your information—and that of your recipients—will be used. If you decide to use the service, set all available privacy settings to your preferences. Some services may, for example, share certain aspects of your transaction activity with other users, such as your social media "friends." If you don't want that to happen, evaluate whether the service's privacy settings allow you to turn off that feature. Because a P2P service provider's privacy practices can change, periodically check its policies and your privacy settings to ensure they still are set in the way you want.

Funds availability: Know when the money you send will be charged to your credit card or deducted from your account. Also be clear on when that money will be available to the recipient. "It may be quick to make a P2P payment, but that doesn't mean the recipient can access the funds right away," said Khalil. "When money is available can vary depending on which P2P service you're using."

Your rights and dispute resolution: Know what the service's user agreement says about resolving errors and disputes. For example, what will happen if the service pays the wrong person or the wrong amount? And, what if you caused the error by mistyping the recipient's e-mail address or the amount you wanted to send? That can easily happen, especially when you're typing on a small mobile phone.

"If the payment is drawn from your checking or savings account, or a credit card, you will have rights under federal law to have the error resolved," said Richard Schwartz, Counsel in the FDIC's Legal Division. "But if the payment comes from somewhere else, like funds you have on hold in an account with the payment service provider, you might not have the same legal protections. Instead, you might have to rely on the service's own policies or perhaps state laws applicable to money transfers. In any case, find out what the service provider's user agreement says will happen if something goes wrong."

Bank or nonbank: "If you're interested in using P2P payments, ask your bank whether it offers the service. And if your bank doesn't, try other banks," Khalil said. "While a number of nonbank companies also offer P2P payments, there can be benefits to working with a bank, such as the opportunity to maintain a financial relationship and obtain other products and services at reasonable rates." another potential benefit is that funds held in your bank account are FDIC-insured, which may not be the case with a nonbank P2P account.

(Source: "Person-To-Person (P2P) Payments Online: What to Know before You Click and Send That Money," Federal Deposit Insurance Corporation (FDIC).)

Disclosures

To understand your rights and responsibilities for your EFTs, read the documents you get from the financial institution that issued your "access device"—the card, code or other way you access your account to transfer money electronically. Although the method varies by institution, it often involves a card and/or a PIN. No one should know your PIN but you and select employees at your financial institution. You also should read the documents you receive for your bank account, which may contain more information about EFTs.

Before you contract for EFT services or make your first electronic transfer, the institution must give you the following information in a format you can keep.

- A summary of your liability for unauthorized transfers

- The phone number and address for a contact if you think an unauthorized transfer has been or may be made, the institution's "business days" (when the institution is open to the public for normal business), and the number of days you have to report suspected unauthorized transfers

- The type of transfers you can make, fees for transfers, and any limits on the frequency and dollar amount of transfers

- A summary of your right to get documentation of transfers and to stop payment on a preauthorized transfer, and how you stop payment

- A notice describing how to report an error on a receipt for an EFT or your statement, to request more information about a transfer listed on your statement, and how long you have to make your report

- A summary of the institution's liability to you if it fails to make or stop certain transactions

- Circumstances when the institution will share information about your account with third parties

- A notice that you may have to pay a fee charged by operators of ATMs where you don't have an account, for an EFT or a balance inquiry at the ATM, and charged by networks to complete the transfer.

You also will get two more types of information for most transactions: terminal receipts and periodic statements. Separate rules apply to deposit accounts from which preauthorized transfers are drawn. For example, preauthorized transfers from your account need your written or similar authorization, and a copy of that authorization must be given to you. Additional information about preauthorized transfers is in your contract with the financial institution for that account. You're entitled to a terminal receipt each time you initiate an electronic transfer, whether you use an ATM or make a point-of-sale electronic transfer, for transfers over $15. The receipt must show the amount and date of the transfer, and its type, like "from savings to checking." It also must show a number or code that identifies the account, and list the terminal location and other information. When you make a point-of-sale transfer, you'll probably get your terminal receipt from the salesperson.

You won't get a terminal receipt for regularly occurring electronic payments that you've preauthorized, like insurance premiums, mortgages, or utility bills. Instead, these transfers will appear on your statement. If the preauthorized payments vary, however, you should get a notice of the amount that will be debited at least 10 days before the debit takes place.

You're also entitled to a periodic statement for each statement cycle in which an electronic transfer is made. The statement must show the amount of any transfer, the date it was credited or debited to your account, the type of transfer and type of account(s) to or from which funds were transferred, the account number, the amount of any fees charged, the account balances at the beginning and end of the statement cycle, and the address and phone number for inquiries. You're entitled to a quarterly statement whether or not electronic transfers were made.

Keep and compare your EFT receipts with your periodic statements the same way you compare your credit card receipts with your monthly credit card statement. This will help you make the best use of your rights under federal law to dispute errors and avoid liability for unauthorized transfers.

Errors

You have 60 days from the date a periodic statement containing a problem or error was sent to you to notify your financial institution. The best way to protect yourself if an error occurs is to notify the financial institution by certified letter. Ask for a return receipt so you can prove that the institution got your letter. Keep a copy of the letter for your records.

Under federal law, the institution has no obligation to conduct an investigation if you miss the 60-day deadline.

Once you've notified the financial institution about an error on your statement, it has 10 business days to investigate. The institution must tell you the results of its investigation within three business days after completing it, and must correct an error within one business day after determining that the error has occurred. An institution usually is permitted to take more time—up to 45 days—to complete the investigation, but only if the money in dispute is returned to your account and you're notified promptly of the credit. At the end of the investigation, if no error has been found, the institution may take the money back if it sends you a written explanation.

An error also may occur in connection with a point-of-sale purchase with a debit card. For example, an oil company might give you a debit card that lets you pay for gas directly from your bank account. Or you may have a debit card that can be used for various types of retail purchases. These purchases will appear on your bank statement. In case of an error on your account, however, you should contact the card issuer (for example, the oil company or bank) at the address or phone number provided by the company for errors. Once you've notified the company about the error, it has 10 business days to investigate and tell you the results. In this situation, it may take up to 90 days to complete an investigation, if the money in dispute is returned to your account and you're notified promptly of the credit. If no error is found at the end of the investigation, the institution may take back the money if it sends you a written explanation.

Lost or Stolen ATM or Debit Cards

If your credit card is lost or stolen, you can't lose more than $50. If someone uses your ATM or debit card without your permission, you can lose much more.

- If you report an ATM or debit card missing to the institution that issues the card before someone uses the card without your permission, you can't be responsible for any unauthorized withdrawals. But if unauthorized use occurs before you report it, the amount you can be responsible for depends on how quickly you report the loss to the card issuer.

- If you report the loss within two business days after you realize your card is missing, you won't be responsible for more than $50 of unauthorized use.

- If you report the loss within 60 days after your statement is mailed to you, you could lose as much as $500 because of an unauthorized transfer.

If you don't report an unauthorized use of your card within 60 days after the card issuer mails your statement to you, you risk unlimited loss; you could lose all the money in that account, the unused portion of your maximum line of credit established for overdrafts, and maybe more.

If an extenuating circumstance, like lengthy travel or illness, keeps you from notifying the card issuer within the time allowed, the notification period must be extended. In addition, if state law or your contract imposes lower liability limits than the federal EFT Act, the lower limits apply.

Once you report the loss or theft of your ATM or debit card to the card issuer, you're not responsible for additional unauthorized use. Because unauthorized transfers may appear on your statements, though, read each statement you receive after you've reported the loss or theft. If the statement shows transfers that you didn't make or that you need more information about, contact the card issuer immediately, using the special procedures it provided for reporting errors.

Overdrafts for One-Time Debit Card Transactions and ATM Cards

If you make a one-time purchase or payment with your debit card or use your ATM card and don't have sufficient funds, an overdraft can occur. Your bank must get your permission to charge you a fee to pay for your overdraft on a one-time debit card transaction or ATM transaction. They also must send you a notice and get your opt-in agreement before charging you.

For accounts that you already have, unless you opt-in, the transaction will be declined if you don't have the funds to pay it, and you can't be charged an overdraft fee. If you open a new account, the bank can't charge you an overdraft fee for your one-time debit card or ATM transactions, either, unless you opt-in to the fees. The bank will give you a notice about opting-in when you open the account, and you can decide whether to opt-in. If you opt-in, you can cancel any time; if you don't opt-in, you can do it later.

These rules do not apply to recurring payments from your account. For those transactions, your bank can enroll you in their usual overdraft coverage. If you don't want the coverage (and the fees), contact your bank to see if they will let you discontinue it for those payments.

Limited Stop-Payment Privileges

When you use an electronic fund transfer, the EFT Act does not give you the right to stop payment. If your purchase is defective or your order isn't delivered, it's as if you paid cash: It's up to you to resolve the problem with the seller and get your money back.

One exception: If you arranged for recurring payments out of your account to third parties, like insurance companies or utilities, you can stop payment if you notify your institution at least three business days before the scheduled transfer. The notice may be written or oral, but the institution may require a written follow up within 14 days of your oral notice. If you don't follow up in writing, the institution's responsibility to stop payment ends.

Although federal law provides limited rights to stop payment, financial institutions may offer more rights or state laws may require them. If this feature is important to you, shop around to be sure you're getting the best "stop-payment" terms available.

Additional Rights

The EFT Act protects your right of choice in two specific situations: First, financial institutions can't require you to repay a loan by preauthorized electronic transfers. Second, if you're required to get your salary or government benefit check by EFT, you can choose the institution where those payments will be deposited.

Chapter 33

Ways to Make Money Online

At one time, teens looking to earn extra money had relatively few, poor-paying jobs available to them. But now, online sources provide a wide variety of opportunities to earn a good income.

Money is tight. It always is. Many high-school students are saving for college, need to help pay expenses, or just want extra cash for movies, video games, or other incidentals. College students have to think about tuition, books, lab fees and other education-related costs, as well as spending money for entertainment, snacks, and miscellaneous expenses that give them a greater degree of independence.

And, sure, there are a lot of traditional jobs for teens, such as waiting tables, working at a grocery store, mowing lawns, or working at a fast-food restaurant, and these kinds of activities still provide good opportunities for millions of students every year. But enterprising, creative young people have a wealth of other opportunities available to them in the online world. And this kind of work has a number of advantages:

- You can work from home, a dorm room, or nearby cafe, so there are no transportation issues.

- The Internet provides a level playing field; there, you're not seen as a kid earning pocket change but are judged on the quality of your work, like everyone else.

- You're also paid the same as everyone else.

- You can make money with skills learned from a hobby or special area of interest.

About This Chapter: "Ways to Make Money Online," © 2017 Omnigraphics.

- Most often, your time is your own, and you can schedule work in between classes, sports, and other activities.

So, although there's nothing wrong with bussing tables or working in a convenience store if that's what you'd like to do, consider few ways to earn money online listed below.

Taking Surveys

A really easy way to begin making some cash on the Internet is to take online surveys. Each individual survey may not pay much, but there are a lot of survey sites out there, and working with them gives you a chance to express your opinion about various topics or products and perhaps influence others. However, some of these sites can be scams trying to get personal information, so it pays to be careful. Some of the better-known survey sites include GlobalTestMarket, InBoxDollars, i-Say, MySurvey, and Toluna.

Starting a Blog or Video Blog

One way to begin is to create a website, blog, or video blog focused on something you're passionate and knowledgeable about—a hobby, sport, school subject, or other areas of interest. If you're not up to building your own website, there are a number of existing sites that will host your written blog for free, including Tumblr, Weebly, Blogger, and WordPress. Video blogs can be uploaded to sites like YouTube or Vimeo. Turning your blog into a money-making operation may take time, since you'll need to build a following, which translates into ad dollars. But once you get enough people reading or viewing your blog, platforms like Google's AdSense can help funnel money your way.

> At age 14, Ashley Qualls started Whateverlife.com, an informational website for teens. Through advertising sales, she made $1 million by the time she was 17. This success has allowed her to pursue new online interests that benefit other people and her community.

Selling Products Online

The advent of sites like eBay, Amazon, and Etsy has opened up a world of opportunity for people to sell things online. Global markets are no longer just the domain of multinational corporations. Everyone, including students, can now find worldwide buyers for everything from junk to collectibles to crafts. Even stuff that's been in your closet for years—old toys, video games, clothing, obsolete electronics—likely has value to someone, somewhere.

Testing Websites

Web developers, designers, and companies with their own sites are always looking for feedback from users, and some are willing to pay for it. If you have a good eye for detail, can identify poor navigation, design, and content, and are able to express your opinions in a clear and logical fashion, you could be an excellent candidate for testing websites. The best way to get started is to sign up at an online service that specializes in providing testers for many websites. One of the best known is UserTesting. Others include TryMyUI, Userlytics, and UserZoom. The best strategy is to sign up with as many services as possible to maximize income.

Writing for a Website

Site owners want their content refreshed regularly to keep users coming back, and that translates into opportunity for students who have the ability to write clearly and concisely on a variety of topics. A good way to begin is to approach the owners of sites you visit regularly for school, a hobby or other area of interest and ask if they need writers. Or, better yet, propose an article on a particular topic. Another option is to sign up as a writer at an online service that provides content for websites. Some of these include Iwriter, Scripted, and Writerbay. There are also sites like Articlesale that allow you to upload your own articles and make them available for sale.

Reviewing Music

Everyone has opinions about the music they listen to, so it makes sense to try to make some money reviewing songs. And since young people comprise a large segment of the listening audiences, many websites welcome the opinions of younger reviewers. At sites like MusicXray, Slicethepie, Radioloyalty, and Hitpredictor you can sign up to give a rating or write a review of songs by a variety of artists in many genres. Most don't pay much per song, but if you listen to a lot of music, the income can add up.

Programming

If you're good at programming, there are numerous opportunities for online work. Sites like Freelancer and Upwork allow you see available projects on their sites and bid on them.

In order to win the projects, you'll either need to be known to the client or submit a very low bid. But by bidding low you'll gain experience and make contacts, which will help get future jobs. There are also programming contests for various languages, in which you compete against others for prizes. Companies and web developers watch these contests to scout for new talent, so the competition can lead to money-making opportunities. And if you can develop interesting apps for mobile devices, there are many online avenues for selling them.

Data Entry

Okay, so maybe you're not a programmer, but almost anyone can key, and there are online services that pay people for data entry. This area is rife with scams, so be careful. But if you're a reasonably fast, accurate keyer there are a number of reputable services you can sign up for, including VirtualBee, SmartLocating, and Microworkers.

Selling Photography

Students who take a lot of photos for their enjoyment may not think of their pictures as a money-makers, but there are a number of online outlets that regularly buy photographs, and, as a rule, they generally don't care if the photographer is a professional or an amateur as long as the quality is good and the subject matter fits into their agenda. Some of the better known sites include Shutterstock, iStockPhoto, 500pxPrime, SmugMugPro, and Dreamstime.

Tutoring Online

If you have an outstanding skill or excel at a particular subject, you can sign up to be an online tutor. Even if you don't have formal training or an education degree, there are sites where you can register to share your knowledge. Some of these include Tutor.com, Home-workTutoring, MyTutor24, Homeworkhelp, and Tutorvista. Many online tutoring jobs take place via video chat, so a reliable webcam may be required, but others are handled by sending documents back and forth. Almost all of them offer flexible hours and the ability to pick the jobs you're interested in.

These are just some of the possible ways for students to make money online. Once you start thinking about it, many more are likely to occur to you. The main thing is to be creative, be persistent, and concentrate on areas where you have the most interest. That way the work you find will be both profitable and enjoyable. Just be sure to use common sense when it comes to online security. As with almost anything else in the cyberworld, online money-making opportunities present a lot of ways for unscrupulous people to take advantage of others.

> In addition to making money, working online also gives you the chance to try different things, make contacts for possible future work, and build your résumé.

References

1. Ahmad, Basheer. "The Best Online Jobs for College Students in 2017," CollegeStudentJobs.com, n.d.

2. Clarke, Oliver. "18 Legit Ways to Make Real Cash as a Teenager (Online)," 101Geek.com, 2016.

3. Dube, Ryan. "Best Websites for Teens to Earn Money Online," MakeUseOf.com, October 22, 2015.

4. Joseph, Frank. "How to Make Money Online for Teenagers in 2017," MoneyHome-Blog.com, January 22, 2017.

5. Satpathy, Sweta. "30 Secrets for Teens and Adults to Make Money Quickly Sitting at Home," Fedobe.com, n.d.

6. VanDerLaan, John. "12 Easy Ways for Teens to Make Money Online," Jvanderlaan.com, July 28, 2016.

Chapter 34

Develop a Financial Plan

Define Your Goals

Knowing how to secure your financial well-being is one of the most important things you can do for yourself. You don't have to be a genius to do it. You just need to know a few basics, form a plan, and be ready to stick to it.

To end up where you want to be, you need a financial plan. Ask yourself what you want. List your most important goals first. Decide how many years you have to meet each specific goal, because when you save or invest, you'll need to find an option that fits your time frame. Here are some tools to help you decide how much you'll need to save for various needs.

- The Ballpark Estimate, created by the American Savings Education Council (ASEC), can help you calculate what you'll need to save each year for retirement.

- The Financial Industry Regulatory Authority (FINRA) has a college savings calculator.

Figure out Your Finances

Take an honest look at your entire financial situation—what you own and what you owe. This is a "net worth statement." On one side, list what you own. These are your "assets. " On the other side, list what you owe. These are your "liabilities" or debts. Subtract your liabilities from your assets. If your assets are larger than your liabilities, you have a "positive" net worth. If your liabilities are larger than your assets, you have a "negative" net worth.

About This Chapter: This chapter includes text excerpted from "Define Your Goals," Investor.gov, U.S. Securities and Exchange Commission (SEC), August 25, 2016.

Drawing a Personal Financial Roadmap

Before you make any investing decision, sit down and take an honest look at your entire financial situation—especially if you've never made a financial plan before.

The first step to successful investing is figuring out your goals and risk tolerance—either on your own or with the help of a financial professional. There is no guarantee that you'll make money from your investments. But if you get the facts about saving and investing and follow through with an intelligent plan, you should be able to gain financial security over the years and enjoy the benefits of managing your money.

(Source: "Financial Navigating in the Current Economy: Ten Things to Consider before You Make Investing Decisions," U.S. Securities and Exchange Commission (SEC).)

You'll want to update your "net worth statement" every year to keep track of how you are doing. Don't be discouraged if you have a negative net worth—following a financial plan will help you turn it into positive net worth.

The next step is to keep track of your income and expenses. Write down what you and others in your family earn and spend each month, and include a category for savings and investing. If you are spending all your income, and never have money to save or invest, start by cutting back on expenses. When you watch where you spend your money, you will be surprised how small everyday expenses can add up. Many people get into the habit of saving and investing by paying themselves first. An easy way to do this is to have your bank automatically deposit money from your paycheck into a savings or investment account.

Small Savings Add up to Big Money

How much does a daily candy bar cost? Would you believe $465.84? Or more?

If you buy a candy bar every day for $1, it adds up to $365 a year. If you saved that $365 and put it into an investment that earns 5 percent a year, it would grow to $465.84 by the end of five years, and by the end of 30 years, to $1,577.50. That's the power of "compounding."

With compound interest, you earn interest on the money you save and on the interest that money earns. Over time, even a small amount saved can add up to big money.

If you buy on impulse, make a rule that you'll always wait 24 hours before buying anything. You may lose your desire to buy it after a day. Also, try emptying your pockets at the end of each day and putting spare change aside. You'll be surprised how quickly those nickels and dimes add up.

Pay Off Credit Cards or Other High Interest Debt

No investment strategy pays off as well as, or with less risk than, eliminating high interest debt. Most credit cards charge high interest rates—as much as 18 percent or more—if you don't pay off your balance in full each month. If you owe money on your credit cards, the wisest thing you can do is pay off the balance in full as quickly as possible. Virtually no investment will give you returns to match an 18 percent interest rate on your credit card. That's why you're better off eliminating all credit card debt before investing. Once you've paid off your credit cards, you can budget your money and begin to save and invest.

Here are some tips for avoiding credit card debt:

Put Away the Plastic

- Avoid a credit card unless you know you'll have the money to pay the bill when it arrives.

Know What You Owe

- It's easy to forget how much you've charged on your credit card. Every time you use a credit card, track how much you have spent and figure out how much you'll have to pay that month. If you know you won't be able to pay your balance in full, try to figure out how much you can pay each month and how long it'll take to pay the balance in full.

Pay Off the Card with the Highest Rate

- If you've got unpaid balances on several credit cards, you should first pay down the card that charges the highest rate. Pay as much as you can toward that debt each month until your balance is once again zero, while still paying the minimum on your other cards. The same advice goes for any other high-interest debt (about 8% or above), which does not offer any tax advantages.

Save for a Rainy Day

Savings are usually put into safe places that allow you access to your money at any time. Examples include savings accounts, checking accounts, and certificates of deposit. Your money may be insured by the Federal Deposit Insurance Corporation (FDIC) or National Credit Union Administration (NCUA). But there's a tradeoff between security and availability; your money earns a low interest rate.

Most smart investors put enough money in savings to cover an emergency, like sudden unemployment. Some make sure they have up to six months of their income in savings so that they know it will absolutely be there for them when they need it.

But how "safe" is a savings account if the interest it earns doesn't keep up with inflation? Let's say you save a dollar when it can buy a loaf of bread. But years later when you withdraw that dollar plus the interest you earned, it might only be able to buy half a loaf. That is why many people put some of their money in savings, but look to investing so they can earn more over longer periods of time.

Understand What It Means to Invest

When investing, you have a greater chance of losing your money than when you save. Unlike FDIC-insured deposits, the money you invest in securities, mutual funds, and other similar investments are not federally insured. You could lose your "principal," which is the amount you've invested. That's true even if you purchase your investments through a bank. But when you invest, you also have the opportunity to earn more money. On the other hand, investing involves taking on some degree of risk.

Diversify Your Investments

Diversification can be neatly summed up as, "Don't put all your eggs in one basket." The idea is that if one investment loses money, the other investments will make up for those losses. Diversification can't guarantee that your investments won't suffer if the market drops. But it

Consider Dollar Cost Averaging

Through the investment strategy known as "dollar cost averaging," you can protect yourself from the risk of investing all of your money at the wrong time by following a consistent pattern of adding new money to your investment over a long period of time. By making regular investments with the same amount of money each time, you will buy more of an investment when its price is low and less of the investment when its price is high. Individuals that typically make a lump-sum contribution to an individual retirement account either at the end of the calendar year or in early April may want to consider "dollar cost averaging" as an investment strategy, especially in a volatile market.

(Source: "Financial Navigating in the Current Economy: Ten Things to Consider before You Make Investing Decisions," U.S. Securities and Exchange Commission (SEC).)

can improve the chances that you won't lose money, or that if you do, it won't be as much as if you weren't diversified.

Gauge Your Risk Tolerance

What are the best saving and investment products for you? The answer depends on when you will need the money, your goals, and whether you will be able to sleep at night if you purchase a risky investment (one where you could lose your principal).

For instance, if you are saving for retirement, and you have 35 years before you retire, you may want to consider riskier investment products, knowing that if you stick to only the "savings" products or to less risky investment products, your money will grow too slowly. Or, given inflation and taxes, you may lose the purchasing power of your money. A frequent mistake people make is putting money they will not need for a very long time in investments that pay a low amount of interest.

On the other hand, if you are saving for a short-term goal, five years or less, you don't want to choose risky investments, because when it's time to sell, you may have to take a loss.

Learn about Investment Options

While the U.S. Securities and Exchange Commission (SEC) cannot recommend any particular investment product, a vast array of investment products exists, including stocks, mutual funds, corporate and municipal bonds, annuities, exchange-traded funds (ETFs), money market funds, and U.S. Treasury securities.

Stocks, bonds, mutual funds and ETFs are the most common asset categories. These are among the asset categories you would likely choose from when investing in a retirement savings program or a college savings plan. Other asset categories include real estate, precious metals and other commodities, and private equity. Some investors may include these asset categories within a portfolio. Investments in these asset categories typically have category-specific risks.

Before you make any investment, understand the risks of the investment and make sure the risks are appropriate for you. You'll also want to understand the fees associated with the buying, selling, and holding the investment.

Chapter 35

How to Save and Invest

The Habit of Saving or Investing

Many people get into the habit of saving or investing by following this advice: pay yourself first. Students can do this by dividing their allowance and putting some in the bank for the long term. Once they have a job, they can continue to save a portion of each paycheck.

There are many different ways for the students to save and invest. Some savings products include:

- **Savings accounts.** If you have money in a savings account, you receive interest on the account balance, and you can easily get your money whenever you want it. At most banks, your account will be insured by the Federal Deposit Insurance Corporation (FDIC). At most credit unions, your account is insured by the National Credit Union Administration (NCUA).

- **Insured bank money market accounts.** These accounts tend to offer higher interest rates than savings accounts and often give you check-writing privileges. As with other bank accounts, many bank money market accounts are insured by the FDIC. Note that bank money market accounts are not the same as money market mutual funds, which are not FDIC-insured.

- **Certificates of deposit (CD).** You can earn higher interest if you put your money in a bank certificate of deposit, or CD, which also is federally insured. When you put funds

About This Chapter: Text beginning with the heading "The Habit of Saving or Investing" is excerpted from "How to Save and Invest," Investor.gov, U.S. Securities and Exchange Commission (SEC), March 6, 2011; Text under the heading "Five Questions to Ask before You Invest" is excerpted from "Five Questions to Ask before You Invest," Investor.gov, U.S. Securities and Exchange Commission (SEC), December 17, 2009.

into a CD, you promise that you're going to keep your money in the CD for a certain amount of time. Penalties typically apply to early withdrawals.

Suggested Student Activities

Have students find current interest rates on savings accounts, bank money market accounts, and certificates of deposit. Students should notice that interest rates are higher the longer the bank or credit union holds their money. Ask them to explain why that is the case. Once people have sufficient savings, they can look to investing. Students need to understand the different types of investments, also called asset classes.

- **Stocks.** Ask students: have you ever thought that you'd like to own part of a computer company, or the company that makes the shoes on your feet? That's what happens when you buy stock in a company—you become one of the owners. How much you own of the company depends on how many shares of the company's stock you purchase.

- **Bonds.** Many companies and governments borrow money by selling bonds. When you buy a bond, you're lending your money to the company or government that issued it. The bond issuer promises to pay you interest and to return your money on a date in the future.

- **Mutual funds.** A mutual fund is an investment pool run by professional managers who research investment opportunities and select the stocks, bonds, or other investments they think are best suited for the mutual fund. Investors who buy shares of the fund will see their shares rise or fall in value as the value of the investments held by the fund rise or fall. Suggested student activities:

Have students begin learning about companies by listing items they buy or use all the time, such as food, clothing, and games. Ask them to research the parent company that makes those products. (This is called "buy what you know.") Suggest students use Electronic Data Gathering, Analysis, and Retrieval (EDGAR), the U.S. Securities and Exchange Commission's (SEC) free, online database, to help them with their research, for instance, by reviewing quarterly and annual reports filed by public companies.

- Based on the research, have students decide if these companies would be good investments.

- Once students have selected companies they believe would be a good investment, have them find and follow each company's stock price and chart if it is going up or down.

Risk and Return

Students should understand that every savings and investment product has different risks and returns. Differences include how readily investors can get their money when they need it, how fast their money will grow, and how safe their money will be.

Savings Products

Savings accounts, insured money market accounts, and CDs are viewed as very safe because they are federally insured. You can easily get to the money in savings if you need it for any reason. But there's a tradeoff for security and ready availability. The interest rate on savings generally is lower compared with investments.

While safe, savings are not risk-free: the risk is that the low-interest rate you receive will not keep pace with inflation. For example, with inflation, a candy bar that costs a dollar today could cost two dollars ten years from now. If your money doesn't grow as fast as inflation does, it's like losing money, because while a dollar buys a candy bar today, in ten years it might only buy half of one.

Investment Products

Stocks, bonds, and mutual funds are the most common investment products. All have higher risks and potentially higher returns than savings products. Over many decades, the investment that has provided the highest average rate of return has been stocks. But there are no guarantees of profits when you buy stock, which makes stock one of the most risky investments. If a company doesn't do well or falls out of favor with investors, its stock can fall in price, and investors could lose money.

You can make money in two ways from owning a stock. First, the price of the stock may rise if the company does well; the increase is called a capital gain or appreciation. Second, companies sometimes pay out a part of profits to stockholders, with a payment that's called a dividend.

Bonds generally provide higher returns with higher risk than savings, and lower returns than stocks. But the bond issuer's promise to repay principal generally makes bonds less risky than stocks. Unlike stockholders, bondholders know how much money they expect to receive, unless the bond issuer declares bankruptcy or goes out of business. In that event, bondholders may lose money. But if there is any money left, corporate bondholders will get it before stockholders.

The risk of investing in mutual funds is determined by the underlying risks of the stocks, bonds, and other investments held by the fund. No mutual fund can guarantee its returns, and no mutual fund is risk-free.

Always remember: the greater the potential return, the greater the risk. One protection against risk is time, and that's what young people have. On any day the stock market can go up or down. Sometimes it goes down for months or years. But over the years, investors who've adopted a "buy and hold" approach to investing tend to come out ahead of those who try to time the market.

Suggested Student Activities

- Now that students understand the concept of risk, how would they invest their money and why?

- If students already have selected a stock that they are following, have them chart how the stock has performed for the past two years, five years and 20 years. If an investor started with 100 shares, how much more—or less—money would she or he have now?

What Is Diversification?

One of the most important ways to lessen the risks of investing is to diversify your investments. It's common sense: don't put all your eggs in one basket. If you buy a mix of different types of stocks, bonds, or mutual funds, your overall holdings will not be wiped out if one investment fails. If you had just one investment and it went down in value, then you would lose money. But if you had ten different investments and one went down in value, you could still come out ahead.

Five Questions to Ask before You Invest

Whether you're a first-time investor or have been investing for many years, there are some basic questions you should always ask before you commit your hard-earned money to an investment.

Question 1: Is the Seller Licensed?

Research shows that con artists are experts at the art of persuasion, often using a variety of influence tactics tailored to the vulnerabilities of their victims. Smart investors check

Things to Consider before You Invest

If you want to pay for retirement, college, or a home, you may decide to invest your money to fund your goals. Before you invest, make sure you have answers to all of these questions:

- **What type of earnings can you expect on your investment?** Will you get income in the form of interest, dividends, or rent?

- **How quickly can you get your money if you need to sell or cash in your investment?** Stocks, bonds, and shares in mutual funds can usually be sold at any time, but there is no guarantee you'll get back all the money you invested. Other investments, such as certificates of deposit (CDs) or IRAs, often limit when you can cash out.

- **What can you expect to earn on your money?** Bonds generally promise a fixed return. Earnings on most other securities go up and down with market changes. Keep in mind, just because an investment has done well in the past doesn't guarantee it will do well in the future.

- **How much risk is involved?** With any investment, there is always the risk that you will not get your money back or the earnings promised. There is usually a trade-off between risk and reward—the higher the potential return, the greater the risk. While the U.S. government backs U.S. Treasury securities, it does not protect against loss on any other investments.

- **Are your investments diversified?** Putting your money in a variety of investment options--diversifying--can reduce your risk. Some investments perform better than others in certain situations. For example, when interest rates go up, bond prices tend to go down. One industry may struggle while another prospers.

- **Are there any tax advantages to a particular investment?** U.S. savings bonds are exempt from state and local taxes. Municipal bonds are exempt from federal income tax and, sometimes, state income tax as well. Tax-deferred investments for special goals, such as paying for college and retirement, let you postpone or even avoid paying income taxes.

(Source: "Saving and Investment Options," USA.gov.)

the background of anyone promoting an investment opportunity, even before learning about opportunity itself.

- **Researching brokers:** Details on a broker's background and qualifications are available for free on Financial Industry Regulatory Authority's (FINRA) BrokerCheck website.

- **Researching investment advisers:** The Investment Adviser Public Disclosure website provides information about investment adviser firms registered with the SEC and most state-registered investment adviser firms.

- **Researching SEC actions:** The SEC Action Lookup—Individuals allows you to look up information about certain individuals who have been named as defendants in SEC federal court actions or respondents in SEC administrative proceedings.

If you are not sure who to contact or have any questions regarding checking the background of an investment professional, call the SEC's toll-free investor assistance line at 800-732-0330.

Question 2: Is the Investment Registered?

Any offer or sale of securities must be registered with the SEC or exempt from registration. Registration is important because it provides investors with access to key information about the company's management, products, services, and finances.

Smart investors always check whether an investment is registered with the SEC by using the SEC's EDGAR database or contacting the SEC's toll-free investor assistance line at 800-732-0330.

Question 3: How Do the Risks Compare with the Potential Rewards?

The potential for greater returns comes with greater risk. Understanding this crucial trade-off between risk and reward can help you separate legitimate opportunities from unlawful schemes.

Investments with greater risk may offer higher potential returns, but they may expose you to greater investment losses. Keep in mind every investment carries some degree of risk and no legitimate investment offers the best of both worlds.

Many investment frauds are pitched as high return opportunities with little or no risk. Ignore these so-called opportunities or, better yet, report them to the SEC.

Question 4: Do You Understand the Investment?

Many successful investors follow this rule of thumb: Never invest in something you don't understand. Be sure to always read an investment's prospectus or disclosure statement carefully. If you can't understand the investment and how it will help you make money, ask a trusted financial professional for help. If you are still confused, you should think twice about investing.

Question 5: Where Can You Turn for Help?

Whether checking out an investment professional, researching an investment, or learning about new products or scams, unbiased information can be a great advantage when it comes to investing wisely. Make a habit of using the information and tools on securities regulators' websites. If you have a question or concern about an investment, please contact the SEC, FINRA, or your state securities regulator for help.

Chapter 36

Managing Money in the Real World

As a teen, you're beginning to make some grown-up decisions about how to save and spend your money. That's why learning the right ways to manage money . . . right from the start . . . is important. Here are suggestions.

- **Save some money before you're tempted to spend it.** When you get cash for your birthday or from a job, automatically put a portion of it—at least 10 percent, but possibly more—into a savings or investment account. This strategy is what financial advisors call "paying yourself first." Making this a habit can gradually turn small sums of money into big amounts that can help pay for really important purchases in the future.

Also, put your spare change to use. When you empty your pockets at the end of the day, consider putting some of that loose change into a jar or any other container, and then about once a month put that money into a savings account at the bank.

"Spare change can add up quickly," said Luke W. Reynolds, Chief of the Federal Deposit Insurance Corporation's (FDIC) Community Affairs Outreach Section. "But don't let that money sit around your house month after month, earning no interest and at risk of being lost or stolen."

If you need some help sorting and counting your change, he said, find out if your bank has a coin machine you can use for free. If not, the bank may give you coin wrappers.

About This Chapter: This chapter includes text excerpted from "How to Ace Your First Test Managing Real Money in the Real World," Federal Deposit Insurance Corporation (FDIC), April 9, 2018.

Some supermarkets and other nonbanking companies have self-service machines that quickly turn coins into cash, but expect to pay a significant fee for the service, often close to 10 cents for every dollar counted, plus you still have to take the cash to the bank to deposit it into your savings account.

- **Keep track of your spending.** A good way to take control of your money is to decide on maximum amounts you aim to spend each week or each month for certain expenses, such as entertainment and snack food. This task is commonly known as "budgeting" your money or developing a "spending plan." And to help manage your money, it's worth keeping a list of your expenses for about a month, so you have a better idea of where your dollars and cents are going.

"If you find you're spending more than you intended, you may need to reduce your spending or increase your income," Reynolds added. "It's all about setting goals for yourself and then making the right choices with your money to help you achieve those goals."

- **Consider a part-time or summer job.** Whether it's babysitting, lawn mowing or a job in a "real" business, working outside of your home can provide you with income, new skills, and references that can be useful after high school or college. Before accepting any job, ask your parents for their permission and advice.

- **Think before you buy.** Many teens make quick and costly decisions to buy the latest clothes or electronics without considering whether they are getting a good value.

"A $200 pair of shoes hawked by a celebrity gets you to the same destination at the same speed as a $50 pair," said Reynolds. "Before you buy something, especially a big purchase, ask yourself if you really need or just want the item, if you've done enough research and comparison-shopping, and if you can truly afford the purchase without having to cut back on spending for something else.

Identity Theft

Identity (ID) theft is a crime where a thief steals your personal information, such as your full name or social security number, to commit fraud. The identity thief can use your information to fraudulently apply for credit, file taxes, or get medical services. These acts can damage your credit status, and cost you time and money to restore your good name. You may not know that you are the victim of ID theft until you experience a financial consequence (mystery bills, credit collections, denied loans) down the road from actions that the thief has taken with your stolen identity.

(Source: "Scams and Frauds—Identity Theft," USA.gov.)

- **Protect yourself from crooks who target teens.** Even if you're too young to have a checking account or credit card, a criminal who learns your name, address and Social Security number (SSN) may be able to obtain a new credit card using your name to make purchases.

One of the most important things you can do to protect against identity theft is to be very suspicious of requests for your name, Social Security number, passwords or bank or credit card information that come to you in an e-mail or an Internet advertisement, no matter how legitimate they may seem.

"Teens are very comfortable using e-mail and the Internet, but they need to be aware that criminals can be hiding at the other end of the computer screen," said Michael Benardo, manager of the FDIC's financial crimes section. These types of fraudulent requests can also come by phone, text message or in the mail.

- **Be smart about college.** If you're planning to go to college, learn about your options for saving or borrowing money for what could be a major expense—from tuition to books, fees, and housing. Also, consider the costs when you search for a school. Otherwise, when you graduate, your college debts could be high and may limit your options when it comes to a career path or where you can afford to live.

Avoid Borrowing Money

Understand that borrowing money comes with costs and responsibilities. When you borrow money, you generally will repay the money monthly and pay interest. Always compare offers to borrow money based on the Annual Percentage Rate (APR). The lower the APR, the less you will pay in interest. And, the longer you take to repay a debt, the more you will pay in interest. If you miss loan payments, you can expect to pay fees and have a hard time borrowing money at affordable rates for some time into the future.

(Source: "For Young Adults and Teens: Quick Tips for Managing Your Money," Federal Deposit Insurance Corporation (FDIC).)

- **Be careful with credit cards.** Under most state laws, you must be at least 18 years old to obtain your own credit card and be held responsible for repaying the debt. If you're under 18, though, you may be able to qualify for a credit card as long as a parent or other adult agrees to repay your debts if you fail to do so.

An alternative to a credit card is a debit card, which automatically deducts purchases from your savings or checking account. Credit cards and debit cards offer convenience, but they also come with costs and risks that must be taken seriously.

Chapter 37

Managing Money/Financial Empowerment

Borrowing Money
Higher Education Loans

If You Need to Borrow for Higher Education, do your homework and have a repayment plan. College or graduate degrees can provide career options and higher income, but they also can be expensive. If you need to borrow for school, carefully consider your options, keep the loan amount as low as possible, and have a clear repayment plan. Here are strategies to keep in mind.

Obtaining a Student Loan

- **First look into your eligibility for grants and scholarships.** Many students qualify for some aid, so start by filling out the *Free Application for Federal Student Aid (FAFSA®)* on the U.S. Department of Education's (ED) website at www.studentaid.gov.

- **Know how much you need to borrow and that you can make the monthly payments.** Your anticipated costs (tuition, textbooks, housing, food, transportation) minus your education savings, family contributions, income from work-study or a job, scholarships and/or grants will help determine how much you may need to borrow. Again, your goal should be to limit the amount you borrow, even if you are approved for a larger loan, because the more you borrow, the more money you will owe.

About This Chapter: This chapter includes text excerpted from "For Young Adults and Teens: Quick Tips for Managing Your Money," Federal Deposit Insurance Corporation (FDIC), 2012.

Also consider the minimum you will owe each month to pay off your loans, including interest, after you graduate and how it compares to your projected earnings. To help you project your future salary in the lines of work you're considering, look at the U.S. Department of Labor's (DOL) statistics on wages in more than 800 occupations (www.bls.gov/oes). Your monthly repayment amount also will generally depend on your interest rate and the term of your loan, which can vary from 10 years to more than 20 years.

"Even though most student loans won't require you to begin monthly payments until after you graduate—generally six to nine months later—a student loan is a serious commitment," said Matt Homer, a Federal Deposit Insurance Corporation (FDIC) policy analyst. He noted, for example, that many adults who borrowed more than they could afford to repay have faced serious debt problems for many years following their graduation. Unlike some other loans, federal and private student loans generally cannot be discharged through bankruptcy. Borrowers who fail to pay their student loans could be referred to debt collection agencies, experience a drop in their credit score (which will make credit more expensive and perhaps make it harder to find a job), and have a portion of their wages withheld.

If you need help deciding how much to borrow, consider speaking with a specialist at your school (perhaps a school counselor at your high school or an admissions or financial aid officer at your college). A college budget calculator also can be helpful, and you can use one from the U.S. Department of Education (ED) by going to http://go.usa.gov/YhFC and clicking on "Manage Your Spending."

- **Consider federal loans first if you need to borrow.** Experts say that, in general, federal loans are better than private student loans, and that you should only consider private loans if you've reached your borrowing limit with federal loans. Why? The interest rates on federal loans are fixed, meaning they won't change over time. But the interest rates on private loans, which are often significantly higher, could be either fixed or variable (they can fluctuate). Federal student loans also offer more flexible repayment plans and options to postpone your loan payments if you are having financial problems.

When You Are in School

Set up direct deposit for your student aid money. Although some schools or financial institutions may encourage you to select a certain debit card or prepaid card for receiving part of your student loan or other aid (the part left after your school has subtracted tuition and fees), carefully weigh all of your options. School-preferred products may come with high fees and inconvenient ATM locations. Remember that you can always deposit federal loan proceeds anywhere you choose.

Keep track of the total amount you have borrowed and consider reducing it, if possible. For example, if your loan accrues interest while you're in school, you may be able to make interest payments while still in school, and this can reduce the amount owed later on. You could also repay some of the principal (the amount borrowed) before the repayment period officially begins.

Paying Off Your Loan

- **Select your repayment plan.** Federal loans offer a variety of repayment options and you can generally change to a different repayment plan at any time. For Example, one type of loan starts off with low payment amounts that increase over time. Another is the "Pay as You Earn" program that the U.S. Department of Education (ED) will soon make available, in which your monthly payment amount will be 10 percent of your "discretionary" income (defined by the Department's regulations but generally what you have left over after paying key expenses). In addition, it may be possible to have any remaining balance forgiven after 20 years of payments. In contrast, private loans generally require fixed monthly payments over a period of time.

With federal loans, you also may qualify for special loan forgiveness benefits if you pursue certain careers in public service. Remember, though, that the longer you take to repay any loan, the more you pay in interest (although in some cases you may receive a tax benefit for the interest you pay).

- **Make your loan payments on time.** "Student loans are typically reported to credit bureaus, so paying on time can help build a good credit history, and paying late can harm your credit history," said Elizabeth Khalil, a Senior Policy Analyst in the FDIC's Division of Depositor and Consumer Protection (DCP). To help you stay on schedule, consider having your payments automatically deducted from your bank account or arranging for e-mail or text message reminders.

Also, make sure your loan servicer—the company that collects your payments and administers your loan—has your current contact information so you don't miss important correspondence, such as a change in a due date.

- **Consider making extra payments to pay off your loan faster.** If you are able to, start by paying the student loans with the highest interest rates. If you have more than one student loan with a particular servicer, make it clear that you want to apply any extra payments to reduce the balance of the higher-rate loans.

- **Look into refinancing opportunities.** You may be able to obtain a lower interest rate and even consolidate multiple loans of the same type into one loan. However, be aware that if you consolidate or refinance a federal loan into a private loan, you may lose important benefits associated with the federal loan (such as loan forgiveness for entering public service). In some cases, even consolidating one type of federal loan into a different kind of federal loan can result in loss benefits.

- **Contact your loan servicer immediately if you're having difficulty repaying.** Repaying student loans can be challenging, especially during tough economic times. "Remember that if you have a federal student loan that you're having trouble paying, you have options that could help. Private loan borrowers may be able to get some assistance as well," noted Jonathan Miller, Deputy Director In the FDIC's Division of Division of Depositor and Consumer Protection (DCP).

Auto Loans: How to Get a Good Deal

Many young people look forward to getting their own car but overlooks what they may need to do to comfortably afford it, especially if they'll be borrowing money. Here are strategies to consider well before you go to the dealership.

- **Start saving early.** "The more money you put down, the less you have to borrow—and that means the less money you'll pay in interest on a loan, if you need to borrow at all," said Phyllis Pratt, an FDIC community affairs specialist.

- **Decide how much you can afford to spend each month on a car.** In addition to car payments, consider how much you'll need for insurance, taxes, registration fees, routine maintenance and unexpected repairs. Online calculators can help you figure out what you can afford.

- **Remember that there are alternatives to buying a car.** Lease Payments may sometimes appear lower than loan payments, but at the end of the lease you will not own the car and you may have to pay more money for excess mileage or body repairs. If You need a car only once in a while, consider using a service that rents cars for periods as short as an hour.

- **Shop for a loan at your bank as well as several other lenders.** Compare the offers based on the annual percentage rate (APR) you're quoted by each lender. The APR reflects the total cost of the loan, including interest and certain fees, as a yearly rate. Then consider getting "prequalified" by the lender offering the best deal. That's not the same as a loan approval, but it will expedite the process once you find a car you like. Before you start shopping for a loan, review your credit report to correct wrong information, which can help you qualify for a lower interest rate In addition, a dealer's special financing (such as zero-percent interest) may not be the best value if it means foregoing an extra discount on the car. In that situation, you may come out ahead if you borrow from a financial institution, even at a higher interest rate, and save on the purchase price. Also, don't purchase a more expensive car than you feel you can comfortably afford, even if you qualify for a larger loan.

- **Whether you are buying or leasing, negotiate with the dealer based on the total cost of the car, not the monthly payment.** Why? "By extending the length of the loan, a dealer can offer a more expensive vehicle with the same monthly loan payment you were quoted for a less expensive car, but you will pay more in interest costs," said Luke W. Reynolds, Acting Associate Director of the FDIC's Division of Depositor and Consumer Protection.

Build a Good Credit Record: It's Important for Loan and Job Applications

As you become responsible for paying your own debts—for credit card purchases, rent, car or student loans, and other obligations—you are building a credit history. In general, the better your credit history and the resulting credit score (a number summarizing your credit record prepared by companies called credit bureaus), the better your chances of getting a loan with a good interest rate. A strong credit score also can help when you apply for a job, an insurance policy, or for an apartment. How can you build and maintain a good credit history?

- **Pay your loans, bills, and other debts on time.** This will show you are responsible with your finances.

- **If you have a credit card, try to charge only what you can afford to pay off immediately or very soon.** If You can't pay your credit card bill in full, try to pay more than the minimum balance due so that you can minimize the interest payments. Also be aware that your credit score will likely fall if you owe a significant amount on your credit card compared to the card's credit limit. Applying for multiple cards also can lower your credit score.

- **Review your credit reports for errors.** Correcting wrong information in your credit history may improve your credit report and score. To obtain a free copy of your credit report from each of the three major credit bureaus, visit www.annualcreditreport.com or call toll-free 877-322-8228. If you are unable to resolve a dispute with a credit bureau over wrong information in your file, you can submit a complaint online at www.consumerfinance.gov/complaint.

Saving Money
Simple Ways to Rev Up Your Savings

You can meet your goals with automated deposits and investments. Many people starting out in their careers find themselves burdened with lots of debt (perhaps from student loans, credit cards, and car loans) and very little savings for future needs. But there are simple strategies for gradually building small savings or investments into large sums, even during your school years, and often with the help of automated services that make it easy. Here are key examples.

- **Save for specific goals.** You Should have a savings plan for large future expenses that you anticipate—perhaps education costs, a home or car purchase, starting a small business, or preparing for retirement (even though that may be many years away). And, young adults just starting to be responsible for their own expenses should build up an "emergency" fund that would cover at least six months of living expenses to help get through a difficult time, such as a job loss, major car repairs or unexpected medical expenses not covered by insurance.

- **Commit to saving money regularly.** This is important for everyone, but especially if you are supporting yourself financially. "Even if you don't make a big salary or have a steady source of income, the combination of consistently adding to savings and the compounding of interest can bring dramatic results overtime," said Luke W. Reynolds, Acting Associate Director of the FDIC Division of Division of Depositor and Consumer Protection (DCP).

Aim to save a minimum of 10 percent of any money you earn or otherwise receive. Putting aside a designated amount is known as "paying yourself first," because you are saving before you're tempted to spend.

- **Put your savings on autopilot.** Make saving money quick and easy by having your employer direct-deposit part of your paycheck into a federally insured savings account. Your employer your financial institution may be able to set this up for you. If you don't yet have a steady job, you can still set up regular transfers into a savings account.

- **Make use of tax-advantaged retirement accounts and matching funds.** Look into all your retirement savings options at work, which may come with matching contributions from your employer. "Chances are your retirement savings will hardly reduce your take-home pay because of what you'll save in income taxes, and the sooner you start in your career, the more you can take advantage of compound growth," Reynolds said.

If you've contributed the maximum at work or if your employer doesn't have a retirement savings program, consider establishing your own individual retirement account (IRA) with a financial institution or investment firm and make regular transfers into it. Remember that you can set up an automatic transfer from a checking account into savings or investments for retirement or any purpose.

- **Decide where to keep the money intended for certain purposes.** For example:

  - Consider keeping emergency savings in a separate federally insured savings account instead of a checking account so that you can better resist the urge to raid the funds for everyday expenses. Be sure to develop a plan to replenish any withdrawals from your emergency fund.

  - For large purchases, you hope to make years from now, consider certificates of deposit and U.S. savings bonds, which generally earn more interest than a basic savings account because you agree to keep the funds untouched for a minimum period of time.

  - For other long-term savings, including retirement savings, young adults may want to consider supplementing their insured deposits with low-fee, diversified mutual funds (a professionally managed mix of stocks, bonds and so on) or similar investments that are not deposits and are not insured against loss by the FDIC. With nondeposit investments, you assume the risk of loss for the opportunity to have a higher rate of return over many years.

  - For future college expenses, look into "529 plans," which provide an easy way to save for college expenses and may offer tax benefits.

  - For healthcare, find out whether you are eligible for a "health savings account," a tax-advantaged way for people enrolled in high-deductible health insurance plans to save for medical expenses.

  - Think about ways to cut your expenses and add more to savings. For your financial services, research lower-cost checking accounts at your bank and some competitors. And if you are paying interest on credit cards fees for spending more money than you have available in your checking account, develop a plan to stop. More Broadly, look at your monthly expenses for everything from food to phones and think about ways to save.

Your Bank Accounts
For Everyday Banking: Choosing the Best Account for You

Whether you're a 20-something just starting a career or a family or you're still in school, a checking or other transaction account will be essential to making payments and managing your income and budget. These tips can save you time and money.

- Look for a bank account that offers the services you want and low fees. Contact multiple institutions and determine which accounts are considered best for young adults or students. Look at services you are most likely to use and the related fees, including any penalties if the balance drops below a minimum. One service you should expect to use is direct deposit of your paycheck. "With direct deposit, you don't have to worry about getting to the bank to deposit the funds because it will be done automatically for you," said Nancy Tillman, an FDIC Consumer Affairs Specialist. Direct deposit will arrive at your bank fast, and it may save you money on your bank account.

For guidance on what an affordable transaction account or savings account for a young consumer could look like, aspects of some low-cost accounts suggested by the FDIC may be helpful.

- Consider a low-cost banking account before settling for a prepaid card. Reloadable prepaid cards that can be used at merchants and ATMs are sometimes marketed as alternatives to traditional bank transaction accounts. While prepaid cards may be useful in some situations, they generally cannot match a well-managed, properly selected, low-cost, insured deposit account when it comes to federally-guaranteed consumer protections, the safety of deposit insurance, monthly charges and transaction fees, and the flexibility to save money and conduct a wide range of everyday banking transactions.

"Before you get a prepaid card, you should carefully read the cardholder agreement, which should be readily available on the card's website, to make sure you understand the terms and fee schedule," suggested Susan Welsh, FDIC Consumer Affairs Specialist.

Also be aware that the funds you place on a prepaid card may or may not be protected by FDIC insurance if the bank that holds the money (for you and other customers) were to fail. If you have questions, call the FDIC toll-free at 877-ASK-FDIC (877-275-3342).

- Debit cards provide a great service, but understand the pros, cons, and costs. Debit cards, which deduct funds directly from your checking or savings account, offer a convenient way to pay for purchases and to access cash at stores or ATMs. "Debit cards can help you stay within budget as long as you don't overdraw your account. Then you are spending money, not money you have borrowed," said Alberto Navarrete, an FDIC Consumer Affairs Specialist.

But debit cards can be costly if you're not careful. For example, expect fees if you drop below a minimum required account balance or you use the card at another bank's ATM. Also, you should report a lost or stolen card immediately to minimize your liability for unauthorized transactions. Welsh Added that consumers who lose a debit card they rely on for all their transactions can ask for speedy delivery of a replacement card.

- Avoid overdraft costs. Ask your bank if it can link your checking account to your savings account and automatically transfer money between accounts if you empty your checking account. The transfer fee will probably be considerably less than a regular overdraft fee. Also review your account frequently, if not daily, online. "Many Banks have online banking services that send text or e-mail alerts when your balance reaches below a certain dollar amount that you can set," advised Joni Creamean, Chief of the FDIC Consumer Response Center.

Also, think carefully before you "opt in" (agree) to an overdraft program, which can be costly. In general, opting in means that if you swipe your debit card and don't have enough funds to cover the transaction, the bank will charge you an overdraft fee to let the transaction go through. That could result in a $5 purchase, such as a cup of coffee and a muffin, costing you an extra $35.

"Remember that your decision whether or not to opt in only applies to everyday debit card transactions. The bank could still charge a significant fee if, for instance, you write a check when you don't have enough money in your account to cover it," cautioned Jonathan Miller, Deputy Director in the FDIC's Division of Depositor and Consumer Protection.

You can also avoid unexpected fees by keeping a close watch on your balance before spending money from your checking account.

Finally, if you are billed an overdraft fee that you believe is incorrect, contact your bank immediately. If The institution will not refund the fee, contact its federal regulator for assistance. "If you are not sure who regulates the bank, you may always file your complaint with the FDIC and we will make sure it gets forwarded to the correct agency for investigation," said Creamean. You can submit your complaint online at www2.fdic.gov/StarsMail/index.asp.

- If you're a college student receiving financial aid, do your homework before choosing an account and a debit card. "Before Your financial aid is disbursed, check out the program offered through your school. You need to understand the terms of that product before you are committed to use it to access your financial aid," Tillmon said. "If you have an existing bank account with a debit card that you will be using on campus, you may be better off having the financial aid money deposited there."

Where to Begin: Saving and Managing Your Own Money

As a teen, you start taking more responsibility for handling money and choosing how you want to save or use it. Here are a few ideas to help make your decisions easier... and better.

- Consider a part-time or summer job. A job can provide you with additional money as well as new skills, and connections to people who may be helpful after you graduate.

If you are filling out a job application for a company with a local office, experts say it's generally safe to provide information such as your date of birth and Social Security number (which may be needed for a background check). If you are applying in person, hand the application to the manager (not just any employee), and if you are applying online, make sure you are using the company's legitimate website.

"But be very suspicious of online job applications for part-time, work-from-home jobs offered by unfamiliar companies without a local office," warned Michael Bernardo, Manager of the FDIC's Cyber Fraud And Financial Crimes Section. "They May only want to commit identity theft, not hire you."

- Open a savings account and put money in it for specific goals. "Some Goals will be for the next few weeks or months, while others are for several years away, such as college," said Irma Matias, an FDIC Community Affairs Specialist. Get in the habit of putting at least 10 percent of any gifts or earnings in a savings account right away. Saving a certain percentage of your income before you're tempted to spend it is what financial advisors call "paying yourself first."

Also, think about where you can add to savings by cutting back on spending. "Money you spend today is money you won't have for future wants or needs," added Matias.

- If you're ready for a checking account, choose one carefully. Many banks offer accounts geared to teens or other students that require less money to open and charge lower fees than their other accounts. "Even if the account appears to be attractive, think about how you're going to use it—for example, if you mostly want to bank online or with your smartphone—and look into how much that account is likely to cost monthly," said Luke

W. Reynolds, acting associate director of the FDIC's Division of Depositor and Consumer Protection. "The shop around and compare this account to what is offered by several other institutions."

When you open an account that comes with a debit card, you will decide how you want the bank to handle an everyday debit card transaction for more than what you have in the account. If you "opt in" (agree) to a bank overdraft program, it will cover these transactions but will charge you fee of as much as $40 each time. "One Overdraft can easily lead to another and become very costly," Reynolds explained. "If you don't opt in, your transactions will be declined, but you won't have to face these penalty fees."

You may also be able to arrange with your bank to automatically transfer money from a savings account to cover the purchase. You'll probably pay a fee, but it will likely be much less than an overdraft fee.

- If you're thinking about using a prepaid card instead of a bank account, understand the potential drawbacks. Prepaid cards often do not offer you the same federal consumer protections as credit or debit cards if, for example, the prepaid card is lost or stolen and used by someone else. And, while prepaid cards may advertise no monthly fee, they may charge for making withdrawals, adding money to the card or checking the balance. "It's hard for a prepaid card to beat a well-selected, well-managed checking account for everyday transactions and allowing easy transfers into a savings account," Reynolds concluded.

- Once you have a bank account, keep a close eye on it. Watch your balance the best way you can. For Example, keep receipts and record expenses so you don't spend more money than you have in your account and run the risk of overdraft costs.

- Take precautions against identity theft. Even if you don't have a credit card, you can be targeted by a criminal wanting to use your name to get money or buy goods. So, be very suspicious of requests for your name, Social Security Number, passwords, or bank or credit card information.

"Don't fall for an e-mail, call, or text message asking you for financial information," Benardo cautioned. "Never give out any personal information unless you have contacted the company first and you are sure it is legitimate."

- Understand that borrowing money comes with costs and responsibilities. When you borrow money, you generally will repay the money monthly and pay interest. Always compare offers to borrow money based on the annual percentage rate (APR). The lower the APR, the less you will pay in interest. And, the longer you take to repay a debt, the more you will pay in interest. If you miss loan payments, you can expect to pay fees and have a hard time borrowing money at affordable rates for some time into the future.

Chapter 38

Financial Checkup

Any time of year, but particularly the start of a new year, is a good time to reflect on how you are managing your finances and to consider whether you would benefit from some changes. Here's a checklist of questions and suggestions that can help you better evaluate and meet your goals.

Saving
What Are My Current Short- and Long-Term Financial Goals?

Write them down. They may include paying off a debt, buying a home or a car, or financing a child's college education. "With goals and target dollar amounts in mind, you may be more motivated to save money and achieve your objectives," said Luke W. Reynolds, Chief of the Federal Deposit Insurance Corporation's (FDIC) Outreach and Program Development Section.

Can I Do Better Making Automatic Transfers into Savings?

"Arranging for your bank or employer to automatically transfer funds into savings or retirement accounts is a great way to build savings, but don't just set it and forget it," said Keith Ernst, Associate Director of the FDIC's Division of Depositor and Consumer Protection in charge of consumer research. "Ask yourself whether you should increase the amount you are automatically saving."

About This Chapter: This chapter includes text excerpted from "Is It Time for Your Financial Checkup?" Federal Deposit Insurance Corporation (FDIC), October 15, 2014.

Do I Have Enough Money in an Emergency Savings Fund?

The idea is to cover major unexpected expenses or a temporary reduction in income without borrowing money. Figure out how much you would need to pay for, say, three to six months of essential expenses (housing, transportation, medical costs and so on). If you don't have that much money in a savings account, start setting aside what you would need. For anyone struggling to build a "rainy day fund" or reach any major savings target, setting up automatic transfers is a steady way to work toward that goal.

Do My Checking and Savings Account Choices Meet My Needs at a Reasonable Cost?

Start by talking to a representative at your current bank and/or visiting your bank's website. That's because some banks only offer certain deals in their branches but not online, or vice versa. "If you paid checking account overdraft fees recently, look into ways to avoid them, starting with keeping a closer eye on your balance," said Luke W. Reynolds, Chief of the FDIC's Outreach and Program Development Section. "And for money you don't need in the near future, remember that nondeposit investment products may have the potential for a higher return but you can also lose some or all of the money you invest." He added that if you have multiple accounts, consider whether consolidating them may save you money and time in monitoring transactions.

Taking Precautions
Am I Adequately Insured?

Having enough life, health, disability, property, and other insurance is essential to protect your finances from a sudden shock. You may find savings on your existing policies by getting updated quotes from your current insurer and comparing them to quotes from at least two other companies.

Am I Prepared Financially in Case of a Fire, Flood, or Other Emergency?

In addition to having your most important possessions insured, ask yourself how your most important documents would be saved from ruin.

Is the Personal Information on My Computer And/Or Smartphone Properly Protected?

Use and automatically update anti-virus software and a firewall to secure your computer. Arrange for your computer or phones to regularly download and install any "patches" (system updates) the manufacturers produce to address security weaknesses. For unlocking your computer and mobile devices and for logging into websites and apps, create "strong" IDs and passwords with combinations of upper- and lowercase letters, numbers and symbols that are hard to guess, and then change the passwords regularly. "Try not to use the same password at more than one site," advised Michael Benardo, manager of the FDIC's Financial Crimes Section. "And if you feel a need to keep a written list of passwords, which is not recommended, try instead to use word and number combinations that vary slightly between sites, which may be easier for you to remember."

Am I Taking Precautions with My Personal Information When I Go to Social Networking Sites?

Scammers try to collect even minor details about an individual, such as a pet's name or a high school mascot, in hopes that they can use this information to reset the passwords on a bank or investment account and commit fraud. Social media sites are places where criminals can often find this information.

Am I Keeping the Right Financial Records?

When it comes to paper versions of records like old bank statements, credit card bills and receipts, consider keeping only those you may need to protect yourself in the event of, say, a tax audit or a dispute with a merchant or manufacturer. Documents you don't need can be discarded, but shred or otherwise securely destroy records that contain personal information. It's also good to keep a list of your financial accounts and personal documents in one secure place, so that a loved one responsible for your affairs could easily find it.

Spending
Do I Have a Good Plan for How I Spend My Money?

Start by listing how much money you take in over a typical four-week period, what expenses you need to pay, and how much goes to savings. Include any large expenses you pay annually or semiannually, such as taxes or insurance premiums. Also pay attention to small expenses, from entertainment to snack food, which can take a toll on your finances. Then jot down ways you can control your spending. Online tools also can help you develop a more comprehensive budget.

Are All the Expenses I'm Paying for Automatically Each Month Really Worth It?

Some expenses you've put on auto-pilot may look small but can add up over the course of a year. Start by reviewing your credit card and checking account statements for expenses that get charged on a recurring basis. Consider whether you still get value from each product or service. Also find out if you may already be receiving the same benefits elsewhere or if you can negotiate a better deal with the company.

"Examples of spending you might be able to reduce could include memberships, extras on your cable TV subscription, or certain options on a cellphone package," said Reynolds. "And, if you are paying for identity theft or credit protection plans [products that would postpone or make your loan payments if you die or become ill or unemployed] ask yourself whether you get the value you pay for them. Keep in mind that federal law affords you considerable protections in the event of fraudulent activity involving your bank accounts or credit cards."

Borrowing
Am I Reviewing My Credit Reports for Accuracy?

Correcting errors may help you improve your credit history and credit score, which can save you money when you need to borrow money. And reviewing your credit reports can help you detect identity theft or errors that could cause you other hassles, such as higher insurance premiums.

Federal law gives you the right to one free copy of your credit report every 12 months. There are three major nationwide consumer reporting agencies (also called "credit bureaus")— Equifax, Experian and TransUnion—and each one issues its own report. Go to www.Annual-CreditReport.com, or call toll-free 877-322-8228, to order your free credit reports from each agency. There also are "specialty" credit bureaus that, for example, track a person's history of handling a checking account or prepare risk profiles that insurers may use when determining your insurance premium.

Is There More That I Can Do to Cut the Costs of a Mortgage Loan?

For example, if you have an adjustable-rate mortgage with an interest rate about to go up, find out if there are lower rates for which you might qualify. Also inquire about your options for refinancing into a different, better loan. You also can research the pros and cons of making additional payments to principal (to pay off the loan sooner) or even paying off the mortgage outright.

Can I Do More to Reduce the Interest I'm Paying on Other Debts?

Any reduction of outstanding debts, particularly those that charge you the highest interest rate, will bring you savings in interest expenses. For example, look into paying all—or at least more—of your credit card balance.

Am I Truly Benefiting from My Credit Card Rewards Programs?

These features can be beneficial, but you have to know what to do to earn extra cash or keep "points" or miles. A rewards program also may have changed since you last looked at it. Also, don't let the allure of rewards be the only factor in choosing a card. "It's not just cash back or points that can make a card appealing. Features like a low interest rate and minimal or no fees can also be beneficial," said Elizabeth Khalil, a Senior Policy Analyst at the FDIC.

If you're considering closing a credit card account that you've managed well for a long time, instead consider the alternative of keeping the card but not using it. That's because closing the account could adversely affect your credit score, which lenders often use to determine your interest rate. According to Jonathan Miller, Deputy Director for Policy and Research in the FDIC Division of Depositor and Consumer Protection, "If you do keep the account open and continue to use the card occasionally, be careful to keep it in a secure place and periodically monitor the account to make sure a fraudster isn't using it instead."

Your Rights to Financial Privacy: How to Stay Informed

You're probably used to receiving privacy notices from your financial institutions explaining how they handle and share your personal information. Federal law requires that you receive a notification about your privacy rights when you open an account, then at least annually, and again if the institution changes its privacy policy. And, in some cases, these privacy statements are available for review at any time online. Unfortunately, many consumers don't review these disclosures, which describe how your information will be used, whether you can choose to "opt out" or say "no" to some sharing of your personal financial information, and how you can do so.

"The privacy notices include important descriptions of rights you may have to limit information sharing with other parts of the same company as well as with unaffiliated companies," said Beverly Shuck, Acting Chief of the FDIC's Consumer Response Center. "If you want to control information sharing, you should take these mailings seriously.

The privacy notices also will explain what you can't prevent from being shared. This is likely to include customer information provided to outside firms that market your financial company's own products, handle data processing services or mail out monthly statements to customers. Banks that limit their sharing to these circumstances will provide a privacy notice stating that, as well as the fact that the customers don't have the right to opt out of any data sharing.

In October 2014, the Consumer Financial Protection Bureau (CFPB) adopted a rule that allows financial institutions that do not engage in certain types of information-sharing to post their annual privacy notices online rather than delivering them individually. In these circumstances, consumers also must be able to call a toll-free number to request a paper copy of the privacy disclosure. Contact your financial institution if you have questions or concerns about its privacy policy. If you're not satisfied with the answers, you may wish to contact the institution's primary federal or state regulator.

"Remember that privacy practices differ at various financial institutions," said Ed Nygard, a Senior Consumer Affairs Specialist at the FDIC. "If you are uncomfortable with the way your information will be treated at one institution, you may wish to shop around for a different one." You also have the right to prohibit credit bureaus from providing information about you to lenders and insurers that want to send you unsolicited offers of credit or insurance.

(Source: "Your Rights to Financial Privacy: How to Stay Informed," Federal Deposit Insurance Corporation (FDIC).)

Part Five
Smart Spending

Chapter 39

Online Shopping: A Guide for E-Consumers

You can buy virtually anything online today, from clothing and electronics to handmade craft items and groceries. No matter what you're looking for, you are likely to find a website that sells it. The infinite variety of goods available on the Internet, along with the ease and convenience of online shopping, has led to tremendous growth in electronic commerce (e-commerce). *Fortune* magazine reported that 190 million Americans shopped online in 2016, and online shopping accounted for 51 percent of overall purchases. While online shopping is very popular and offers many benefits, you still need to be careful to choose reputable sellers, protect your privacy, and avoid scams.

> Amazon is the undisputed leader of online shopping. The company earned $82.7 billion in sales revenue in 2016, an increase of nearly 16 percent from the previous year.

Benefits of Online Shopping

Online shopping has grown tremendously as consumers have recognized the many benefits it offers, which include the following:

- **Convenience**—you can shop from home on your computer or from anywhere on your smartphone or laptop, at any time of the day or night.

- **Time savings**—you don't have to drive to the store or wait in a checkout line, and the product will be delivered right to your doorstep.

About This Chapter: "Online Shopping: A Guide for E-Consumers," © 2017 Omnigraphics.

- **Comparison shopping**—you can easily compare the prices and selection available on different websites.

- **Cost savings**—you can find clearance sales or research online coupons to save money.

- **Product reviews**—you can ask questions or read reviews posted by other people who have purchased a product.

- **Wide selection**—you can buy specialty items that are difficult to find or out of season.

- **Customer support**—many websites offer online customer service via e-mail or chat functions.

- **Easy returns and exchanges**—most reputable online sellers have generous return policies that allow you to simply put the item back in the box and drop it off at a nearby shipping location.

Types of Online Shopping Sites

Once you've made the decision to shop online, the next step is to figure out what type of online store to visit. The different types of shopping websites available include the following:

Online Marketplaces

Amazon is the world's largest online retailer, offering more than 480 million products for sale on its website and serving more than 300 million customers worldwide. Many other online shopping sites provide one-stop shopping for a variety of general merchandise, including Target, WalMart, Overstock.com, and Wayfair.

Manufacturer Websites

Many companies that produce consumer goods, like clothing or electronics, offer their products for sale on their own websites. Buying direct from the manufacturer often provides better product information, customer service, and warranties, but you may be able to find better prices elsewhere.

Price Comparison Websites

A number of search engine sites are available to help consumers compare the deals available through various online retailers. Sites like PriceGrabber, NexTag, Bizrate, and Shopzilla gather information from multiple online stores in one location, although advertising some-times influences what sites are listed.

Online Auction Sites

A wide variety of goods are available at bargain prices on auction sites like eBay, Listia, uBid, and ShopGoodwill. Name-brand merchandise is sometimes listed at deep discounts, and vendors often have collector items and hard-to-find pieces for sale as well. To participate in an auction, you simply register as a user and place your bids. The security risk is somewhat higher than manufacturer sites, but most auction sites provide ratings to help you evaluate sellers' past history.

Online Classifieds

Sites like Craigslist and Recycler are similar to the classified advertisements that appear in newspapers. People place ads for items that they wish to buy or sell and connect with others online to complete the transaction. Although these sites may provide good deals on used merchandise, you should proceed with caution because it can be difficult to evaluate the honesty of the seller.

Online shopping has gone mobile: 44 percent of smartphone owners used their phones to make an online purchase in 2016.

Making an Online Purchase

Once you have found an item that you are interested in buying online, there are a number of important steps to follow before you complete your purchase, such as:

- **Read the fine print**

  Be sure to read and understand all the terms and conditions of the sale. Double check the product description, price, taxes, delivery date, and shipping costs. See if the product comes with a warranty, if the seller accepts returns, and how the retailer handles complaints or disputes.

- **Look for secure checkout**

  Before entering a credit card number or other personal information, make sure the online shopping site offers secure checkout. You might see a padlock next to the URL in your browser's status bar, or the website might begin with https (with the "s" meaning secure). Most online shopping sites use Secure Sockets Layer (SSL) technology to encrypt your payment details as the information travels through the Internet.

- **Check the privacy policy**

  Reputable websites provide customers with access to a privacy policy that outlines exactly what personal information is collected, how it is used, and whether it is stored or shared with third parties. Many websites use "cookies," or small files that are placed on your computer, to store information about you and your browsing habits. Some retailers sell customer information and buying preferences to market research firms or telemarketers.

- **Choose a payment method**

  Many experts recommend using credit cards for online purchases since they offer cardholder protections against unauthorized or fraudulent transactions. If you don't feel safe giving your credit card number to online retailers, third-party payment services like PayPal can be a good option. These services allow you to send money directly to anyone through the Internet and to link your payment account to a bank account or credit card. PayPal also provides automatic currency conversions for international transactions.

Staying Safe while Shopping Online

Despite the many benefits of online shopping, many people continue to voice concerns about the security of their personal information. They worry that shopping online might expose them to data breaches, identity theft, credit card fraud, hacking, or scams. To protect your privacy and shop online safely, experts recommend taking the following precautions:

- Stick with familiar, reputable, trusted websites whenever possible. When visiting an online retailer for the first time, check their customer satisfaction ratings and read the user comments. The Better Business Bureau is a good resource to find out whether sellers have complaints lodged against them for product, delivery, or return issues.

- Go directly to the online shopping website through your Internet browser, rather than clicking on coupon links or product advertisements that may have originated from a different source. Be sure to type in the website name correctly, because misspellings sometimes lead to fake "copycat" sites that try to trick you into giving away your personal information.

- Never make online purchases from public computers, like the ones at the library or the computer lab at school. If you must use a shared machine, make sure no one is looking over your shoulder when you input payment information, and be sure to log out of the store website and clear the browser history, cookies, and page cache when you're done. Otherwise, the next person who uses the computer could gain access to all of your private information.

- Only provide the minimum information required to complete the transaction. Never give online retailers your Social Security number, birthday, mother's maiden name, or other data that could be used to steal your identity.

- Keep your computer, tablet, and smartphone updated and protected against viruses and malware. Be sure to use strong passwords when creating accounts on e-commerce sites, and never share your passwords with anyone.

- Use private browsing while online shopping to avoid cookies and pop-up ads related to your product searches.

- Keep track of your online purchases and save a copy of your receipts and any correspondence with retailers. Check the online statements for your credit card, debit card, and bank accounts regularly for any suspicious or fraudulent charges. Notify your bank or credit card company immediately if you notice any problems.

- Order a free copy of your credit report annually and check carefully for mistakes or fraudulent accounts.

- Use common sense to avoid falling victim to scams. If an online shopping site offers a deal that seems too good to be true, it probably is.

References

1. Alford, Catherine. "The Ultimate Guide to Online Shopping," Simple Dollar, May 15, 2015.

2. Farber, Madeline. "Consumers Are Now Doing Most of Their Shopping Online," Fortune, June 8, 2016.

3. Griffith, Eric. "Eleven Tips for Safe Shopping Online," PC Magazine, November 21, 2011.

4. Kollmorgen, Andy. "Stretch Your Shopping Dollar Further Online," Choice, September 3, 2014.

5. O'Donnell, Andy. "Ten Tips for Shopping Safely Online," Lifewire, December 30, 2016.

Chapter 40

Using Debit and Credit Cards

What Is a Debit Card?

Debit cards are a way to pay for things. You get a debit card from your bank or credit union when you open a checking account. Sometimes a debit card is free to use. Sometimes you will pay a fee to use the card. Debit cards look like credit cards. But they do not work the same way. Credit cards use money that you borrow. Debit cards use money that is already in your checking account.

Why Would I Use a Debit Card?

- Debit cards let you buy things without carrying cash. You can use your debit card in most stores to pay for something. You just swipe the card and enter your PIN number on a keypad.

- Debit cards take money out of your checking account immediately.

- Debit cards let you get cash quickly. You can use your debit card at an automated teller machine, or automated teller machine (ATM), to get money from your checking account. You also can get cash back when you use a debit card to buy something at a store.

What Is a Personal Identification Number (PIN)?

A "PIN" is a security code that belongs to you. "PIN" stands for personal identification number. A bank or credit union gives you a PIN when you get a debit card. You can change

About This Chapter: Text beginning with the heading "What Is a Debit Card?" is excerpted from "Using Debit Cards," Consumer.gov, Federal Trade Commission (FTC), September 28, 2012; Text beginning with the heading "Choose a Credit Card" is excerpted from "Credit Cards," USA.gov, May 29, 2018.

your PIN to a number you will remember. When you use your debit card, you need to enter your PIN on a keypad. This is one way the bank tries to stop dishonest people from using your debit card to get your money. Never share your PIN with anyone. Remember it. Do not keep it in your wallet or on your card.

How Do Debit Cards Work?

When you open a checking account at a bank or credit union, you usually get a debit card. A debit card lets you spend money from your checking account without writing a check.

- You can use your debit card to buy things in a store.

- You can use it at an ATM to get cash.

When you pay with a debit card, the money comes out of your checking account immediately. There is no bill to pay later.

How Do I Know Where I Used My Debit Card?

Your bank or credit union gives you a statement every month. Your statement shows:

- Where you paid with your debit card and how much you spent

- Where you used the ATM, how much you withdrew, and what fees you paid

- Who you wrote a check to and for how much

Your statement can help you track your spending and create a budget.

How Is a Debit Card Different from a Credit Card?

When you buy something with a credit card, you are borrowing money from the credit card company. The credit card company will send you a bill every month for the money you borrowed to buy things. When you use a debit card, you are using money in your checking account to buy things. For example, with debit cards:

- You can get a debit card from the bank when you open a checking account.

- Money comes out of your checking account when you pay with a debit card.

- You don't pay extra money in interest when you pay with a debit card.

- You can use a debit card at an ATM to get money from your checking account.

- You do not build a credit history using a debit card.

With credit cards:

- You apply for a credit card at a bank or store.

- You get a bill once a month for everything you buy with a credit card.

- You might pay extra money in interest if you don't pay all of your credit card bills every month.

- You can use a credit card as a safer way to pay for things online.

- You can build a credit history using a credit card if you pay the whole bill every month when it is due.

Can I Use My Debit Card to Buy Things Online?

Your debit card will work online. But debit cards are not a good way to pay when you shop online. Credit cards are safer to use when you buy things online:

- You might have a problem with something you buy online. It is easier to get your money back if you use a credit card.

- Someone might steal your credit card number online. The law says you can lose only $50 if you report it right away.

- Someone might steal your debit card number online. The thief can take all your money out of your bank account.

What If I Use All the Money in My Checking Account?

You might not have enough money in your checking account. That means your debit card will be "declined." You will not be able to buy things. Some banks and credit unions might let you sign up for "overdraft protection." That means you can use your debit card even when you do not have enough money to pay for the things you are buying. But you might have to pay a fee to the bank. Some banks might charge this fee for every purchase until you put enough money in your account to pay for the things you are buying.

For Example

- I did not know my checking account balance was $1.78.

- I used my debit card three times. I paid for groceries, coffee, and my cable bill.

- My bank charged a $25 overdraft fee every time I used my card.

- The good part: My debit card was never declined. I could buy what I wanted.

- The bad part: Now I owe the bank $75, plus the money I spent.

How Do I Choose a Debit Card?

A bank or credit union usually gives you a debit card when you open a checking account. Compare the services and fees at a few banks and credit unions. Go to the website or visit in person. Find out what the fee is if you:

- Have a checking account

- Use a debit card

- Get cash from ATMs at other banks

- Have less money in your account than the bank requires

- Spend more money than you have in your account

Compare the answers. Find the bank or credit union that meets your needs.

How Can I Protect My Debit Card?

- Keep your debit card number and PIN private.

- Do not use your debit card to buy things online.

- If you lose your debit card, report it to your bank or credit union right away. Ask your bank to cancel the card and send you another card.

- Ask for account alerts by e-mail or text message. This can let you know if your account has less money in it than you think.

How Can I Keep Track of My Money?

To keep track of your money:

- Write down how much money you spend with your debit card.

- Write down how much money you take out of the ATM. Remember to add the fees.

- Use your monthly budget to schedule payments for regular bills.

- Look at your bank statement whenever it comes. Make sure it is what you expected.

- Ask your bank or credit union to send you e-mail or text alerts. Some banks contact you if your balance goes below an amount you set.

Choose a Credit Card

When applying for credit cards, it's important to shop around. There are many credit cards with various features, but there is no one single best card. When you're trying to find the credit card that best suits your needs, consider these factors:

- **Annual percentage rate (APR).** The APR is a measure of the cost of credit, expressed as a yearly interest rate. If the interest rate is variable, ask how it is determined and when it can change.

- **Periodic rate.** This is the interest rate used to determine the finance charge on your balance each billing period.

- **Annual fee.** While some credit cards have no annual fee, others expect you to pay an amount each year for being a cardholder.

- **Rewards programs.** Can you earn points for flights, hotel stays, and gift certificates to your favorite retailers? Use online tools to find the card that offers the best rewards for you.

- **Grace period.** This is the number of days you have to pay your bill in full before finance charges start. Without this period, you may have to pay interest from the date you use your card or when the purchase is posted to your account.

- **Finance charges.** Most lenders calculate finance charges using an average daily account balance: the average of what you owed each day in the billing cycle. Look for offers that use an adjusted balance, which subtracts your monthly payment from your beginning balance. Avoid offers that use the previous balance in calculating what you owe; this method has the highest finance charge. Also, find out if there is a minimum finance charge.

- **Other fees.** Are there fees if you get a cash advance, make a late payment, or go over your credit limit? Some credit card companies also charge a monthly fee. Be careful: sometimes companies may also try to upsell by offering other services such as credit protection, insurance, or debt coverage that you may not need.

- **Terms and conditions.** Read the agreement before you apply for the card to make sure that you agree with the requirements, such as mandatory arbitration or repossession clauses.

- **Security features.** Does the card allow you to switch it on or off, receive fraud alerts, or text messages immediately after purchases?

- **Chip and personal identification number (PIN).** Does the card issuer offer chip and PIN security features that use an embedded strip instead of a magnetic strip? You may need this card type if you travel internationally. In 2015, merchants and businesses in the United States were required to add in-store technology and processing systems so you can make a purchase using a chip card.

The Fair Credit and Charge Card Disclosure Act (FCCCDA) requires credit and charge card issuers to include all of the information above on credit applications.

Credit Card Laws

Credit card regulation protects you from unfair practices, gives you the right to dispute charges on your credit card, and allows you to file a complaint with your credit card company.

Credit Cardholders Rights

Often called the Credit Cardholders Bill of Rights, the Credit Card Accountability Responsibility and Disclosure (CARD) Act protects you in two ways:

- **Fairness**—By prohibiting certain practices that are unfair or abusive, such as hiking up the rate on an existing balance, or allowing you to go over limit and then imposing an over-limit fee

- **Transparency**—Making the rates and fees on credit cards more transparent, so you can understand how much you're paying for your credit card

Dispute a Credit Card Charge

Under the Fair Credit Billing Act (FCBA), you have the right to dispute charges on your credit card that you didn't make or are incorrect, or for goods or services you didn't receive. To dispute a charge, follow these guidelines:

- Send a letter to the creditor within 60 days of the postmark of the bill with the disputed charge.

- Include your name and account number, the date and amount of the disputed charge, and a complete explanation of why you're disputing the charge.

- To ensure it is received, send your letter by certified mail with a return receipt requested.

- The creditor or card issuer must acknowledge your letter in writing within 30 days of receiving it and conduct an investigation within 90 days. You do not have to pay the amount in dispute during the investigation.

- If there was an error, the creditor must credit your account and remove any fees.

- If the bill is correct, you must be told in writing what you owe and why. You must pay it along with any related finance charges.

  - If you do not agree with the creditor's decision, file an appeal with the Consumer Financial Protection Bureau (CFPB).

File a Complaint

For problems with your credit card company, call the number on the back of your card or submit a complaint to the CFPB. This includes issues with managing your credit card account, billing disputes, changes to your annual percentage rate (APR), and unauthorized transactions. If you can't resolve the issue, ask for the name, address, and phone number of the card company's regulatory agency.

Credit Card Protections

Did you know that your credit card may offer you other protections that are not typically advertised?

Tax Payment through Debit Card and Credit Card

You can pay by Internet, phone, or mobile device whether you e-file, paper file or are responding to a bill or notice. It's safe and secure—the IRS uses standard service providers and business/commercial card networks, and your information is used solely to process your payment.

Fees and Information
- Your payment will be processed by a payment processor who will charge a processing fee.
- The fees vary by service provider and may be tax deductible.
- No part of the service fee goes to the IRS.
- Your information is used solely to process your payment.

(Source: "Pay Your Taxes by Debit or Credit Card," Internal Revenue Service (IRS).)

When using your credit card for travel purchases, your credit card issuer may offer you travel insurance in certain situations:

- Your trip is delayed

- You have to cancel your trip because you or a family member becomes ill

- Your luggage gets lost during travel

If you rent a car, you may be offered auto insurance coverage as part of the rental. Some credit card networks even offer return assistance programs that extend the window for returning unused merchandise. Keep in mind: the rules vary between cards and the issuers.

Chapter 41

Credit Card Payments and Late Payments

When Is My Credit Card Payment Considered to Be Late?

Under the law, a credit card company generally cannot treat a payment as late if it was received by 5 p.m. on the day that it was due. If the due date was not a day on which the card company receives or accepts mail (for example, Sunday or a holiday), the card company cannot treat a mailed payment as late if it was received by 5 p.m. on the next business day.

Sometimes payments that you make may get delayed in the mail. Card companies consider the day the payment was received and not the date it was mailed. You should contact your card company and ask it to waive the late fee.

(Source: "When Is My Credit Card Payment Considered to Be Late?" Consumer Financial Protection Bureau (CFPB).)

Questions and Answers

I Made a Payment, but It Has Not Shown up on My Credit Card/Home Equity Line of Credit (HELOC)/Personal Lines of Credit Statement. What Can I Do?

You should file a written billing error dispute with the bank at the address specified after "Send Billing Inquiries to:" or similar on the back of the monthly billing statement. This address usually differs from where you send your payment. You should file your written dispute

About This Chapter: This chapter includes text excerpted from "Payments and Late Payments—Answers about Credit Card Payments and Late Payments," HelpWithMyBank.gov, Office of the Comptroller of the Currency (OCC), April 23, 2010.

within 60 days of the date the bank mailed the statement on which you believe the credit should have appeared.

You should be prepared to provide documentation showing that you made the payment, such as a copy of the canceled check or a copy of confirmation of an electronic payment.

I Paid My Credit Card Bill on the 31st Day after the Payment Due Date and the Bank Reported That I Made a Late Payment to a Credit-Reporting Agency. Can the Bank Do That?

Generally, yes. Whether a payment is late is determined by your account agreement, which is the contract governing your account. The bank would have provided this agreement to you when you opened the account. As long as the information is accurate, the bank can report its experience with your credit card account, including late payments, to a credit reporting agency.

My Bank Increased the Minimum Payment on My Credit Card Account. What Should I Do If I Can't Afford It?

If you cannot afford the increase, you should contact your bank directly to discuss a payment plan.

Can I Make Special Payment Arrangements on My Credit Card Account?

You will have to contact your financial institution or credit card company. However, many lenders will work with their customers on an alternate repayment or collection program.

The Bank Is Not Giving Me Enough Time to Make the Payment on My Credit Card Account. How Many Days in Advance of the Due Date Does the Bank Have to Send the Statement?

Credit card issuers must have reasonable procedures in place to make sure that periodic statements are mailed or delivered at least 21 days prior to the payment due date shown on the statement.

A credit card issuer may not treat a required minimum payment as late for any purpose if the minimum payment is received by the card issuer within 21 days after mailing or delivering the credit card statement disclosing the due date for that payment. This means that, if your minimum payment is received by the card issuer within 21 days after the statement is mailed or delivered, the card issuer cannot:

- Increase the annual percentage rate (APR) as a penalty

- Report you as delinquent to a credit-reporting agency

- Assess a late fee

- Terminate benefits (such as rewards on purchases)

- Initiate collection activities

After a Payment Is Made, When Does the Bank Make the Additional Credit Available?

If you are referring to a credit card or other type of loan known as open-end credit, your available credit limit typically increases when the payment is posted to your account. However, the decision of when to replenish the credit limit is up to the bank and, in some circumstances, a bank may delay replenishing a credit line. If the bank delays replenishing a credit line, it cannot charge an over-the-limit fee even if the consumer has opted in to allow over-limit fees. If you are referring to a closed-end credit arrangement, then your payments simply reduce the outstanding balance—with no ability to charge other amounts to it. To learn more about your particular account, consult with your lender.

Can the Bank Charge a Fee for Making Payments, Such as for Making a Payment over the Phone?

Generally, the Credit Card Accountability Responsibility and Disclosure (CARD) Act prohibits creditors from charging a fee for making a payment. However, a fee may be charged if you make a payment using a payment method involving an expedited service by a customer service representative of the creditor.

A payment method involves an expedited service by a customer service representative if a payment is made with the assistance of a live representative of the creditor, whether in person, by telephone, or by electronic means, and applied that same day, or the next day, if received after the creditor's payment cut-off time. Fees cannot be charged for payments made using only a voice response unit, or made at the branch without expedited service, or placed in an office mail slot.

My Payment Is Due on the 4th of the Month, However, This Month the 4th Is a Federal Holiday. I Generally Mail My Payments to the Bank. Why Don't They Change the Due Date on the Bill?

The law requires that:

- The due date must be the same day each month. The due date could be set as the last day of the month or it could be a specific date in the month, such as the fourth.

- The payment cut-off time generally cannot be earlier than 5:00 p.m. on the due date.

- If the payment due date falls on a weekend or a holiday when the bank does not accept or receive mailed payments, then any mailed payment received by the bank before the cut-off time on the next business day would be considered an on-time payment.

Since you mail your payments, you would have until the cut-off time on the next business day to make your timely payment. However, if the bank accepts or receives payments on the due date by a method other than mail, such as electronic or telephone payments, and you make a payment using that other method, you would still need to make the payment by the due date.

If you followed the payment requirements and you were still charged a late payment fee, you can dispute the charge with the bank. Notify your bank in writing using the billing error notice instructions, which should be on the back of the monthly billing statement. Be sure to use the address specified after "Send Billing Inquiries to:" on the back of the billing statement. This is usually not the same address where you send your payment.

I Mailed My Payment Four Days before It Was Due, but the Card Issuer Says It Was Late. What Can I Do?

A card issuer cannot treat a payment as late if it was received by the card issuer's cut off time on the day that it was due at the location specified by the creditor for the receipt of such payments. If the payment was mailed and the due date was not a day on which the issuer receives mail (for example, a holiday), the issuer cannot treat the payment as late if it was received by the cut off time on the next business day. For example, the creditor may specify that payment is due on a Sunday and the creditor does not receive mailed payments on Sundays.

However, if the bank accepts or receives payments on the due date by a method other than mail, such as electronic or telephone payments, and you make a payment using that other method, you would still need to make the payment by the due date.

In general, if a creditor specifies, on or with the periodic statement, requirements for the consumer to follow in making payments as permitted (such as the location at which to mail payments or other requirements), but accepts a payment that does not conform to the requirements, the creditor shall credit the payment within five days of receipt.

Sometimes payments that you make may get delayed in the mail. Card issuers consider the day the payment was received and not the date it was mailed in determining whether or not the payment was timely made. You should contact your card issuer and see if the late fee can be waived.

Can the Bank Delay the Posting of a Payment to My Credit Card Account?

The bank must credit a payment to a customer's account as of the date of receipt of payment. The bank can set reasonable requirements for making payments. Reasonable requirements include:

- Requiring that the account number or payment stub be provided with the payment

- Specifying that only checks or money orders be sent by mail

- Specifying that payment is to be made in U.S. dollars

- Setting reasonable cut-off times for payments received by mail, by electronic means, by telephone, and in person. The cut-off time must be 5 p.m. or later, except for in-person payments at branches that close prior to 5 p.m.

If the bank specified reasonable requirements on the billing statement, but accepts a payment that does not conform to those requirements, the bank must credit the payment within five days of receipt. You should review your monthly billing statement and the account agreement to determine the bank's policies or contact the bank for an explanation.

Can the Bank Apply Payments to the "Purchase Portion" of the Account First and Then to the Cash Advance Balance?

The bank must apply the amount paid in excess of the minimum payment to the balance with the highest interest rate. For example, if the highest interest rate applicable to your account applies to the cash advance balance, the amount of any payment you make in excess of the minimum payment would be applied to the cash advance balance.

There is an exception for deferred interest plans. A deferred interest plan is a payment plan that is typically offered at the time of purchase that permits a consumer to avoid interest charges if the purchase balance is paid in full by a certain date. Often, deterred interest plans are offered in connection with the sale of higher-priced goods, such as furniture or electronics.

For deferred interest plans:

- You may request to apply extra amounts to the deferred interest balance before other balances

- For the two billing cycles prior to the end of the deferred interest period, the credit card company must apply your entire payment in excess of the minimum payment amount to the deferred interest rate balance first.

Why Wasn't My Online Payment Credited to My Credit Card Account on the Same Day I Made It?

The general rule is that the payment must be credited as of the date it is received. The bank may set reasonable requirements for payments, including a cut-off time. The cut-off time on the payment due date generally must be 5 p.m. or later. Payments received after the established cut-off time will generally be credited as of the next business day. If the bank listed reasonable requirements for conforming payments on your billing statement, but accepted a payment you made that did not meet those requirements; the bank must credit the nonconforming payment within five days of receipt. If the bank promoted electronic payment via their website, then generally any payments made via the bank's website prior to the specified cut-off time would be considered a timely payment.

This Month My Due Date Falls on a Sunday. I Mailed My Credit Card Payment and It Has Not Arrived There Yet. If the Payment Is Received on Monday, Will It Be Considered as Late?

If your payment due date falls on a weekend or a holiday when the bank does not accept or receive mailed payments, any mailed payments received by the bank before the cut-off time on the following business day will be considered timely.

For example, if you mailed your payment via U.S. Postal Service (USPS) and the due date is Sunday, March 14th, but the bank does not receive mail on Sundays, then your postal payment would be considered timely if it is received by Monday, March 15th, before 5 p.m. However; it is important to note that:

- If the bank accepts or receives payments made on the due date by a method other than mail, such as an electronic payment

- You make your payment electronically

Then your electronic payment must be received by the bank by the cut-off time on the due date (Sunday, March 14th) in order to be considered timely.

Chapter 42

Mobile Wallet Services Protection

Many consumers use their smartphones, tablets, and other mobile devices as mobile wallets to pay for goods and services, using apps to make both online and in-person purchases. As our use of mobile payment services increases, so does the need to protect mobile devices, apps, and associated data from theft and cyber attacks.

> Mobile payment services typically function by linking to one or more payment sources. Many mobile payment platforms allow consumers to choose among several different funding sources for payment, such as a credit card, debit card, bank account, or mobile phone account. For instance, a particular payment application on a smartphone may be linked to a credit card so that the credit card is charged when the consumer pays using that application. During the workshop, FTC staff presented observations about these various funding sources based upon an examination of the websites of 19 U.S. mobile payment service providers. Staff found that 15 of 19 providers allowed consumers to fund their mobile payments via credit or debit cards, 7 of 19 allowed funding by bank account debit, 4 of 19 allowed billing to a mobile carrier account, and 7 of 19 allowed multiple funding sources.
>
> *(Source: "The Legal Landscape and Resolution of Disputes in Mobile Payment Systems," Federal Trade Commission (FTC).)*

How to Safeguard Your Mobile Wallet

- Never leave your smartphone unattended in a public place or visible in an unattended car.

About This Chapter: Text in this chapter begins with excerpts from "Mobile Wallet Services Protection," Federal Communications Commission (FCC), December 8, 2017; Text beginning with the heading "Wireless Connections and Bluetooth Security Tips" is excerpted from "Wireless Connections and Bluetooth Security Tips," Federal Communications Commission (FCC), October 20, 2017.

- Consider your surroundings and use your smartphone or mobile device discreetly.

- Never use mobile payment services over an unsecured Wi-Fi network.

- Choose unique passwords for all your mobile apps.

- Install and maintain security software on your smartphone. Apps are available to:

  - Locate your smartphone from any computer

  - Lock your smartphone to restrict access

  - Wipe sensitive personal information and mobile wallet credentials from your smartphone

  - Make your smartphone emit a loud sound ("scream") to help you or the police locate it

- Be careful about using social networking apps, which may pose a security risk and may possibly allow unwanted access to personal information, including your mobile financial data.

- Monitor financial accounts linked to in mobile apps for any fraudulent charges. Review the service agreements for these accounts to find out what steps to take if your smartphone is lost, stolen or hacked, and what charges you may be responsible for paying.

- The police may need your smartphone's unique identifying information if it is stolen or lost. Write down the make, model number, serial number, and unique device identification number—either the International Mobile Equipment Identifier (IMEI) or the Mobile Equipment Identifier (MEID) number. Some phones display the IMEI/MEID number when you dial *#06#. The IMEI/MEID also can be found on a label located beneath the phone's battery or on the box that came with the phone.

What to Do If Your Mobile Device Is Lost or Stolen

- If you are not certain whether your smartphone or mobile device has been stolen, or if you have simply misplaced it, try locating the smartphone by calling it or by using the security software's global positioning system (GPS) locator.

- If you have installed security software on your smartphone, use it to lock the device, wipe sensitive personal information, and/or activate the alarm.

- Immediately report the theft or loss to your wireless carrier. If you provide your carrier with the IMEI or MEID number, your carrier may be able to disable your smartphone and mobile payment apps, and block access to your personal information and sensitive data. Request written confirmation from your carrier that you reported the smartphone as missing and that the smartphone was disabled.

- Report the theft to the police—including the make and model, serial and IMEI or MEID number in your report. Some service providers require proof that the smartphone was stolen and a police report can provide that documentation.

- If you are unable to lock your stolen or lost smartphone, change all of your passwords for mobile payment apps and any bank or credit card accounts that you have accessed using your smartphone service, then contact those financial institutions about the loss or theft.

Wireless Connections and Bluetooth Security Tips

Wi-Fi networks and Bluetooth connections can be vulnerable points of access for data or identity theft. Fortunately, there are many ways to decrease your chances of becoming a victim.

Encryption is the best way to keep your personal data safe. It works by scrambling the data in a message so that only the intended recipients can read it. When the address of a website you're visiting starts with "https" instead of "http," that indicates encryption is taking place between your browser and site.

The two most common types of encryption are Wired Equivalent Privacy (WEP), and Wi-Fi Protected Access (WPA). The strongest one commonly available is Wi-Fi Protected Access II (WPA2), so use that if you have the option. Home Wi-Fi systems and public Wi-Fi access points (WAPs), or "hotspots," usually will inform you of the encryption they use.

Public Wi-Fi Access

Many Wi-Fi users prefer to choose to use public networks instead of their devices' data plans for accessing the Internet remotely. But the convenience of public Wi-Fi can be risky. If you're not careful, hackers may quickly access your connection and compromise sensitive information stored on your device and in online accounts. Here are some steps you can take to minimize the risk:

- Check the validity of available Wi-Fi hotspots. If more than one hotspot appears claiming to belong to an establishment that you're in, check with the staff to avoid connecting to an imposter hotspot.

- Make sure all websites you exchange information with have "https" at the beginning of the web address. If so, your transmitted data will be encrypted.

- Install an app add-on that forces your web browsers to use encryption when connecting to websites—even well-known sites that may not normally encrypt their communications.

- Adjust your smartphone's settings so it does not automatically connect to nearby Wi-Fi networks. This gives you more control over where and when you connect.

- If you use public Wi-Fi hotspots on a regular basis, consider using a virtual private network, which will encrypt all transmissions between your device and the Internet. Many companies offer virtual private networks (VPNs) to their employees for work purposes, and individuals may subscribe to VPNs on their own.

- When transmitting sensitive information, using your cellphone data plan instead of Wi-Fi may be more secure.

Bluetooth Security

Bluetooth connections to your mobile devices can be used to connect to wireless headsets, transfer files, and enable hands-free calling while you drive, among other things. Most of the time, a user must allow a Bluetooth connection to occur before data is shared—a process called "pairing"—which provides a measure of data security. But just like Wi-Fi connections, Bluetooth can put your personal data at risk if you are not careful. Here are some steps you may wish to take when using Bluetooth:

- Turn Bluetooth off when not in use. Keeping it active enables hackers to discover what other devices you connected to before, spoof one of those devices, and gain access to your device.

- If you connect your mobile phone to a rental car, the phone's data may get shared with the car. Be sure to unpair your phone from the car and clear any personal data from the car before you return it. Take the same steps when selling a car that has Bluetooth.

- Use Bluetooth in "hidden" mode rather than "discoverable" mode. This prevents other unknown devices from finding your Bluetooth connection.

Home Wireless Network Security

Home wireless networks enable computers and mobile devices to share one broadband connection to the Internet without having to use up minutes on cellular data plans. But like all other wireless network technologies, home wireless networks present vulnerabilities that could be exploited by hackers. To help protect your home wireless network from unwanted users, consider the following steps:

- Turn on encryption. Wireless routers often come out of the box with the encryption feature disabled, so be sure it is enabled soon after the router is installed.

- Change the network's default network name, also known as its service set identifier or "SSID." When a computer with a wireless connection searches for and displays the wireless networks nearby, it lists each network that publicly broadcasts its SSID. Manufacturers usually give all of their wireless routers a default SSID, which is often the company's name. For additional security, choose a unique and hard to guess name as your SSID.

- Change the network's default password. Most wireless routers come with preset passwords for administering a device's settings (this is different from the password used to access the wireless network itself). Unauthorized users may be familiar with the default passwords, so it is important to change the router device's password as soon as it is installed. Longer passwords made up of a combination of letters, numbers and symbols are more secure.

- Consider using the Media Access Control, or "MAC," address filter in your wireless router. Every device that can connect to a Wi-Fi network has a unique identity document (ID) called the "physical address" or "MAC" address. Wireless routers can screen the MAC addresses of all devices that connect to them, and users can set their wireless network to accept connections only from devices with MAC addresses that the router will recognize. To create another obstacle to unauthorized access, consider activating your wireless router's MAC address filter to include your devices only.

- Turn off your wireless router when it will not be in use for any extended period of time.

- Use antivirus and anti-spyware software on your computer, and use similar apps on your devices that access your wireless network.

Passwords

Remembering all of your assorted passwords can be a pain. Web browsers and other programs may offer to remember passwords for you, which can be a significant timesaver. However, certain password shortcuts can leave you less safe secure. The following best practices may help keep your personal information safer:

- Don't use the same password for multiple accounts, especially for the most sensitive ones, such as bank accounts, credit cards, legal, or tax records and files containing medical information. Otherwise, someone with access to one of your accounts may end up with access to many others.

- Don't have your web browser remember passwords and add them for you, particularly for your most important financial, legal, and medical accounts. If an unauthorized person gains access to your computer or smartphone, they could access any account that your browser automatically logs into.

Chapter 43

Online Payment Services

According to a Pew Research Center survey, 80 percent of Americans shop online, and 15 percent do so on a weekly basis. And increasing numbers are using online payment services, like PayPal, to process their transactions. The advantages are clear. From the seller perspective, merchants don't need to set up complicated technology and financial infrastructure to take funds via the web. Instead they pay a fee to the service, which handles the transaction. And buyers enjoy advantages like convenience, payment flexibility and a higher level of information security.

Using Online Payment Services

Online payments can be made in a variety of ways, including with credit cards, debit cards, gift cards, eChecks, and mobile phone apps. But more and more, online payment services are becoming a method of choice, both for individual sellers and for the websites of large companies. Although services vary somewhat, here's how the process generally works:

- Go to the payment service's website and sign up for a free account.

- Link the account to your credit card, debit card, or bank account.

- Send money to anyone with an e-mail address.

- Receive money from anyone who has an account with that service.

When you send money, it's charged to your credit card or deducted from your bank account. When you receive money, it can be deposited directly into your account or you can request

---

About This Chapter: "Online Payment Services," © 2017 Omnigraphics.

a check in the mail. Some services also have their own debit cards that allow you to get cash from an automated teller machine (ATM) or make purchases.

Advantages and Disadvantages of Online Payment Services

Online payment services have become so popular because they offer a number of advantages over other forms of making purchases on the web. Some of these include:

- **Convenience.** Online retailers and auction sites that take payments from services generally link to those services making it easy for you to transfer funds.

- **Security.** Rather than having your credit card number or other financial information held by every online store and individual you do business with, that data can be maintained by just one service.

- **Flexibility.** Most online payment services allow you to shop with online merchants, buy from individual sellers, have money sent to you at college, and send funds to someone who needs it.

- **Easy access to funds.** When you sell something or get money from an individual, you can generally use your payment service account to buy goods and services online, have money sent to you as a check or bank transfer, or, in some cases, get a debit card that can be used anywhere.

Of course, there are some disadvantages, as well, such as:

- **There can be fees.** Most online payment services allow buyers to create an account and conduct certain transactions at no cost, but some have limits on the amount of business that can be transacted for free, after which fees are added. And all of them charge sellers a fee that is usually based on the amount sold.

- **Lack of regulation.** Online payment services function in many ways like a bank, taking in money, holding it, and paying it out when requested. Yet they're not subject to the same regulations as banks. For example, money held by a payment service is not insured by the FDIC (Federal Deposit Insurance Corporation) as it would be when deposited in a bank.

- **Fraud.** Since many transactions handled by payment services are between individual buyers and sellers, rather than through company websites, there is always the possibility that you could find yourself doing business with an unscrupulous person. If you buy something and don't get it, if it's not what you thought you were buying, or if you sell something and don't get your payment, there will be a process for resolving the issue, but it could take some time.

- **Hacking.** While it's true that online payment services offer the security of having your card or bank account information stored in just one place, there's always the chance that the service's system could be invaded by a hacker stealing customer data. In such a case, it's likely that account holders will eventually be compensated, but the process could be complex and take a long time.

- **Slow customer service.** With many payment services, if something goes wrong with a transaction, it can be difficult to speak to a customer-service representative. Most of the services are set up to take complaints online, with automated responses. There's almost always a way to resolve problems, but it can be time-consuming and frustrating.

Some Common Online Payment Services

There are quite a few online payment services available to buyers and sellers. Some are aimed at facilitating individual transactions, like auctions, while others are designed for use by merchants with their own dedicated websites. A few of these services include:

- **PayPal.** With almost 200 million users, PayPal is the main player in online payments. Easy to use, free to set up basic personal accounts, and free to send money in most cases, PayPal functions well for a wide variety of consumer transactions. When merchants make a sale, however, fees are assessed.

- **2Checkout.** Unlike PayPal, this service does not require buyers to register for an account. The customer simply pays with a credit or debit card, or six other payment options. 2Checkout is aimed at small- to medium-sized merchants, so it's getting popular with online sellers. One benefit for some users is that 2Checkout is globally oriented. It serves merchants in 25 countries outside of the United States with 87 different currencies, making it easy to handle international transactions.

- **Amazon payments.** This service is intended to provide additional value, build brand loyalty, and offer a payment alternative for customers of online retail giant Amazon.com. Not limited to Amazon's own website, the service allows customers to make purchases without a fee at many other U.S.-based shopping sites using card information stored in their Amazon accounts. The service has been growing steadily, although some of the major retailers have yet to get on board.

- **Skrill.** Skrill is known for its user-friendly interface, free setup, ease of international transactions, and debit cards that can be used anywhere. The service is free for buyers, but there are fees associated with sending money to an e-mail address or another Skrill user.

- **Dwolla.** This service allows users to send and receive funds via bank transfers anywhere in the world, either individual-to-individual or customer-to-merchant. Its advantages include an easy-to-use interface and the ability to transfer funds to Twitter accounts, phone numbers, e-mail addresses, and business websites.

Online Payment Security

Payment security issues are not the exclusive domain of online transactions, of course—they can also be a problem at physical stores—but online payments cause extra concern on the part of consumers, so it pays to be familiar with some of the steps you can take to protect yourself:

- Do some research before committing to an online payment service. Go to their websites and see what kind of security measures they use. Also, do a web search for reviews of the service to see what other consumers have to say about them.

- Use strong passwords. Even if online payment websites don't require complex passwords, you can create your own by using a combination of numbers, symbols, and a mix of capital and lowercase letters.

- Use different passwords for each online account or payment service. Once a hacker figures out one of your passwords, you don't want the criminal to have access to all of your online accounts. At least use different passwords for online purchases and other financial transactions than you do for e-mail and social media.

- Install antivirus and antimalware software and a firewall on your computer. This is an all-around good practice, but it's especially important if you do any financial transactions online, including sending funds through a payment service.

Online payment services can help secure your personal data, but if you pay directly on a merchant's website, don't create an account and store your card information on the site. It's generally safer to log in as a "guest" and re-enter your card data each time you make a purchase. That way your information isn't being held everywhere you shop.

References

1. Hord, Jennifer. "How Electronic Payment Works," HowStuffWorks.com, October 19, 2005.

2. McIver, Rich. "Online Payment Processing 101," CleverBridge.com, November 4, 2015.

3. O'Brien, Russell. "Online Payment Basics," HubPages.com, December 15, 2016.

4. Smith, Aaron, and Monica Anderson. "Online Shopping and E-Commerce," Pew Research Center, December 19, 2016.

5. Whitehouse, Jordan. "Types of eCommerce Payment Systems," Techwalla.com, March 31, 2015.

Part Six
Saving and Protecting Your Earnings

Chapter 44

Savings and Investing

The thought of starting a savings or investment account can be overwhelming, but it doesn't have to be. No matter how much or how little money you have, you can get started planning your financial future today with just a few basic steps. The important thing is to begin by thinking about what you want to achieve, and then learn about the opportunities that are available to you.

Step One: Make a Plan

Every successful investor or savings account holder started out with one thing in common—they made a financial plan and they were prepared to stick to it. Every savings plan is different, because each person is different and has different goals in life. There is no wrong way to make a financial plan, and your plan doesn't have to stay the same forever. Your financial plan can change as your life changes, and there is no reason to wait for the perfect moment to begin. In fact, the sooner you make your financial plan, the better off you will be in the long run.

Here are some things to consider when thinking about your financial plan:

- What are your financial goals?

- How much money do you want to save, and why?

- Your savings goals can be anything that is important to you. For example: Are you saving to buy a car? Pay for college?

Make a list of your financial goals and then put them in order of importance. Include an estimate of the amount of money needed to reach each goal. Then think about how much time you will have to meet each specific goal. For example, in order to buy a car, how many months will you be able to save for that purchase? Knowing how much money you will need, and when you will need it, are the most important factors that will influence your savings and investment plan. Divide the amount of money you need by the number of weeks until the money is needed to determine how much money you will need to save each week in order to meet your goal. Online savings calculators can also help you figure how much money you will need to save each week or month in order to meet your goal. You can find a wealth of information about savings and investment, including savings calculators and links to other resources online at www.investor.gov.

Quick Tip
Getting started with saving and investing is as easy as 1-2-3!

1. Make a financial plan. What are your goals?
2. Understand your current financial status, including income, expenses, and debt.
3. Start saving and investing as soon as you've paid off your debts.

Step Two: Know Your Financial Status

The second step in getting started in saving and investing is understanding your current financial situation. To do this, you will need to know how much money you owe to others and how much money you currently have. There are worksheets and calculators available online to help you with this step.

Once you have listed all of your debts and all of the money you currently have, you can then move on to examining your current income and expenses. Begin by listing all of your expenses, either monthly or weekly. Then write down how much money you earn. If your income is greater than your expenses, you can begin saving immediately. If your expenses are greater than your income, you will have to do some additional calculations in order to being saving or investing.

When expenses are greater than income, you will need to find ways to reduce your expenses. You can begin this process by writing down how you spend your money. What kinds of things do you buy each day, each week, or each month? Take note of where your money is going. Once you start paying close attention to your spending habits, you might be surprised to see how quickly small everyday purchases add up over time. The next step is to identify where you might be able to cut back on expenses. For example, instead of buying coffee from a coffee shop every day, you could save money by making coffee at home. If you find that you buy lunch fairly often, you might be able to reduce that expense by bringing your own lunch from home instead. There are many ways to cut back on unnecessary expenses, and each person will find different ways to save according to their own priorities.

Once you have found some ways to reduce your expenses, your first priority should be to pay off any existing debts. This is especially important for high-interest debts such as credit card balances. After you have paid those debts, you can start using that money for savings and investments.

Step Three: Start Saving and Investing

When you are ready to begin saving and investing your money, you will need to learn about the different opportunities that are available to you. Saving and investing are two different ways to manage your money. The basic difference between saving and investing is the amount of risk involved.

A savings account is usually considered the safest place to keep your money. With savings accounts, you can generally access your money at any time, for any reason, whenever you need it. Savings account products include bank savings accounts, checking accounts, and credit union accounts. After you have paid off credit cards or other high-interest debts, some financial advisors recommend building a savings account containing the equivalent of up to six months of regular expenses. This amount is recommended because it can be used in case of an emergency, period of unemployment, or other financial need.

An investment is a way to manage money over a longer period of time. Unlike savings accounts, investments may not be as easy to access and there may be fees associated with withdrawing money. The longer-term commitment of an investment, such as in stocks, securities, and mutual funds, also comes with benefits and risks. When you make an investment, you give your money to a company or other enterprise such as a bank, hoping that the organization will be successful and pay you back with more money than you initially invested. The main benefit is that investments generally provide the opportunity to earn greater interest on the money you invest. Interest is the dividend that is paid when, for example, a stock that you purchased increases in value during the time that you own that stock. The main risk of certain investments is that there is a greater chance of losing some of the money you invested, for example, when a stock that you purchased decreases in value during the time that you own it. You will need to understand the relative benefits and risks associated with savings accounts and investments that you consider. You will also need to decide how much risk you are comfortable with in order to make the best investment decisions to meet your overall goals.

A study in which 8,000 teens were surveyed showed that 38 percent reported that they're actively saving money and 22 percent said they are saving more than they did the previous year. Fifty-seven percent of teens said they are saving money for new clothes while 36 percent are socking away cash to buy a car.

References

1. "Saving and Investing: A Roadmap to Your Financial Security through Saving and Investing," Office of Investor Education and Assistance (OIAE), U.S. Securities and Exchange Commission (SEC), June 2011.

2. "Saving and Investing," The Money Advice Service, n.d.

3. "The Facts on Saving and Investing," Office of Investor Education and Assistance (OIAE), U.S. Securities and Exchange Commission (SEC), n.d.

Chapter 45

Banking Basics

Many parents set up bank savings accounts for their children as soon as they're born, so it's possible that you've been dealing with banks for many years. But perhaps you've never done business with a bank, or if you had an account as a child maybe you're ready to transition to an account of your own. In any case, it pays to learn a bit about the banking system so you can understand your choices and make informed decisions.

What Is a Bank?

No one is sure when and where banking first began, but it's a good bet that it started in ancient times, probably in the area around the Mediterranean Sea, when wealthy individuals would back merchants traveling to distant areas to sell goods. In exchange for paying travel expenses, those individuals would take a percentage of the profits, essentially acting as banks loaning money.

It may seem obvious, but a bank is more than the building on the corner with a drive-through cash machine. Odds are that building houses a branch of a much larger organization that consists of many branches and an overarching corporate structure. In some cases, there may be no brick-and-mortar (B&M) building at all. Some banks strictly operate online, with all transactions taking place via a secure website.

Whatever its structure, a bank is a financial institution that provides a wide variety of functions for businesses and individual customers. But its main purpose is to take in funds, pool

About This Chapter: "Banking Basics," © 2017 Omnigraphics.

them together, and use that money for loans and other investments. The money it earns is then paid to depositors in the form of interest.

> The Federal Reserve is the central banking system of the United States. Among other things, it acts a bank for banks, serves as the U.S. government's own bank, and makes policies that govern the amount of cash and credit that will be available in the country's economy.

Bank Services

Most of the many functions performed by banks probably won't concern you at the moment, but it's worthwhile to understand a few of the more common services they provide, including:

- **Savings accounts.** There are simple savings accounts that pay a relatively small amount of interest on your deposits but allow you to withdraw your money at any time. Then there are other types of accounts that earn a higher rate of interest in exchange for leaving your money in the bank for longer periods, such as money market accounts and certificates of deposit (CDs).

- **Checking accounts.** When you open a checking account you deposit funds and receive a book of checks, slips of paper that are a promise to pay a specified amount of money from your account. These days, writing physical checks is becoming something of a rarity, but checking accounts also let you make deposits and withdrawals from an ATM (automated teller machine), pay bills online, and transfer money between accounts.

- **Debit cards.** When you open a savings or checking account, the bank might issue a debit card to you. This card has a magnetic strip and an embedded microchip that can be scanned by readers at ATMs, restaurants, gas stations, and stores, allowing you to conduct transactions using funds in your accounts at the bank.

- **Loans.** One of the primary ways banks make money is by taking funds it receives from depositors and lending it to people who need it. The bank makes money by charging a higher fee for these loans than it pays out in interest.

- **Credit cards.** Credit cards are, essentially, a type of loan. Unlike with a debit card, money for credit-card purchases doesn't automatically come out of the customer's bank account. Rather, the bank is advancing the funds to a merchant or other payee with the understanding that the customer will pay the money back to the bank.

- **Online and mobile banking.** When you open an account, you're typically given a user i.d. and password to get access to the bank's secure website. Then, from any computer with an Internet connection, you can check your balances, transfer funds between accounts, and pay bills. Most banks now also have mobile apps that allow you to perform these same functions from your phone or tablet.

Advantages of Banks

As an informed consumer, it's to your benefit to learn how banks can work for you. Some advantages include:

- **You earn money.** Funds you deposit into a savings account—and some checking accounts—earn interest, which the bank pays you for letting it use your money. Generally, the interest earned on these accounts is not a lot, but it's more than you'd get by keeping it in a drawer.

- **Your money is safe.** The Federal Deposit Insurance Corporation (FDIC), an independent agency created by the U.S. Congress, insures most personal bank deposits up to $250,000. There are some types of bank investments that are not covered, but customers with regular savings and checking accounts know their money is guaranteed to be there.

- **Banks help you budget.** A bank statement, either mailed to you monthly or accessed online, lets you keep track of income and expenses very easily. You can also set up different accounts for different purposes. For example, you might have one savings account where you accumulate money for a car and another for short-term use, such as school expenses.

- **Convenience.** Banks give you option of buying goods and services or paying bills as easily as possible using their various payment methods, including debit cards and online or mobile banking. They also allow you to go to the bank location to make deposits or withdrawals or take advantage of the nearest ATM to perform the same functions.

Banks are highly regulated by the U.S. government, by individual states, and even by some cities. Among other things, these rules ensure that banks reduce risk to depositors by making sound loans and investments, protect customer confidentiality, and maintain adequate cash reserves to cover a minimum percentage of depositor funds.

Bank Fees

Unsurprisingly, banks charge fees for many of their services. These vary depending on the bank and the type of account, so it's smart to shop around. Some bank fees can include:

- **Checking account fees.** Most banks charge a monthly fee for maintaining your checking account, usually between $10 and $20. This can often be avoided by either keeping a minimum balance in that account or by maintaining a minimum balance in a saving account at the same bank.

- **Overdraft charge.** If you use more money than you have in your checking account—either by writing a check or by using your debit card—and the bank covers the difference, you may be charged an overdraft fee of $20 to $40.

- **Returned check fee.** A returned check fee (also called NSF, for nonsufficient funds) is incurred when you write a check without enough money in your account and the bank doesn't cover the difference. The bank may charge as much as $40 in such a case.

- **ATM fees.** Usually, banks don't charge customers for using their own cash machines. But if you use an ATM operated by another bank, the other bank will charge a fee, and in some instances, your own bank may add a fee, as well. The average charge is around $3.

Other bank charges can include foreign transaction fees; paper statement fees, charged by some banks if you want hard-copies mailed to you; inactivity fees, which are sometimes incurred if an account lies dormant for a long time; check-printing fees; and lost debit-card fees.

Choosing a Bank

As with shopping for clothes, a car, or anything else, when selecting a bank it's smart to shop around. Banks vary considerably in such areas as the fees the charge, the amount of interest they pay, and the services they offer, and some are bound to meet your needs better than others. Some factors to consider:

- **Fees.** One of the most important things to learn is how much it's going to cost you to do business with a bank. Ask about account maintenance charges, ATM fees, overdraft fees, and any other charges that may be associated with the accounts you plan to open.

- **Legitimacy.** You want to be sure you're dealing with a reliable, established bank. One of the most important things is to be sure the bank is a member of the FDIC. The bank's website will usually tell you this, but you can also go to FDIC.gov and search their Bank Find tool just to be sure.

- **Location.** Even people who don't actually go to the bank building very often tend to select a bank near where they live or work. If the need arises for a personal visit, you'll appreciate the convenience.

- **Size.** If you travel a lot it could be helpful to do business with a large bank that has branches in several states, or even outside the country.

- **Minimum deposit amount.** Many banks have a minimum amount required to open an account, and this can vary widely.

- **Types of services offered.** Right now, you might only be interested in opening a savings account, but at some point, you may want a checking account, credit card, or car loan. It's good to know your options before you begin doing business with a bank.

- **Technology**. If you plan to make regular use of electronic banking, be sure the bank offers what you need. Ask about online fund transfers, remote deposits, text and e-mail alerts for unusual account activity, and mobile apps.

Finally, when shopping for a bank, use the Internet to your advantage. You can learn a lot about a bank from its website. There you'll find information about interest rates, fees, services they offer, and special promotions they may be running (such as free check-printing for new customers). And, as with pretty much everything these days, you can Google the bank's name and find useful customer reviews and ratings.

References

1. "Banking 101," USTrust.com, 2016.

2. "Banking Basics," Indiana Department of Financial Institutions (IDFI), n.d.

3. "Banking Basics 101: A Quick Lesson in Banking and Saving," CesiSolutions.org, September 21, 2013.

4. Calonia, Jennifer. "Banking," Learnvest.com, June 1, 2012.

5. Campisi, Natalie. "Banking 101 Guide: Tips and Terms to Know before Opening Your First Account," GoBankingRates.com, August 19, 2016.

6. "Selecting a Bank," Teensguidetomoney.com, n.d.

Chapter 46

If Debit or Credit Cards Are Stolen

If your credit, automated teller machine (ATM), or debit card is lost or stolen, federal law limits your liability for unauthorized charges. Your protection against unauthorized charges depends on the type of card—and when you report the loss.

Report Loss or Theft Immediately

Acting fast limits your liability for charges you didn't authorize. Report the loss or theft of your card to the card issuer as quickly as possible. Many companies have toll-free numbers and 24-hour service for such emergencies. Once you report the loss of your ATM or debit card, federal law says you cannot be held liable for unauthorized transfers that occur after that time.

- Follow up with a letter or e-mail. Include your account number, the date, and time when you noticed your card was missing, and when you first reported the loss.

- Check your card statement carefully for transactions you didn't make. Report these transactions to the card issuer as quickly as possible. Be sure to send the letter to the address provided for billing errors.

- Check if your homeowner or renter's insurance policy covers your liability for card thefts. If not, some insurance companies will allow you to change your policy to include this protection.

About This Chapter: This chapter includes text excerpted from "Lost or Stolen Credit, ATM, and Debit Cards," Federal Trade Commission (FTC), August 2012.

How to Report Fraudulent Transactions

- Contact your ATM or debit card issuer.
  - Report the fraudulent transaction.
  - Act as soon as you discover a withdrawal or purchase you didn't make.
- Write a follow-up letter to confirm that you reported the problem.
  - Keep a copy of your letter.
  - Send it by certified mail and ask for a return receipt.
- Update your files.
  - Record the dates you made calls or sent letters.
  - Keep copies of letters in your files.

How to Limit Your Losses

The Fair Credit Billing Act (FCBA) and the Electronic Fund Transfer Act (EFTA) offer protection if your credit, ATM, or debit cards are lost or stolen.

Credit Card Loss or Fraudulent Charges

Under the FCBA, your liability for unauthorized use of your credit card tops out at $50. However, if you report the loss before your credit card is used, the FCBA says you are not responsible for any charges you didn't authorize. If your credit card number is stolen, but not the card, you are not liable for unauthorized use.

ATM or Debit Card Loss or Fraudulent Transfers

If you report an ATM or debit card missing before someone uses it, the EFTA says you are not responsible for any unauthorized transactions. If someone uses your ATM or debit card before you report it lost or stolen, your liability depends on how quickly you report it:

If someone makes unauthorized transactions with your debit card number, but your card is not lost, you are not liable for those transactions if you report them within 60 days of your statement being sent to you.

Table 46.1. ATM Liability

If You Report	Your Maximum Loss
Before any unauthorized charges are made	$0
Within 2 business days after you learn about the loss or theft	$50
More than 2 business days after you learn about the loss or theft, but less than 60 calendar days after your statement is sent to you	$500
More than 60 calendar days after your statement is sent to you	All the money taken from your ATM/debit card account, and possibly more; for example, money in accounts linked to your debit account

How to Protect Your Cards and Account Information
For Credit and ATM or Debit Cards

- Don't disclose your account number over the phone unless you initiate the call.

- Guard your account information. Never leave it out in the open or write it on an envelope.

- Keep a record of your account numbers, expiration dates, and the telephone numbers of each card issuer so you can report a loss quickly.

- Draw a line through blank spaces on charge or debit slips above the total so the amount can't be changed.

- Don't sign a blank charge or debit slip.

- Tear up copies and save your receipts to check against your monthly statements.

- Cut up old cards—cutting through the account number—before you throw them away.

- Open your monthly statements promptly and compare them to your receipts. Report mistakes or discrepancies as soon as possible.

- Carry only the cards you'll need.

For ATM or Debit Cards

- Don't carry your personal identification number (PIN) in your wallet, purse, or pocket—or write it on your ATM or debit card. Commit it to memory.

- Never write your PIN on the outside of a deposit slip, an envelope, or other papers that could be lost or looked at.

- Carefully check your ATM or debit card transactions; the funds for this item will be quickly transferred out of your checking or other deposit accounts.

- Periodically check your account activity, especially if you bank online. Compare the current balance and transactions on your statement to those you've recorded. Report any discrepancies to your card issuer immediately.

---

1. Check your accounts for unauthorized charges or debits and continue monitoring your accounts

If you have online or mobile access to your accounts, check your transactions as frequently as possible. If you receive paper statements, be sure to open them and review them closely. If your provider offers it, consider signing up for e-mail or text alerts. Report even small problems right away. Sometimes thieves will process a small debit or charge against your account and return to take more from your bank account or add more charges to your credit card if the first smaller debit or charge goes through. And keep paying attention—fraudulent charges to your card or fraudulent debits to your bank account might occur many months after the theft of your information during a data breach.

2. Report a suspicious charge or debit immediately

Contact your bank or card provider immediately if you suspect an unauthorized debit or charge. If a thief charges items to your account, you should cancel the card and have it replaced before more transactions come through. Even if you're not sure that PIN information was taken, consider changing your PIN just to be on the safe side. If your physical credit card has not been lost or stolen, you're not responsible for unauthorized charges. You can protect yourself from being liable for unauthorized debit card charges by reporting those charges immediately after you find out about them or they show up on your bank statement.

If you spot a fraudulent transaction, call the card provider's toll-free customer service number immediately. Follow up with a written letter. Your monthly statement or error resolution notice will tell you how and where to report fraudulent charges or billing disputes. When you communicate in writing, be sure to keep a copy for your records. Write down the dates you make follow-up calls and keep this information together in a file. If your card or PIN was lost or stolen, different rules may apply. Your timeline for reporting after your

---

card, PIN, or other access device is lost or stolen is tied to when you discover the loss or theft or when unauthorized transactions show up on your bank statement. Therefore, you should make the report as soon as you know that there is a problem

3. Submit a complaint if you have an issue with your bank or card provider's response

Debit card issuers should investigate the charges (generally within 10 business days) and take action quickly (generally within 3 business days). For your credit card, it can take longer, but you don't have to pay the charge while it's under investigation. You also have a right to see the results of their investigations. If you have an issue with their response, you can submit a complaint online or by calling 855-411-2372. For TTY/TDD, call 855-729-2372. If you have other questions about billing disputes and your debit and credit card protections, you can Ask CFPB.

4. Know when to ignore anyone contacting you to "verify" your account information by phone or e-mail

This could be a common scam, often referred to as "phishing," to steal your account information. Banks and credit unions never ask for account information through phone or e-mail that they initiate. If you receive this type of contact, you should immediately call your card provider (using a customer service number that you get from a different source than the initial call or e-mail) and report it.

(Source: "Four Steps You Can Take If You Think Your Credit or Debit Card Data Was Hacked," Consumer Financial Protection Bureau (CFPB).)

Chapter 47

Beware of Online Perils and Internet Fraud

The Internet has proven to be a major boon for consumers making financial decisions. Information that at one time would've taken days or weeks to ferret out can now be found easily in minutes. Annual reports and other corporate filings are available on SEC.gov, the website of the U.S. Securities and Exchange Commission (SEC). Most companies provide those documents and other valuable investor information on their own sites. In addition, thousands of other sites contain a wealth of data about investments, banks, online stores, and e-mail offers, allowing consumers to perform in-depth research before making financial decisions.

Unfortunately, the web has also been a boon for scammers and has fostered a host of possible ways for people to lose money. It's an easy way for criminals to reach large numbers of people cheaply and without much effort and then lure them into traps using tools like social media, spam e-mails, pop-up ads, newsletters, discussion forums, and fake websites. So it's very important to learn to spot online scammers and fraudulent Internet practices in order to avoid becoming the next victim.

Common Online Investment Scams

There are many thousands of ways unscrupulous individuals can take advantage of investors, and they're inventing more every day. But some have proven so successful that criminals keep using them over and over. A few of the most common ones include:

- **Online investment newsletters.** Online newsletters can provide valuable information for investors, but some are fraudulent. In these cases, companies often pay newsletter

About This Chapter: "Beware of Online Perils and Internet Fraud," © 2017 Omnigraphics.

writers to recommend their stock. This isn't actually illegal if the newsletters follow SEC regulations and disclose who's paying them and how much they're getting. But many fail to do this and pose as unbiased sources of information while they convince the public to make poor investment choices.

- **Online bulletin boards or discussion forums.** These sites allow people to exchange information about investments, ask questions, and share their experiences. The problem is, you don't really know who's doing the posting. It could be a company, or someone it's hired, promoting a certain investment while posing as small investors or perhaps as someone with inside information. This is another cheap and easy way to disseminate false information and get people to buy stock.

- **Spam.** Spam is a fact of life for virtually anyone with an e-mail address. Most people receive multiple messages each day trying to get them to buy products or use a service. Investment spam is one more way for scammers to reach a large audience and spread false information about a company or investment opportunity, usually making it sound much better than it really is.

- **"Pump and dump" schemes.** This term refers to a scheme in which a scammer acquires a large amount of cheap stock and then pumps up the price through the use of false information in e-mails, online discussion groups, and social media, urging people to buy the stock quickly. The sudden burst of promotion increases demand for the stock and drives up the price, at which point the fraudster sells all of his or her shares. Then the stock drops in value, and other investors lose money.

- **High-yield investment scheme.** Also known as "prime bank scams," these are unregistered investments, usually managed by unlicensed brokers, that are almost always fraudulent. They promise to deliver extremely high returns with little or no risk to the investor. Typically a high-yield promoter will use a website or other online means to convince people that their investment will net an annual return of 30–40 percent—or even 100 percent. In reality, it's likely that the scammer will simply take the money and disappear.

- **Advance fee scam.** Here a scammer typically uses spam e-mails to solicit up-front fees for investments. Often these are positioned as a commission, tax, deposit, or underwriting fee, and sometimes victims are told they'll get this money back at a future date. They are almost always accompanied by very official-looking e-mail addresses or website, and often investors are instructed to send the fee to an attorney or another agent. Needless to say, the fraudster will vanish with no further word about the "investment."

- **Fraudulent online offerings.** These scams are instances in which investments in stocks, bonds, or other securities are offered to the public with false information intended to make the investment look better than it is. Usually, this involves the promise of a higher return than is actually possible.

> Use common sense. If an online offer sounds too good to be true, it probably is. Scam artists are experts as using greed as leverage against their victims. If someone is promising you free stuff or large sums of money in exchange for a small investment on your part, your instinct should tell you that something doesn't add up.

Other Online Scams

In addition to investment fraud, there are thousands of other ways criminals use the Internet to take people's money. Here are some common scams:

- **Phishing.** One of the most prevalent fraudulent online practices, phishing e-mails tries to steal your personal information, such as birth date, passwords, and credit card numbers. Typically they trick you into visiting a fake website made to look like a legitimate online store or banking site, often one with which you've done business in the past. There they may ask you to "verify" your personal information or enter financial details, which they can then use to hack into your accounts or steal your identity.

- **Greeting card scams.** Here you receive an e-card in your e-mail box, but when you click on the link to see the card you're taken to a website that's rigged to download a malicious bot to your computer. When downloaded, it can wreak all sorts of havoc, including stealing personal details and financial information.

- **Lottery frauds.** Lots of people dream of winning the lottery, and these scams prey on those hopes and dreams. The scammers send you an e-mail saying you've won a lottery, and to collect the huge prize all you need to do is send them a "processing fee." Of course, there is no lottery, and they keep your fee.

- **Nigerian scam.** This one has been around for almost as long as the Internet, yet it continues to rob people every year. There are many variations of this scheme, which is similar to lottery fraud. An e-mail from Nigerian royalty, or another very wealthy person, asks for your help in getting a large sum of money out of the country. You need to advance a small amount of money, and in return, you're promised a big payoff once the transaction is completed. As with a lottery scam, there is no transaction, except the money you advanced.

- **Guaranteed acceptance fraud.** Here an e-mail tells you that you've been preapproved for a credit card or loan for a large sum of money, and to get it all you need to do is send an up-front "processing fee." These scams are particularly believable because banks and credit-card companies often do send consumers preapproval offers. But in this case, of course, there's no card or loan.

- **Pyramid scheme.** This scam predates the Internet by many years, but where it once was perpetrated by mail, scammers now use e-mail to reach a lot more victims. Pyramid schemes purport to be businesses that sell goods or services with growth accomplished by "associates" (salespeople) recruiting more people into the scheme. Each new associate pays a fee to join. Often no goods or services ever exist, and the people at the top of the pyramid make all the money.

> Sign up to receive regular scam alerts at the Federal Trade Commission (FTC) website, ftc.gov. There you'll also find valuable information on some of the latest scams and how to avoid them.

How to Avoid Becoming a Victim

Fraudsters are clever, and they're always thinking up new ways to separate people from their money. With the Internet at their disposal they're able to reach more victims and can make their schemes look especially tempting with legitimate-appearing websites and e-mails. Young people are particularly susceptible to some of their scams, in part because they may not have been exposed to similar types of fraud in the past. But there are steps you can take to protect yourself from the scammers, such as:

- **Use the Internet to your advantage.** There's a wealth of information available online that can help you investigate investments or e-mail offers before parting with your money. Often a simple Google search will uncover other people who've been victims. When it comes to investments, the SEC website or your state's securities regulation site can also be a valuable source of information about companies and their stocks or bonds.

- **Work with professionals.** When investing, use the services of a reputable broker or financial adviser. They can not only guide you to some of the most stable investments but can also provide assurance that you're putting your money into legitimate sources. If you're investing with an online broker, check out the site thoroughly to be sure it's not a scam.

- **Choose regular investments.** Get-rich-quick e-mail schemes sound tempting, which is why so many people fall for them. But avoid any offers that sound too good to be true, and invest your money in more common securities, like stocks and bonds that are recommended by reputable analysts and advisers. These investments may not seem as exciting, but they're less likely to be scams.

- **Beware of imposters.** Scammers very often pose as a trusted source, such as a bank, a company you do business with, a government agency, or even a friend or family member. Don't send money to anyone until you check them out thoroughly. Typing their name, or the company's name, into a search engine followed by "scam" or "complaint" will often reveal the truth.

- **Don't pay up front.** Never make an advance payment or pay an up-front fee for any unsolicited offers. Scammers send e-mails for everything from prizes to job offers to preapproved credit in order to get you to send money. Be wary of anyone asking for "processing" or "handling" fees.

- **Make a phone call.** If your research into an online offer turns up what appears to be a legitimate business, get the company's phone number and call for more information. If the offer is legitimate, they'll be glad to verify it and give you additional details.

- **Choose a safe online payment method.** The safest way to shop or make payments online is with credit cards, because they have the most built-in fraud protection. Debit cards are less secure; with those you will probably get your money back in case of fraud, but it will be more difficult and take more time. It's especially risky to wire money or use reloadable debit cards; if an online source insists that you use one of these payment methods, that should raise a red flag.

> If you suspect online fraud, you should report it to the Federal Bureau of Investigation (FBI) Internet Crime Complaint Center (IC3) (ic3.gov), the U.S. Government's Online Safety page (usa.gov/online-safety), or the Better Business Bureau's (BBB) Scam Tracker page (bbb.org/scamtracker/us/reportscam).

References

1. "Avoiding Internet Investment Scams: Tips for Investors," U.S. Securities and Exchange Commission (SEC), August 15, 2007.

2. "Internet Fraud: How to Avoid Internet Investment Scams," Findlaw.com, n.d.

3. "Online Scams and Fraud: How Internet Users Can Minimize Exposure," Whoishostingthis.com, n.d.

4. Schock, Lori J. "Don't Get Scammed by Investment Fraud on the Internet," Militarysaves.org, February 3, 2015.

5. Smith, Lisa. "Avoiding Online Investment Scams," Investopedia.com, n.d.

Chapter 48

Identity Theft and Identity Fraud

Identity (ID) theft is a crime where a thief steals your personal information, such as your full name or Social Security number, to commit fraud. The identity thief can use your information to fraudulently apply for credit, file taxes, or get medical services. These acts can damage your credit status, and cost you time and money to restore your good name. You may not know that you are the victim of ID theft until you experience a financial consequence (mystery bills, credit collections, denied loans) down the road from actions that the thief has taken with your stolen identity.

There are several common types of identity theft that can affect you:

- **Child ID theft.** Children's IDs are vulnerable because the theft may go undetected for many years. By the time they are adults, the damage has already been done to their identities.

- **Tax ID theft.** A thief uses your Social Security number to falsely file tax returns with the Internal Revenue Service or state government.

- **Medical ID theft.** This form of ID theft happens when someone steals your personal information, such as your Medicare ID or health insurance member number to get medical services, or to issue fraudulent billing to your health insurance provider.

- **Senior ID theft.** ID theft schemes that target seniors. Seniors are vulnerable to ID theft because they are in more frequent contact with medical professionals who get their medical insurance information, or caregivers and staff at long-term care facilities that have access to personal information or financial documents.

- **Social ID theft.** A thief uses your name, photos, and other personal information to create a phony account on a social media platform.

(Source: "Identity Theft," USA.gov)

About This Chapter: This chapter includes text excerpted from "Identity Theft," U.S. Department of Justice (DOJ), February 7, 2017.

What Are Identity Theft and Identity Fraud?

Identity theft and identity fraud are terms used to refer to all types of crime in which someone wrongfully obtains and uses another person's personal data in some way that involves fraud or deception, typically for economic gain.

What Are the Most Common Ways That Identity Theft or Fraud Can Happen to You?

- In public places, for example, criminals may engage in "shoulder surfing"—watching you from a nearby location as you punch in your telephone calling card number or credit card number—or listen in on your conversation if you give your credit card number over the telephone.

- If you receive applications for "preapproved" credit cards in the mail, but discard them without tearing up the enclosed materials, criminals may retrieve them and try to activate the cards for their use without your knowledge. Also, if your mail is delivered to a place where others have ready access to it, criminals may simply intercept and redirect your mail to another location.

- Many people respond to "spam"—unsolicited e-mail—that promises them some benefit but requests identifying data, without realizing that in many cases, the requester has no intention of keeping his promise. In some cases, criminals reportedly have used computer technology to steal large amounts of personal data.

With enough identifying information about an individual, a criminal can take over that individual's identity to conduct a wide range of crimes. For example:

- False applications for loans and credit cards
- Fraudulent withdrawals from bank accounts
- Fraudulent use of telephone calling cards or online accounts
- Obtaining other goods or privileges which the criminal might be denied if he were to use his real name

What Can You Do If You've Become a Victim of Identity Theft?

- Call the companies where you know the fraud occurred.
- Place a fraud alert and get your credit reports.

- Report identity theft to the Federal Trade Commission (FTC).

- You may choose to file a report with your local police department.

Take steps to protect yourself from identity theft:

- Secure your Social Security number (SSN). Don't carry your Social Security card in your wallet or write your number on your checks. Only give out your SSN when absolutely necessary.

- Don't respond to unsolicited requests for personal information (your name, birthdate, Social Security number, or bank account number) by phone, mail, or online.

- Contact the three credit reporting agencies to request a freeze of your credit reports.

- Collect mail promptly. Place a hold on your mail when you are away from home for several days.

- Pay attention to your billing cycles. If bills or financial statements are late, contact the sender.

- Enable the security features on mobile devices, especially if you have contacts, banking websites and applications saved.

- Update sharing and firewall settings when you're on a public wi-fi network. Consider using a virtual private network, which can give you the privacy of secured private network.

- Review your credit card and bank account statements. Promptly compare receipts with account statements. Watch for unauthorized transactions.

- Shred receipts, credit offers, account statements, and expired credit cards, to prevent "dumpster divers" from getting your personal information.

- Store personal information in a safe place.

- Install firewalls and virus-detection software on your home computer.

- Create complex passwords that identity thieves cannot guess easily. Change your passwords if a company that you do business with has a breach of its databases

- Review your credit report once a year to be certain that it doesn't include accounts that you have not opened. You can order it for free from Annualcreditreport.com.

- Freeze your credit files with Equifax, Experian, Innovis, TransUnion, and the National Consumer Telecommunications and Utilities Exchange, for free. This prevents someone from using your personal information to open a credit account or get utility services.

(Source: "Identity Theft," USA.gov)

What's the U.S. Department of Justice Doing about Identity Theft and Fraud?

The U.S. Department of Justice (DOJ) prosecutes cases of identity theft and fraud under a variety of federal statutes. In the fall of 1998, for example, Congress passed the Identity Theft and Assumption Deterrence Act (ITADA). This legislation created an offense of identity theft, which prohibits "knowingly transfer(ring) or us(ing), without lawful authority, a means of identification of another person with the intent to commit, or to aid or abet, any unlawful activity that constitutes a violation of federal law, or that constitutes a felony under any applicable State or local law." 18 U.S.C. § 1028(a)(7). This offense, in most circumstances, carries a maximum term of 15 years' imprisonment, a fine, and criminal forfeiture of any personal property used or intended to be used to commit the offense.

Schemes to commit identity theft or fraud may also involve violations of other statutes such as identification fraud (18 U.S.C. § 1028), credit card fraud (18 U.S.C. § 1029), computer fraud (18 U.S.C. § 1030), mail fraud (18 U.S.C. § 1341), wire fraud (18 U.S.C. § 1343), or financial institution fraud (18 U.S.C. § 1344). Each of these federal offenses are felonies that carry substantial penalties—in some cases, as high as 30 years' imprisonment, fines, and criminal forfeiture.

Federal prosecutors work with federal investigative agencies such as the Federal Bureau of Investigation (FBI), the U.S. Secret Service (USSS), and the U.S. Postal Inspection Service (USPIS) to prosecute identity theft and fraud cases.

Chapter 49

Telemarketing Scams

When you send money to people you do not know personally or give personal or financial information to unknown callers, you increase your chances of becoming a victim of telemarketing fraud.

Here are some warning signs of telemarketing fraud—what a caller may tell you:

- "You must act 'now' or the offer won't be good."

- "You've won a 'free' gift, vacation, or prize." But you have to pay for "postage and handling" or other charges.

- "You must send money, give a credit card or bank account number, or have a check picked up by courier." You may hear this before you have had a chance to consider the offer carefully.

- "You don't need to check out the company with anyone." The callers say you do not need to speak to anyone including your family, lawyer, accountant, local Better Business Bureau (BBB), or consumer protection agency.

- "You don't need any written information about the company or their references."

- "You can't afford to miss this 'high-profit, no-risk' offer."

If you hear these or similar "lines" from a telephone salesperson, just say "no thank you" and hang up the telephone.

About This Chapter: This chapter includes text excerpted from "Telemarketing Fraud," Federal Bureau of Investigation (FBI), February 1, 2001.

Tips for Avoiding Telemarketing Fraud

It is very difficult to get your money back if you have been cheated over the telephone. Before you buy anything by telephone, remember:

- Don't buy from an unfamiliar company. Legitimate businesses understand that you want more information about their company and are happy to comply.

- Always ask for and wait until you receive written material about any offer or charity. If you get brochures about costly investments, ask someone whose financial advice you trust to review them. But beware—not everything written down is true.

- Always check out unfamiliar companies with your local consumer protection agency, Better Business Bureau, state attorney general, the National Fraud Information Center (NFIC), or other watchdog groups. However, not all bad businesses can be identified through these organizations.

- Obtain a salesperson's name, business identity, telephone number, street address, mailing address, and business license number before you transact business. Some con artists give out false names, telephone numbers, addresses, and business license numbers—verify the accuracy of these items.

- Before you give money to a charity or make an investment, find out what percentage of the money is paid in commissions and what percentage actually goes to the charity or investment.

- Before you send money, ask yourself a simple question: "What guarantee do I really have that this solicitor will use my money in the manner we agreed upon?"

- Don't pay in advance for services; pay only after they are delivered.

- Be wary of companies that want to send a messenger to your home to pick up money, claiming it is part of their service to you. In reality, they are taking your money without leaving any trace of who they are or where they can be reached.

- Always take your time making a decision. Legitimate companies won't pressure you to make a snap decision.

- Don't pay for a "free prize." If a caller tells you the payment is for taxes, she or he is violating federal law.

- Before you receive your next sales pitch, decide what your limits are—the kinds of financial information you will and won't give out on the telephone.

- Be sure to talk over big investments offered by telephone salespeople with a trusted friend, family member, or financial advisor. It is never rude to wait and think about an offer.

- Never respond to an offer you don't understand thoroughly.

- Never send money or give out personal information such as credit card numbers and expiration dates, bank account numbers, dates of birth, or Social Security numbers (SSNs) to unfamiliar companies or unknown persons.

- Be aware that your personal information is often brokered to telemarketers through third parties.

- If you have been victimized once, be wary of persons who call offering to help you recover your losses for a fee paid in advance.

- If you have information about a fraud, report it to state, local, or federal law enforcement agencies.

- Sign up for the National Do Not Call (NDNC) Registry, maintained by the Federal Trade Commission (FTC), to prevent telemarketers from calling (verification does require an e-mail address).
- The National Telemarketing Victim Call Center (NTVCC): 855-322-9218. This program accepts reports of telemarketing fraud and uses peer support to provide follow up in an attempt to prevent subsequent instances of financial fraud.

(Source: "Elder Fraud and Financial Exploitation," StopFraud.gov, Financial Fraud Enforcement Task Force (FFETF).)

Chapter 50

Ten Things You Can Do to Avoid Financial Fraud

Crooks use clever schemes to defraud millions of people every year. They often combine new technology with old tricks to get people to send money or give out personal information. Here are some practical tips to help you stay a step ahead.

1. **Spot imposters.** Scammers often pretend to be someone you trust, like a government official, a family member, a charity, or a company you do business with. Don't send money or give out personal information in response to an unexpected request—whether it comes as a text, a phone call, or an e-mail.

2. **Do online searches.** Type a company or product name into your favorite search engine with words like "review," "complaint," or "scam." Or search for a phrase that describes your situation, like "IRS call." You can even search for phone numbers to see if other people have reported them as scams.

3. **Don't believe your caller ID.** Technology makes it easy for scammers to fake caller ID information, so the name and number you see aren't always real. If someone calls asking for money or personal information, hang up. If you think the caller might be telling the truth, call back to a number you know is genuine.

4. **Don't pay upfront for a promise.** Someone might ask you to pay in advance for things like debt relief, credit and loan offers, mortgage assistance, or a job. They might even say you've won a prize, but first, you have to pay taxes or fees. If you do, they will probably take the money and disappear.

About This Chapter: This chapter includes text excerpted from "10 Things You Can Do to Avoid Fraud," Federal Trade Commission (FTC), August 2018.

5. **Consider how you pay.** Credit cards have significant fraud protection built in, but some payment methods don't. Wiring money through services like Western Union or MoneyGram is risky because it's nearly impossible to get your money back. That's also true for reloadable cards (like MoneyPak or Reloadit) and gift cards (like iTunes or Google Play). Government offices and honest companies won't require you to use these payment methods.

6. **Talk to someone.** Before you give up your money or personal information, talk to someone you trust. Con artists want you to make decisions in a hurry. They might even threaten you. Slow down, check out the story, do an online search, consult an expert—or just tell a friend.

7. **Hang up on robocalls.** If you answer the phone and hear a recorded sales pitch, hang up and report it to the Federal Trade Commission (FTC). These calls are illegal, and often the products are bogus. Don't press #1 to speak to a person or to be taken off the list. That could lead to more calls.

8. **Be skeptical about free trial offers.** Some companies use free trials to sign you up for products and bill you every month until you cancel. Before you agree to a free trial, research the company, and read the cancellation policy. And always review your monthly statements for charges you don't recognize.

9. **Don't deposit a check and wire money back.** By law, banks must make funds from deposited checks available within days, but uncovering a fake check can take weeks. If a check you deposit turns out to be a fake, you're responsible for repaying the bank.

10. **Sign up for free scam alerts from the FTC.** Get the latest tips and advice about scams sent right to your inbox. If you spot a scam, report it at ftc.gov/complaint. Your reports help the FTC and other law enforcement investigate scams and bring crooks to justice.

If you would like to report financial fraud to the FBI, please contact at 202.324.3000 or online at https://tips.fbi.gov.

You may also wish to contact the U.S. Attorney's Office where you are located or where the fraud was committed. Visit the Offices of the U.S. Attorneys for a list of the 93 U.S. Attorney's Offices and links to their websites.

In addition, certain government agencies target particular types of financial fraud.

(Source: "Report Financial Fraud," StopFraud.gov, Financial Fraud Enforcement Task Force (FFETF).)

Part Seven
Looking Ahead

Chapter 51

Self-Employment

What's the best thing about being self-employed? Angella Luyk, owner of two businesses in Rochester, New York, doesn't hesitate to answer. "No one can tell me what to do, because I'm the boss," she says. "I'm in charge of my own future."

Luyk is one of nearly 15 million workers identified as self-employed in April 2014, according to the U.S. Bureau of Labor Statistics (BLS). These workers accounted for about 10 percent of the overall workforce.

But Luyk cautions that working for yourself isn't for everyone. "It can get tough and scary," she says, "because everything relies on you." Success takes preparation, determination, and time—and it's not guaranteed.

Is Self-Employment for You?

People choose to become self-employed for many reasons, including greater independence and flexibility. But they also consider the downsides, such as the long hours and lack of benefits.

As part of your decision-making process, you should weigh the pros and cons of starting a business, along with your own reasons for seeking self-employment. For example, hoping to make a lot of money quickly can lead you into trouble. But if you feel passionate about developing an idea, self-employment may be right for you.

About This Chapter: This chapter includes text excerpted from "Self-Employment: What to Know to Be Your Own Boss," U.S. Bureau of Labor Statistics (BLS), U.S. Department of Labor (DOL), June 2014.

Rewards

For many self-employed workers, autonomy is the biggest reward. They are able to make their own decisions, such as what kind of work they do, whom they do it for, where and when they do it—and even how much to pay themselves.

Self-employed workers usually take on many different tasks, learning to do each as the need arises. For example, a self-employed barber needs to find a suitable location for opening a shop, attract clients, and price services, in addition to cutting hair.

Many workers find that self-employment allows them not only to expand their professional skills, but also to enrich themselves personally. "I learned a lot more about business and life than I ever expected," says Megan Lebon, a physician who owns a practice in Atlanta, Georgia.

Self-employment can bring other rewards, too. Some workers enjoy creating a new business and watching it grow. They feel good about working for something they believe in.

Challenges

Self-employment is hard work, especially during the first few years. Workers may have difficulty finding clients, earning a steady income, securing business loans, and navigating laws. These challenges add up to financial risk and uncertainty.

And, with income frequently unpredictable, workers may try to handle all or most parts of the business themselves. "You end up working a lot more than you think, oftentimes way more than when you were working for someone else," says Vicki James, owner of a marketing business in Rochester, New York. This schedule can make balancing work and personal life difficult.

Another challenge with self-employment is lack of benefits. Public and private employers typically contribute to retirement, health, and other benefits, offering affordable options to their employees. But self-employed workers must find these benefits and pay for them entirely out of pocket. And there is no paid leave for vacation or illness: A day off work is a day without pay. These types of burdens may overstretch limited financial resources.

Get Started

Even after you choose an occupation for starting a business, becoming self-employed isn't as easy as deciding to work for yourself. You need certain skills and a lot of preparation before you can focus on setting up and growing a business.

But if getting started seems daunting, remember that you don't have to do everything at once and that help is available. Focus on taking one step at a time.

Skills and Knowledge

One of the most important requirements for self-employment, business experts say, is having the technical skills and knowledge you need to do the work you want to do. For example, a graphic design freelancer needs to know color theory and how to use design software. It's a bad idea to start a business in something you don't understand well.

Other technical skills, such as bookkeeping and marketing, are helpful for operating a business. You can learn these skills in a class, at school, with the help of a mentor, or on your own. Higher education, although not a prerequisite for success, is often useful.

Some occupations have specific entry requirements, regardless of whether workers are self-employed. Physicians, for example, must have a bachelor's degree and complete a medical degree program, residency, and licensure requirements. And real estate agents need to become licensed in their state.

Experts suggest that, in addition to having technical skills, you focus on improving "soft" skills, such as time management and people skills. And, regardless of what you do, having a passion for the work is key.

Time management. Self-employed workers often have multiple responsibilities and keep long hours. Being able to manage time efficiently—for example, through multitasking and scheduling—is crucial. These skills help you determine how much time you need to complete tasks and whether you can take on additional work.

People skills. Good people skills, such as communication and customer service, help you attract and retain both employees and clients—especially in the beginning. "Early on, you're the chief salesperson," says Dennis Wright, a small-business mentor in Santa Ana, California. "You have to sell people on your abilities and the value of your product or service."

Passion. Experts say that a passion for what you do can give you the belief, motivation, and commitment you need to overcome the challenges that self-employment may present. "You must like and be committed to what you're doing," Wright says, "or you're likely to give up when you hit bumps in the road."

Preparation

No matter how skilled and knowledgeable you are about the product or service you want to sell, you still need to prepare to ensure success in self-employment. Experts recommend that before you invest any money, you take some time to figure out what motivates you to become self-employed, do your research, and ask for help as you plan your business.

Understand why. Experts say that self-employed workers often feel discouraged, especially when just getting started. Understanding your motivations for becoming self-employed can help sustain you in times of struggle. "The reasons why are the catalyst that will push you forward," says James. "They will help you overcome the moments of doubt."

The reasons for becoming self-employed differ for everyone. Consider what your reasons are, and make note of them. Then, refer to them when you face challenges, to remind yourself of why you pursued self-employment.

Research. Researching your potential business is a way of evaluating whether your idea is marketable. Through research, you can also learn more about your potential customers, competitors, and collaborators. Experts suggest examining the prospective market for your product or service so that you can answer essential questions, such as the following:

- Who and where is the customer?

- How can your potential customers benefit from the product or service you are offering?

- Who are your competitors?

- What will set you apart from your competition?

Professional journals, focus groups, surveys, business clubs, seminars, and current business owners are among the sources that can provide answers to these questions. You may even find reports written by people who have done similar research.

But not every business idea is a winner. Experts suggest moving on when your research shows that an idea won't work. Your next idea might be the right one.

And be careful not to let research stop you from actually getting started. "I thought I first needed to know everything about running a business," James says. "Find the courage to make mistakes, and learn from them as you go."

Ask for help. Many of the principles of business are the same, so people who have already had success with self-employment are often good sources of information to those who are considering it. They may share tips and mistakes, experts say, or make valuable suggestions you hadn't considered. "Learn from people smarter and more experienced than you," says Luyk.

Another possible advantage in asking for help is finding a mentor: someone who offers guidance, encouragement, advice, and emotional support throughout the life of your business. You may meet a potential mentor informally or through a business organization.

Setting up Shop

After you've determined that your business idea is viable, it's finally time to set up shop, right? Not quite; you still have work to do. For starters, you need to write a business plan, ensure that you meet all legal and tax requirements, and prepare to limit your legal and financial liability. These steps also apply if you decide to freelance, even if you get started quickly out of your own home.

Write Your Business Plan

A business plan is an essential roadmap for business success. This living document generally projects 3–5 years ahead and outlines the route a company intends to take to grow revenues.

For a more in-depth look at writing a business plan go to: www.sba.gov/starting-business/write-your-business-plan

The process of setting up a business can be confusing and difficult. You'll need to complete a lot of paperwork to ensure that you're complying with different laws and regulations, for example. Experts recommend consulting an accountant and a lawyer for help, and they say that this investment in your future business is money well spent. "Be upfront about what you want and what you can afford," says Luyk. "These professionals will save you money in the end."

Another difficulty is a lack of money early on. Experts suggest that, before you get started, you should save up enough money to last a couple of years so that you avoid financial pitfalls.

Write a business plan. A business plan describes what service you'll provide or product you'll make, along with how and when you'll do it. "If you don't set goals, you won't achieve them," says business mentor Jack Bernard. "You'll just chase your tail." Use your research to set goals for the business within specific timeframes. Your business plan should explain in detail every part of your business, including the following:

- Your business values and vision for the future

- Your business's strengths, weaknesses, opportunities, and threats

- Financial projections

- The experience and achievements of key staff.

Business plans are important when you seek funding, which may include loans and grants. Most reputable creditors require applicants to have a business plan, a solid credit score, and a criminal background check before agreeing to lend or invest money in a business startup.

There are plenty of free resources available to help you write your plan. For example, you can find step-by-step guides and templates online or at your local library. And some business organizations offer individualized business counseling.

Meet legal requirements. To legally operate a business, you need a business license, as well as permits from the city and county, or both, in which the business is located. Local governments have many different requirements, but common ones include health and zoning permits.

You also need to meet Internal Revenue Service requirements. These include registering for an employer identification number, reporting wages and taxes withheld, and verifying employees' eligibility to work in the United States.

Other federal requirements may apply, depending on your business product or service. For example, a business that sells produce throughout the country needs a permit from the U.S. Department of Agriculture (USDA)to ensure that the food is safe.

Limit liability. The way you structure your business affects your legal and financial responsibilities. For example, a sole proprietor is someone who owns a business and is accountable for all of its assets, obligations, and so on. And sole proprietors take a great risk by assuming all responsibility for their business; lenders can take control of personal assets of a sole proprietor who fails to repay a business loan.

Some business structures are designed to limit personal liability. The most common are a limited liability company (LLC) and an S corporation. Both of these arrangements protect personal assets by risking only what is invested in the business. Generally speaking, an LLC is easier to set up and manage, but an S Corporation allows for the sale of business stock to investors.

Loans guaranteed by the U.S. Small Business Administration (SBA) range from small to large and can be used for most business purposes, including long-term fixed assets and operating capital. Some loan programs set restrictions on how you can use the funds, so check with an SBA-approved lender when requesting a loan. Your lender can match you with the right loan for your business needs.

(Source: "The SBA Helps Small Businesses Get Loans," U.S. Small Business Administration (SBA).)

Growing the Business

After you've completed the necessary steps for self-employment, you'll need to focus on growing the business. Networking, staying competitive, making adjustments, and working through challenges will increase your chances of success.

Network. Experts say that networking is one of the best ways for self-employed people to spend their time. Among other benefits it provides, networking offers opportunities for self-employed workers to reach potential clients, meet business mentors, and test ideas to gauge interest. "You have to make yourself visible to your market," Lebon says. "People can only do business with you if they can find you first."

People usually network at business events, clubs, and meetings. Volunteering with a professional organization or serving on a community board also can be useful. And networking doesn't have to be formal. "Sometimes I just have coffee with people and share ideas, without worrying about business," says Ryan Schwartz, a freelance communications specialist in Portland, Oregon.

Some self-employed workers also use traditional marketing tools, such as creating a website or advertising in a local paper, to attract clients. But experts caution against relying too heavily on marketing, which often is expensive and yields mixed results. "There is no better form of advertising than word of mouth," Wright says. "Give your customers a positive experience, and they'll come back with a friend."

Stay competitive. Competition is a part of being in business. To stay competitive with other businesses that are like yours, you have to stand out in areas such as price, quality, and service. "If you can't define what makes you better," says Bernard, "your customers certainly won't know, and they will take their business elsewhere."

Updating your research will help keep you informed about competition in your market. After starting her cleaning business, for example, Luyk asked potential clients what they liked and disliked about their existing cleaning service. She used their feedback to improve her business.

When trying to set yourself apart from other small businesses, don't compete on price, say experts. Large businesses often offer lower prices because they have some advantages, such as the ability to buy in bulk at reduced cost, that small businesses do not. Lowering prices also reduces profit, which makes it harder to stay in business. "There's always someone willing to undercut your prices," says James. "Be better in other ways."

Make adjustments. As your business evolves, it may outgrow your original vision. Keep up with developments by making adjustments as necessary. For example, you may have planned to run your business from home for several years, but brisk sales might allow you to rent office space sooner than expected.

Experts often recommend adding workers to your payroll as one of the first tweaks you make after your business is established. "Hire people to help you as soon as you can afford them," says Luyk. "Then you can spend your time working on your business—not in the business."

It's important to hire employees who have experience and skills that you don't have. For example, opening an eatery to showcase your culinary skills can be risky if you have never run a restaurant. Employing a manager will offset your lack of management experience and let you focus on your strengths, such as cooking or designing the menu.

Persevere. Working for yourself is not easy. The business might take longer than you expect to turn a profit, for example, or you might have trouble making rent or paying your employees.

As most self-employed workers will tell you, it takes lots of preparation, determination, and time to achieve success in a new business. "This is a marathon," Lebon says. "Temper your expectations, take things one step a time, and don't give up."

Remember, experts say, you don't have a chance for success unless you take the first step. "People are so afraid to fail that they become paralyzed," says Luyk. "But you can learn a lot from failure. And if you don't try, you'll always wonder what could have been."

Chapter 52

Investing Wisely

Investing on Your Own

The first step to investing, especially investing on your own, is to make sure you have a financial plan. How much are you going to invest? For how long? What are your financial goals? Do you understand your tolerance for risk? All investments carry some risk. The next step is research, research, research. When investing on your own, you are responsible for your decisions. How will you select one stock, bond, or mutual fund over others? Always make sure that all securities are registered with the Securities and Exchange Commission (SEC), using the SEC's electronic data gathering, analysis, and retrieval system (EDGAR) database. Don't purchase solely on stock tips from others. There are several ways you can invest on your own, including Online Investing, Direct Investing, and Dividend Reinvestment Plans.

(Source: "Investing on Your Own," U.S. Securities and Exchange Commission (SEC).)

Ten Things to Consider before You Make Investing Decisions

Given the market events, you may be wondering whether you should make changes to your investment portfolio. The U.S. Securities and Exchange Commission's (SEC) Office of Investor Education and Advocacy (OIEA) is concerned that some investors, including bargain

About This Chapter: Text under the heading "Ten Things to Consider before You Make Investing Decisions" is excerpted from "Ten Things to Consider before You Make Investing Decisions," U.S. Securities and Exchange Commission (SEC), October 27, 2008; Text under the heading "Don't Fall for 'All or Nothing' Investment Schemes" is excerpted from "Don't Fall for 'All or Nothing' Investment Schemes," Investor.gov, U.S. Securities and Exchange Commission (SEC), July 28, 2018.

hunters and mattress stuffers, are making rapid investment decisions without considering their long-term financial goals. While SEC can't tell you how to manage your investment portfolio during a volatile market, they are issuing this Investor Alert to give you the tools to make an informed decision. Before you make any decision, consider these areas of importance:

1. **Draw a personal financial roadmap.**

   Before you make any investing decision, sit down and take an honest look at your entire financial situation—especially if you've never made a financial plan before.

   The first step to successful investing is figuring out your goals and risk tolerance—either on your own or with the help of a financial professional. There is no guarantee that you'll make money from your investments. But if you get the facts about saving and investing and follow through with an intelligent plan, you should be able to gain financial security over the years and enjoy the benefits of managing your money.

2. **Evaluate your comfort zone in taking on risk.**

   All investments involve some degree of risk. If you intend to purchase securities—such as stocks, bonds, or mutual funds—it's important that you understand before you invest that you could lose some or all of your money. Unlike deposits at Federal Deposit Insurance Corporation (FDIC)-insured banks and National Credit Union Administration (NCUA)-insured credit unions, the money you invest in securities typically is not federally insured. You could lose your principal, which is the amount you've invested. That's true even if you purchase your investments through a bank.

   The reward for taking on risk is the potential for a greater investment return. If you have a financial goal with a long time horizon, you are likely to make more money by carefully investing in asset categories with greater risk, like stocks or bonds, rather than restricting your investments to assets with less risk, like cash equivalents. On the other hand, investing solely in cash investments may be appropriate for short-term financial goals. The principal concern for individuals investing in cash equivalents is inflation risk, which is the risk that inflation will outpace and erode returns over time.

3. **Consider an appropriate mix of investments.**

   By including asset categories with investment returns that move up and down under different market conditions within a portfolio, an investor can help protect against significant losses. Historically, the returns of the three major asset categories—stocks, bonds, and cash—have not moved up and down at the same time. Market conditions that cause one asset category to do well often cause another asset category to have average or poor returns. By investing in more than one asset category, you'll reduce the risk that you'll lose money and your portfolio's overall investment returns will have a smoother ride. If one asset category's investment return falls, you'll be in a position to counteract your losses in that asset category with better investment returns in another asset category.

In addition, asset allocation is important because it has a major impact on whether you will meet your financial goal. If you don't include enough risk in your portfolio, your investments may not earn a large enough return to meet your goal. For example, if you are saving for a long-term goal, such as retirement or college, most financial experts agree that you will likely need to include at least some stock or stock mutual funds in your portfolio.

4. **Be careful if investing heavily in shares of employer's stock or any individual stock.**

One of the most important ways to lessen the risks of investing is to diversify your investments. It's common sense: don't put all your eggs in one basket. By picking the right group of investments within an asset category, you may be able to limit your losses and reduce the fluctuations of investment returns without sacrificing too much potential gain.

You'll be exposed to significant investment risk if you invest heavily in shares of your employer's stock or any individual stock. If that stock does poorly or the company goes bankrupt, you'll probably lose a lot of money (and perhaps your job).

5. **Create and maintain an emergency fund.**

Most smart investors put enough money in a savings product to cover an emergency, like sudden unemployment. Some make sure they have up to six months of their income in savings so that they know it will absolutely be there for them when they need it.

6. **Pay off high-interest credit card debt.**

There is no investment strategy anywhere that pays off as well as, or with less risk than, merely paying off all high-interest debt you may have. If you owe money on high-interest credit cards, the wisest thing you can do under any market conditions is to pay off the balance in full as quickly as possible.

7. **Consider dollar cost averaging.**

Through the investment strategy known as "dollar cost averaging," you can protect yourself from the risk of investing all of your money at the wrong time by following a consistent pattern of adding new money to your investment over a long period of time. By making regular investments with the same amount of money each time, you will buy more of an investment when its price is low and less of the investment when its price is high. Individuals that typically make a lump-sum contribution to an individual retirement account either at the end of the calendar year or in early April may want to consider "dollar cost averaging" as an investment strategy, especially in a volatile market.

8. **Take advantage of "free money" from the employer.**

In many employer-sponsored retirement plans, the employer will match some or all of your contributions. If your employer offers a retirement plan and you do not contribute enough to get your employer's maximum match, you are passing up "free money" for your retirement savings.

9. **Consider rebalancing portfolio occasionally.**

Rebalancing is bringing your portfolio back to your original asset allocation mix. By rebalancing, you'll ensure that your portfolio does not overemphasize one or more asset categories, and you'll return your portfolio to a comfortable level of risk.

You can rebalance your portfolio based either on the calendar or on your investments. Many financial experts recommend that investors rebalance their portfolios on a regular time interval, such as every six or twelve months. The advantage of this method is that the calendar is a reminder of when you should consider rebalancing. Others recommend rebalancing only when the relative weight of an asset class increases or decreases more than a certain percentage that you've identified in advance. The advantage of this method is that your investments tell you when to rebalance. In either case, rebalancing tends to work best when done on a relatively infrequent basis.

10. **Avoid circumstances that can lead to fraud.**

Scam artists read the headlines, too. Often, they'll use a highly publicized news item to lure potential investors and make their "opportunity" sound more legitimate. The SEC recommends that you ask questions and check out the answers with an unbiased source before you invest. Always take your time and talk to trusted friends and family members before investing.

Don't Fall for "All-or-Nothing" Investment Schemes

Do you like making high-stakes decisions? Are you tempted by "all or nothing" investments?

If you have been researching investments in search of high-yield, low-risk investments, you may have come across something called, "binary options." You may have even been sent an e-mail or a message on social media asking you to look at a sales pitch.

You should be aware these pitches are often nothing more than frauds using flashy, high-pressure sales tactics to try to rob you of your hard-earned money.

There are unique characteristics and risks associated with all or nothing investment opportunities and there are several warning signs that might indicate the investment you are considering is really a scam. Taking a few minutes to educate yourself can prevent you from losing your life savings.

The Basics—A binary option or all or nothing type of options contract involves a payout that depends entirely on the outcome of a yes-or-no proposition. When the option expires, the investor receives either a set amount of cash, or nothing at all. For example, you might pay $50 for a binary option contract that promises a 50-percent return if the company's stock price goes above $5 when the option expires. So what happens if the stock doesn't go above $5 by the time the option expires? Put simply, you lose all or nearly all of the money you invested, very fast. You take a huge risk when investing in these kinds of options, and you have to be comfortable with that level of risk.

Consider This—Be aware that binary-options operators may not comply with the federal securities laws. That could mean they offer unregistered securities or operate as an unregistered broker–dealer or securities exchange. But the biggest risk is that binary options operators may actually be trying to scam you.

Red Flags—The investment you are considering may actually be a scam if the seller:

- Promises you a high return on your investment with no risk

- Requests photocopies of personal documents such as your passport or utility bills

- Uses aggressive sales tactics or threats to try to get you to invest more money

- Pretends to be your friend as a way to gain your trust and encourage you to invest more money

- Strings you along and puts up roadblocks when you try to withdraw your money

- Refuses to pay out your winnings

Many fraudulent exchanges are offshore and unregulated by U.S. laws, which can ultimately mean that they are beyond the reach of U.S. law enforcement. If you get scammed by one of these operators, it may be virtually impossible to get your money back.

Big Takeaways

- All-or-nothing investments involve a high degree of risk, and many binary-options promotions on the Internet are frauds.

- Internet fraudsters may use binary options or other trendy investment buzzwords as a lure for investors when they really intend to rip you off.

Chapter 53

Your Credit History

What Is a Credit History?

Sometimes, people talk about your credit. What they mean is your credit history. Your credit history describes how you use money:

- How many credit cards do you have?

- How many loans do you have?

- Do you pay your bills on time?

If you have a credit card or a loan from a bank, you have a credit history. Companies collect information about your loans and credit cards. Companies also collect information about how you pay your bills. They put this information in one place: your credit report.

What Is a Credit Report?

Your credit report is a summary of your credit history. It lists:

- Your name, address, and Social Security number (SSN)

- Your credit cards

- Your loans

- How much money you owe

- If you pay your bills on time

About This Chapter: This chapter includes text excerpted from "Your Credit History," Consumer.gov, Federal Trade Commission (FTC), September 28, 2012.

Why Do I Have a Credit Report?

Businesses want to know about you before they lend you money. Would you want to lend money to someone who pays bills on time? Or to someone who always pays late? Businesses look at your credit report to learn about you. They decide if they want to lend you money, or give you a credit card. Sometimes, employers look at your credit report when you apply for a job. Cell phone companies and insurance companies look at your credit report, too.

Who Makes My Credit Report?

A company called a credit reporting company collects your information. There are three big credit reporting companies:

- TransUnion

- Equifax

- Experian

These companies write and keep a report about you.

Can I See My Credit Report?

You can get a free copy of your credit report every year. That means one copy from each of the three companies that writes your reports.

The law says you can get your free credit reports if you:

- call Annual Credit Report at 877-322-8228 or

- go to AnnualCreditReport.com

Someone might say you can get a free report on another website. They probably are not telling the truth.

What Is a Credit Score?

A credit score is a number. It is based on your credit history. But it does not come with your free credit report unless you pay for it. A high credit score means you have good credit. A low credit score means you have bad credit. Different companies have different scores. Low scores are around 300. High scores are around 700–850.

Do I Need to Get My Credit Score?

It is very important to know what is in your credit report. But a credit score is a number that matches your credit history. If you know your history is good, your score will be good. You can get your credit report for free. It costs money to find out your credit score. Sometimes a company might say the score is free. But if you look closely, you might find that you signed up for a service that checks your credit for you. Those services charge you every month. Before you pay any money, ask yourself if you need to see your credit score. It might be interesting. But is it worth paying money for?

What If I Do Not Have Credit?

You might not have a credit history if:

- You have not had credit card
- You have not gotten a loan from a bank or credit union

Without a credit history, it can be harder to get a job, an apartment, or even a credit card. It sounds crazy: You need credit to get credit.

How Do I Get Credit?

Do you want to build your credit history? You will need to pay bills that are included in a credit report.

- Sometimes, utility companies put information into a credit report. Do you have utility bills in your name? That can help build credit.
- Many credit cards put information into credit reports.
  - Sometimes, you can get a store credit card that can help build credit.
  - A secured credit card also can help you build your credit.

Why Is My Credit Report Important?

Businesses look at your credit report when you apply for:

- Loans from a bank
- Credit cards

- Jobs

- Insurance

If you apply for one of these, the business wants to know if you pay your bills. The business also wants to know if you owe money to someone else. The business uses the information in your credit report to decide whether to give you a loan, a credit card, a job, or insurance.

What Does "Good Credit" Mean?

Some people have good credit. Some people have bad credit. Some people do not have a credit history. Businesses see this in your credit report. Different things happen based on your credit history:

I have good credit.

- I pay my bills on time.

- I do not have big loans.

That means:

- I have more loan choices.

- It is easier to get credit cards.

- I pay lower interest rates.

- I pay less for loans and credit cards.

I have bad credit.

- I pay my bills late.

- I owe a lot of money.

That means:

- I have fewer loan choices.

- It is harder to get credit cards.

- I pay higher interest rates.

- I pay more for loans and credit cards.

I do not have credit.

- I never borrowed money from a bank or credit union.

- I never had a credit card.

That means:

- I have no bank loan choices.
- It is very hard to get credit cards.
- I pay high-interest rates.
- Loans and credit cards are hard to get and cost a lot.

All this information is in your credit report.

Why Should I Get My Credit Report?

An important reason to get your credit report is to find problems or mistakes and fix them:

- You might find somebody's information in your report by mistake.
- You might find information about you from a long time ago.
- You might find accounts that are not yours. That might mean someone stole your identity.

You want to know what is in your report. The information in your report will help decide whether you get a loan, a credit card, a job or insurance.

If the information is wrong, you can try to fix it. If the information is right—but not so good— you can try to improve your credit history.

Where Do I Get My Free Credit Report?

You can get your free credit report from Annual Credit Report. That is the only free place to get your report. You can get it online at AnnualCreditReport.com, or by phone: 877-322-8228.

You get one free report from each credit reporting company every year. That means you get three reports each year.

What Should I Do When I Get My Credit Report?

Your credit report has a lot of information. Check to see if the information is correct. Is it your name and address? Do you recognize the accounts listed?

If there is wrong information in your report, try to fix it. You can write to the credit reporting company. Ask them to change the information that is wrong. You might need to send proof that the information is wrong—for example, a copy of a bill that shows the correct information. The credit reporting company must check it out and write back to you.

How Do I Improve My Credit?

Look at your free credit report. The report will tell you how to improve your credit history. Only you can improve your credit. No one else can fix information in your credit report that is not good, but is correct.

It takes time to improve your credit history. Here are some ways to help rebuild your credit.

- Pay your bills by the date they are due. This is the most important thing you can do.

- Lower the amount you owe, especially on your credit cards. Owing a lot of money hurts your credit history.

- Do not get new credit cards if you do not need them. A lot of new credit hurts your credit history.

- Do not close older credit cards. Having credit for a longer time helps your rating.

After six to nine months of this, check your credit report again. You can use one of your free reports from Annual Credit Report.

How Does a Credit Score Work?

Your credit score is a number related to your credit history. If your credit score is high, your credit is good. If your credit score is low, your credit is bad. There are different credit scores. Each credit reporting company creates a credit score. Other companies create scores, too. The range is different, but it usually goes from about 300 (low) to 850 (high). It costs money to look at your credit score. Sometimes a company might say the score is free. But usually, there is a cost.

What Goes into a Credit Score?

Each company has its own way to calculate your credit score. They look at:

- How many loans and credit cards you have

- How much money you owe

- How long you have had credit

- How much new credit you have

They look at the information in your credit report and give it a number. That is your credit score.

It is very important to know what is in your credit report. If your report is good, your score will be good. You can decide if it is worth paying money to see what number someone gives your credit history.

How Do I Check My Credit Report by Telephone?

Your credit history is important. It tells businesses how you pay your bills. Those businesses then decide if they want to give you a credit card, a job, an apartment, a loan, or insurance. Find out what is in your report. Be sure the information is correct. Fix anything that is not correct.

This is easy to do by phone:

- Call Annual Credit Report at 877-322-8228.

- Answer questions from a recorded system. You have to give your address, Social Security number (SSN), and birth date.

- Choose to only show the last four numbers of your Social Security number. It is safer than showing your full Social Security number on your report.

- Choose which credit reporting company you want a report from. (You get one free report from each company every year.)

That company mails your report to you. It should arrive two to three weeks after you call.

What Do I Do with My Credit Report?

Read it carefully. Make sure the information is correct:

- **Personal information**—are the name and address correct?
- **Accounts**—do you recognize them?
  - Is the information correct?
- **Negative information**—do you recognize the accounts in this section of the report?
  - Is the information correct?
- **Inquiries**—do you recognize the places you applied for credit? (If you do not, maybe someone stole your identity.)

The report will tell you how to improve your credit history. Only you can improve your credit history. It will take time. But if any of the information in your report is wrong, you can ask to have it fixed.

How Do I Fix Mistakes in My Credit Report?

- Write a letter. Tell the credit reporting company that you have questions about the information in your report.

- Explain which information is wrong and why you think so.

- Say that you want the information corrected or removed from your report.

- Send a copy of your credit report with the wrong information circled.

- Send copies of other papers that help you explain your opinion.

- Send this information Certified Mail. Ask the post office for a return receipt. The receipt is proof that the credit reporting company got your letter.

The credit reporting company must look into your complaint and answer you in writing.

Credit Freeze

Placing a credit freeze allows you to restrict access to your credit report. This is important after a data breach or identity theft when someone could use your personal information to apply for new credit accounts. Most creditors look at your credit report before opening a new account. But if you've frozen your credit report, creditors can't access it, and probably won't approve fraudulent applications. You have the right to place or lift a credit freeze for free. You can place a freeze on your own credit files and on those of your children age 16 or younger.

Place a Credit Freeze

Contact each credit reporting agency to place a freeze on your credit report. Each agency accepts freeze requests online, by phone, or by postal mail.

(Source: "Credit Reports and Scores," USA.gov)

Chapter 54

Credit Scores and Why They Matter

Ever wonder how a lender decides whether to grant you credit? For years, creditors have been using credit scoring systems to determine if you'd be a good risk for credit cards, auto loans, and mortgages. These days, other types of businesses—including auto and homeowners insurance companies and phone companies—are using credit scores to decide whether to issue you a policy or provide you with a service and on what terms. A higher credit score is taken to mean you are less of a risk, which, in turn, means you are more likely to get credit or insurance—or pay less for it.

What Is Credit Scoring?

Credit scoring is a system creditors use to help determine whether to give you credit. It also may be used to help decide the terms you are offered or the rate you will pay for the loan. Information about you and your credit experiences, like your bill-paying history, the number and type of accounts you have, whether you pay your bills by the date they're due, collection actions, outstanding debt, and the age of your accounts, is collected from your credit report. Using a statistical program, creditors compare this information to the loan repayment history of consumers with similar profiles. For example, a credit scoring system awards points for each factor that helps predict who is most likely to repay a debt. A total number of points—a credit score—helps predict how creditworthy you are: how likely it is that you will repay a loan and make the payments when they're due.

About This Chapter: Text in this chapter begins with excerpts from "Credit Scores," Federal Trade Commission (FTC), September 2013; Text under the heading "Why Your Credit Score Matters" is excerpted from "Why Your Credit Score Matters," Federal Trade Commission (FTC), September 7, 2016.

Some insurance companies also use credit report information, along with other factors, to help predict your likelihood of filing an insurance claim and the amount of the claim. They may consider this information when they decide whether to grant you insurance and the amount of the premium they charge. The credit scores insurance companies use sometimes are called "insurance scores" or "credit-based insurance scores."

Credit Scores and Credit Reports

Your credit report is a key part of many credit scoring systems. That's why it is critical to make sure your credit report is accurate. Federal law gives you the right to get a free copy of your credit reports from each of the three national credit reporting companies once every 12 months.

The Fair Credit Reporting Act (FCRA) also gives you the right to get your credit score from the national credit reporting companies. They are allowed to charge a reasonable fee for the score. When you buy your score, you often get information on how you can improve it.

To order your free annual credit report from one or all of the national credit reporting companies, and to purchase your credit score, visit www.annualcreditreport.com, call toll-free 877-322-8228, or complete the Annual Credit Report Request Form and mail it to:

Annual Credit Report Request Service

P.O. Box 105281

Atlanta, GA 30348-5281

How Is a Credit Scoring System Developed?

To develop a credit scoring system or model, a creditor or insurance company selects a random sample of customers and analyzes it statistically to identify characteristics that relate to risk. Each of the characteristics then is assigned a weight based on how strong a predictor it is of who would be a good risk. Each company may use its own scoring model, different scoring models for different types of credit or insurance, or a generic model developed by a scoring company.

Under the Equal Credit Opportunity Act (ECOA), a creditor's scoring system may not use certain characteristics—for example, race, sex, marital status, national origin, or religion—as factors. The law allows creditors to use age, but any credit scoring system that includes age must give equal treatment to applicants who are elderly.

What Can You Do to Improve Your Score?

Credit scoring systems are complex and vary among creditors or insurance companies and for different types of credit or insurance. If one factor changes, your score may change—but improvement generally depends on how that factor relates to others the system considers. Only the business using the system knows what might improve your score under the particular model they use to evaluate your application.

Nevertheless, scoring models usually consider the following types of information in your credit report to help compute your credit score:

- **Have you paid your bills on time?** You can count on payment history to be a significant factor. If your credit report indicates that you have paid bills late, had an account referred to collections, or declared bankruptcy, it is likely to affect your score negatively.

- **Are you maxed out?** Many scoring systems evaluate the amount of debt you have compared to your credit limits. If the amount you owe is close to your credit limit, it's likely to have a negative effect on your score.

- **How long have you had credit?** Generally, scoring systems consider your credit track record. An insufficient credit history may affect your score negatively, but factors like timely payments and low balances can offset that.

- **Have you applied for new credit lately?** Many scoring systems consider whether you have applied for credit recently by looking at "inquiries" on your credit report. If you have applied for too many new accounts recently, it could have a negative effect on your score. Every inquiry isn't counted; for example, inquiries by creditors who are monitoring your account or looking at credit reports to make "prescreened" credit offers are not considered liabilities.

- **How many credit accounts do you have and what kinds of accounts are they?** Although it is generally considered a plus to have established credit accounts, too many credit card accounts may have a negative effect on your score. In addition, many scoring systems consider the type of credit accounts you have. For example, under some scoring models, loans from finance companies may have a negative effect on your credit score.

Scoring models may be based on more than the information in your credit report. When you are applying for a mortgage loan, for example, the system may consider the amount of your down payment, your total debt, and your income, among other things.

Improving your score significantly is likely to take some time, but it can be done. To improve your credit score under most systems, focus on paying your bills in a timely way, paying down any outstanding balances, and staying away from new debt.

Are Credit Scoring Systems Reliable?

Credit scoring systems enable creditors or insurance companies to evaluate millions of applicants consistently on many different characteristics. To be statistically valid, these systems must be based on a big enough sample. They generally vary among businesses that use them.

Properly designed, credit scoring systems generally enable faster, more accurate, and more impartial decisions than individual people can make. And some creditors design their systems so that some applicants—those with scores not high enough to pass easily or low enough to fail absolutely—are referred to a credit manager who decides whether the company or lender will extend credit. Referrals can result in discussion and negotiation between the credit manager and the would-be borrower.

Companies use a mathematical formula called a scoring model to create your credit score from the information in your credit report. Some factors that make up a typical credit score include:

- Your bill-paying history
- Your current unpaid debt
- The number and type of loan accounts you have
- How long you have had your loan accounts open
- How much of your available credit you are using
- New applications for credit
- Whether you have had a debt sent to collection, a foreclosure, or a bankruptcy, and how long ago

(Source: "What Is a Credit Score?" Consumer Financial Protection Bureau (CFPB).)

What If I Am Denied Credit or Insurance, or Don't Get the Terms I Want?

If you are denied credit, the ECOA requires that the creditor give you a notice with the specific reasons your application was rejected or the news that you have the right to learn the reasons if you ask within 60 days. Ask the creditor to be specific: Indefinite and vague reasons for denial are illegal. Acceptable reasons might be "your income was low" or "you haven't been employed long enough." Unacceptable reasons include "you didn't meet our minimum standards" or "you didn't receive enough points on our credit scoring system."

Sometimes you can be denied credit or insurance—or offered less favorable terms—because of information in your credit report. In that case, the FCRA requires the creditor or insurance company to give you a notice that includes, among other things, the name, address, and phone number of the credit reporting company that supplied the information. If a credit score was a factor in the decision to deny you credit or to offer you terms less favorable than most other customers receive, the notice also will include that credit score. If you receive one of these notices, you are entitled to a free copy of your credit report. Contact the company to find out what your report said. The credit reporting company can tell you what's in your report, but only the creditor or insurance company can tell you why your application was denied.

If a creditor or insurance company says you were denied credit or insurance because you are too near your credit limits on your credit cards, you may want to reapply after paying down your balances. Because credit scores are based on credit report information, a score often changes when the information in the credit report changes.

If you've been denied credit or insurance or didn't get the rate or terms you want, ask questions:

- Ask the creditor or insurance company if a credit scoring system was used. If it was, ask what characteristics or factors were used in the system, and how you can improve your application.

- If you receive a notice explaining that you are being offered less favorable credit terms than those offered to most other consumers, ask the creditor or insurance company why you aren't getting its best offer.

- If you are denied credit or not offered the best rate available because of inaccuracies in your credit report, be sure to dispute the inaccurate information with the credit reporting company.

Why Your Credit Score Matters

When you apply for credit, insurance, phone service, or even to rent a place to live, providers want to know if you're a good risk. They use credit scores to help them decide.

A credit score is a number. A high credit score means you have good credit. A low credit score means you have bad credit. A higher score means you're less of a risk, and are more likely get the product or service—or pay less for it.

Here's how it works: Lenders pull information from your credit report, like your bill-paying history, how long you've had your accounts, outstanding debt, and collection actions. A scoring system awards points for each factor that helps predict who is most likely to repay a debt. The total number of points—a credit score—helps predict the likelihood that you'll repay a loan and make payments on time.

Credit scores can be used in a variety of ways. Here are some examples.

Insurance companies may use information from your credit report, along with other factors, to help predict your likelihood of filing an insurance claim and the amount you might claim. They consider this information when deciding whether to give you insurance and how much to charge.

Utility companies use credit scores to decide if a new customer has to make a deposit for service. Cellphone providers and landlords also use scores when considering a new customer or tenant.

Different companies have different scoring systems, and the scores may be based on more than the information in your credit report. When you apply for a mortgage, for example, the system may consider the amount of your down payment, your total debt, and your income.

To improve your credit score, focus on paying your bills on time, paying down outstanding balances, and staying away from new debt.

Chapter 55

Ways to Establish and Maintain a Healthy Credit Score for Your Startup or Small Business

Establishing good credit is essential if you intend to apply for a business loan. But it's not just for loans anymore—a good credit score can also help you:

- Secure a business credit card

- Open a merchant account

- Benefit from lower insurance premiums

- Build relationships and get flexible payment terms from suppliers

- Rent commercial property

- Lease or buy business vehicles

But how do you establish and maintain a healthy business credit score? What if your personal credit score isn't as good as it should be? Can that impact your ability to build business credit? This chapter includes tips for building your small business credit score.

First, however, you need to understand how business credit is measured.

How Business Credit Is Measured

Business credit is calculated using what's known as your Paydex Score—the business equivalent of an individual's Fair Isaac Corporation (FICO) score. Creditors and banks will check

About This Chapter: This chapter includes text excerpted from "6 Ways to Establish and Maintain a Healthy Credit Score for Your Startup or Small Biz," U.S. Small Business Administration (SBA), September 23, 2016.

Got Bad Credit?—Steer Clear of Credit Repair Scams

You see the ads in newspapers, on TV, and online. You hear them on the radio. You get fliers in the mail, e-mail messages, and maybe even calls offering credit repair services. They all make the same claims:

- Credit problems? No problem!
- We can remove bankruptcies, judgments, liens, and bad loans from your credit file forever!
- We can erase your bad credit—100 percent guaranteed.
- Create a new credit identity—legally

Do yourself a favor and save some money, too. Don't believe these claims: they're very likely signs of a scam. Indeed, attorneys at the Federal Trade Commission (FTC), the nation's consumer protection agency, say they've never seen a legitimate credit repair operation making those claims. The fact is there's no quick fix for creditworthiness. No one can legally remove accurate and timely negative information from a credit report. You can improve your credit report legitimately, but it takes time, a conscious effort, and sticking to a personal debt repayment plan.

(Source: "Building a Better Credit Report," Federal Trade Commission (FTC).)

---

your Paydex score to see if you are a risky investment before they'll extend loans and credit. But what is Paydex?

Maintained by Dun & Bradstreet (D&B), a Paydex score is "…D&B's unique dollar-weighted numerical indicator of how (a) business paid its bills over the past year, based on trade experiences reported to D&B by various vendors." Unlike your personal credit score, which is determined by several different factors, Paydex scores your business solely on whether or not you paid your bills promptly and within agreed-upon terms. Paydex is used by business credit bureaus to rate your business credit, although these organizations (D&B, Experian, and Equifax) also take into consideration other factors when weighing your overall score.

How to Build and Manage Your Business Credit Score

There are several practical steps you can take to establish and build both your Paydex score and general business credit score:

1. Register for a Tax Identification Number

If you are a sole proprietor, consider incorporating your business. This will legally separate your personal finances from those of your business so that you can build a separate credit history. Next, apply for a tax identification number from the Internal Revenue Service (IRS). You'll use this to file your taxes as an incorporated business and to register your business with credit bureaus such as D&B.

2. Get a Data Universal Number System (DUNS) Number

If you are starting a business, get a jumpstart on building your credit history by applying online for a DUNS number at D&B's small business iUpdate portal. This nine-digit code is used by D&B and other credit bureaus to identify your business and maintain a credit file against it. If you already have a business credit file with D&B be sure to review it and correct any inaccurate information.

3. Apply for Credit from Suppliers

According to business credit specialist Marco Carbajo, the best place to start building credit as a startup is with suppliers. You can do this by applying for lines of credit to finance purchases such as office supplies, computers, inventory and so on, with flexible payment terms of net 30 or 60 days. Carbajo advises that you choose suppliers who you'll likely deal with on a regular basis so that you can continue to build and maintain your credit (as long as you pay them on time!).

4. Separate Personal and Business Finances

Further, separate your business and personal finances and start building a business credit score by opening a business bank account and putting expenses in your business name. You should also apply for a business credit card. Start by approaching your existing bank or credit card issuer—since you already have a relationship with them, approvals should be easier. This chapter has some tips and considerations to be aware of before choosing a card.

5. Pay Your Bills on Time!

Since your Paydex score is based on your bill payment habits, never miss a payment date. If your cash flow can tolerate it, you could also consider paying your bills ahead of time to increase your Paydex score!

6. Monitor Your Score

According to D&B, the credit score of about one in three businesses declines over just a three-month period. So, plan on monitoring your credit once a quarter so that you are aware of what's happening and how it might affect relationships with suppliers and lenders. It's also a good habit to review your credit file to make sure it's current and accurate. Any changes to your business, such as location, number of employees, outstanding suits/liens, and revenue—can impact your credit rating.

Chapter 56

Using Credit Wisely

The responsible use of credit can have a major impact on a student's future. Obviously, you need to have an established, healthy credit history if you plan to buy a car or home and make other large purchases, but the way you handle credit can also have other significant implications. For example, landlords review credit history before they'll rent you an apartment, and many employers check your credit record as part of the hiring process. The smart thing to do is to begin building a positive credit history now, taking small steps to demonstrate your ability to handle money effectively. A good record of repayment will not only make it easier to get the credit you need in the future but will also result in lower interest rates when you do borrow money.

Credit Score

When someone checks your credit history, what they're looking at is your credit score. This is a number, generally from 300–850, tallied by large credit reporting agencies (CRAs) using information about past purchases and repayment that is obtained from various retailers and other creditors. The three largest CRAs are Equifax, Experian, and TransUnion, and prospective lenders use their scores as predictors of your likelihood to default on future credit.

There can be more than 30 factors that go into calculating a credit score, but these are generally grouped together into five major categories:

- **Credit history.** This is the most important factor and makes up 35 percent of your credit score. Unsurprisingly, lenders want to know that you regularly pay back the money you owe.

About This Chapter: "Using Credit Wisely," © 2017 Omnigraphics.

- **Total indebtedness.** This makes up 30 percent of the score and is important because having a lot of debt can make it hard to pay it all back. The ratio of debt to available credit is also critical. Having a lot of available credit but only using a small amount is good; using up all or most of your available credit hurts your score.

- **Length of credit history.** Accounting for 15 percent of the total score, this includes both how long you have had a credit record and how long individual accounts have been open. A longer history gives potential lenders a better idea of how you handle credit.

- **Type of credit.** This generally makes up 10 percent of the score, although it is more important for individuals with a short credit history. A mix of different kinds of credit shows potential lenders that you can handle various types of indebtedness responsibly.

- **New credit.** This makes up another 10 percent of the total and includes newly opened accounts as well as "hard inquiries," which go on your record any time you apply for credit, whether you actually borrow money or not. (Soft inquiries, such as when you check your own credit record, have no impact on your score.) Lenders may see too much new credit—or applying for new credit—as an indication that you'll be adding more indebtedness in the near future.

Building a Credit Record

Students building a credit history will need to start small and take carefully measured steps to demonstrate fiscal responsibility. One of the first things to do is to check your current credit history, if you have one. There are several online sites that allow you to do this, including Freecreditreport.com, Annualcreditreport.com, and Creditkarma.com, as well as the three major CRAs. Here are some suggestions for next steps:

- **Open savings and checking accounts.** It's always good to have some savings in the bank, and the regular use of a checking account and debit card shows that you can budget and handle money responsibly.

- **Pay your monthly bills.** Regular payment of phone, electric, and cable bills is another indicator of prudent financial management.

- **Pay your student loans.** Most students need loans to help pay for college, and making payments on time shows that you take your responsibilities seriously.

- **Get a student credit card.** One of the best ways to begin building credit is to select a suitable card with a low credit limit, then use it regularly and make payments in full each month. To start with, you may need a joint card with a parent or other person with established credit.

Note that not all of these go directly into a credit score. For example, the use of a debit card won't have an impact on the total. But each of these steps provides an indication of financial responsibility and helps develop good money-management habits.

> Take advantage of technology. Most banks and credit-card issuers have mobile apps that make it easier to conduct transactions and keep track of spending. Many also offer text messages for low-balance alerts, overdrafts, and payment-due reminders.

Types of Credit

There are a number of kinds of credit that are commonly available to students, and it's important to understand how they work. Unless you have an established credit history, it's likely that you'll need a co-signer or joint account holder, but as long as your name is on the account, you'll be building a positive credit history.

- **Credit cards.** These are cards, such as Visa, Mastercard, and Discover, issued by a bank or other financial institution that you can use to purchase goods or services. The card-issuer pays the merchant or service provider, then you pay back the money to the issuer. About one-third of college students have a credit card of some kind, because they're a convenient way to pay expenses and buy things on campus. But if you don't pay off the entire balance each month, a finance charge will be added, and this will continue to build until the balance is paid off. Look for a card with no annual fee and the lowest interest rate possible.

- **Retail cards.** Also called "store cards," these are usually issued by department stores for use at their retail locations or online. They have limited use, since they can only be used with one retailer, and for that reason, they're not as common as they once were. (Most retailers now partner with a major credit-card issuer for a store-branded card that can be used anywhere.) But retail cards have the advantage of generally being easier to get than a major credit card, so they can be a good way to start building credit history.

- **Gasoline cards.** Another type of retail card, these are issued by gasoline companies for use at their own stations. Like store cards, they tend to be easier to get than major credit-card brands, and they're a good way for students with cars to keep track of fuel and maintenance expenses and build a good credit score.

- **Student loans.** Education loans most often come from government-backed sources. Some are based on need and some are open to anyone. Most of the time, repayment is deferred until you graduate or leave school, and interest may also not begin accruing until then. Other student loans come from private sources and work like any other credit instrument, such as a car loan. In either case, maintaining a regular schedule of repayment works to build a strong credit history.

Consider a secured credit card. This is a card that requires a cash deposit in the amount of the credit limit. So if you deposit $200, you can spend up to $200 with the card. They're easy to get, although some carry an annual fee, and most allow you (or your parents) to add funds to the account on a regular basis. And, unlike prepaid cards, secured cards help build your credit score.

Good Credit Practices

Many people get into trouble by not using credit wisely. Developing solid credit practices while avoiding some common pitfalls can help ensure that you build and maintain a good credit score and create financial health. Here are some tips:

- **Shop for credit.** Fees and interest rates vary widely, and they can really add up. Speak to several lenders and examine their websites carefully before signing anything.

- **Read the fine print.** Credit applications contain a lot of detail. Be sure you know if, for example, you're signing up for a low introductory interest rate that goes up after a period of time.

- **Don't borrow more than you can pay back.** It may seem strange, but lenders will often loan you more money than you can repay. Know your finances and live within your budget.

- **Use cash or a debit card when possible.** Credit cards are convenient, but they let you spend more than you have. Sticking to cash or debit cards limits you to the funds you have on hand.

- **Have only one credit card.** Credit-card offers are tempting, but with multiple cards you run the risk of overextending your debt, and applying for them negatively affects your credit score.

- **Avoid annual fees.** Some credit cards come with an annual fee, but so many of them don't that there's no need to pay for the privilege of having a card.

- **Avoid late fees.** If you don't make payments on time, you'll be assessed a late fee. This not only costs money, it also negatively affects your credit score and may result in a higher interest rate.

- **Pay your balance every month.** By paying off the amount you charge each month, you'll avoid accruing interest, which costs you money. Note: There's a common myth that paying the balance each month has a negative impact on your credit score. This is false. It will help build your score.

- **Don't get cash advances.** Read the fine print. Cash advances on credit cards almost always come with higher interest rates and possibly some additional fees.

- **Take advantage of points and other perks.** When shopping for a credit card, look for one that offers reward points, travel rewards, discounts, and other perks. These can save you money.

- **Check your monthly statements.** You want to be sure the lender's accounting is accurate and that there are no charges you didn't initiate. If you find a discrepancy, call the lender immediately.

- **Check your credit score at least annually.** Make sure it's accurate and there are no accounts listed that you didn't open. If something looks wrong, contact the lender and the CRA right away.

Keep in touch with your creditors. If you can't make a payment on time, for example, ask for an extension. There's usually not a problem doing this (once, anyway), and it might help you avoid a late fee. If payments are due at a bad time of month for you, ask for a revised due date.

References

1. "10 Tips for Using Credit Wisely," BusinessWire.com, April 7, 2015.

2. "Credit Basics: Using Credit Wisely," CapitolOne.com, 2017.

3. "How to Use Credit Cards Wisely," CollegeBoard.org, 2017.

4. Irby, LaToya. "Dos and Don'ts of Using Credit Cards Wisely," TheBalance.com, June 26, 2016.

5. "Using Credit Wisely," Greenpath.com, n.d.

6. "Using Credit Wisely," HandsOnBanking.org, n.d.

Chapter 57

Credit Report and Credit Report Errors

Your credit history is important to a lot of people: mortgage lenders, banks, utility companies, prospective employers, and more. So it's especially important that you understand your credit report, credit score, and the companies that compile that information, credit bureaus. This chapter provides answers to some of the most common, and most important, questions about credit.

Your Credit Report
What Is a Credit Report?

A credit report is a record of your credit history that includes information about:

- **Your identity.** Your name, address, full or partial Social Security number (SSN), date of birth (DOB), and possibly employment information.

- **Your existing credit.** Information about credit that you have, such as your credit card accounts, mortgages, car loans, and student loans. It may also include the terms of your credit, how much you owe your creditors, and your history of making payments.

- **Your public record.** Information about any court judgments against you, any tax liens against your property, or whether you have filed for bankruptcy.

- **Inquiries about you.** A list of companies or persons who recently requested a copy of your report.

About This Chapter: This chapter includes text excerpted from "Credit Reports and Credit Scores," Board of Governors of the Federal Reserve System, November 10, 2010.

Why Is a Credit Report Important?

Your credit report is important because lenders, insurers, employers, and others may obtain your credit report from credit bureaus to assess how you manage financial responsibilities. For example:

- Lenders may use your credit report information to decide whether you can get a loan and the terms you get for a loan (for example, the interest rate they will charge you).

- Insurance companies may use the information to decide whether you can get insurance and to set the rates you will pay. Employers may use your credit report, if you give them permission to do so, to decide whether to hire you.

- Telephone and utility companies may use information in your credit report to decide whether to provide services to you.

- Landlords may use the information to determine whether to rent an apartment to you.

Who Collects and Reports Credit Information about Me?

There are three major credit bureaus—Equifax, Experian, and TransUnion—that gather and maintain the information about you that is included in your credit report. The credit bureaus then provide this information in the form of a credit report to companies or persons that request it, such as lenders from whom you are seeking credit.

Where Do Credit Bureaus Get Their Information?

Credit bureaus get information from your creditors, such as a bank, credit card issuer, or auto finance company. They also get information about you from public records, such as property or court records. Each credit bureau gets its information from different sources, so the information in one credit bureau's report may not be the same as the information in another credit bureau's report.

How Can I Get a Free Copy of My Credit Report?

You can get one free credit report every twelve months from each of the nationwide credit bureaus—Equifax, Experian, and TransUnion—by

- Visiting www.annualcreditreport.com, or

- Calling 877-322-8228.

You will need to provide certain information to access your report, such as your name, address, Social Security number, and date of birth. You can order one, two, or all three reports at the same time, or you can request these reports at various times throughout the year. The option you choose will depend on the goal of your review. A report generated by one of the three major credit bureaus may not contain all of the information pertaining to your credit history. Therefore, if you want a complete view of your credit record at a particular moment, you should examine your report from each bureau at the same time. However, if you wish to detect any errors and monitor changes in your credit profile over time, you may wish to review a single credit report every four months.

Who Else Is Allowed to See My Credit Report?

Because credit reports contain sensitive personal information, access to them is limited. Credit bureaus can provide credit reports only to lenders from whom you are seeking credit:

- lenders that have granted you credit
- telephone, cell phone, and utility companies that may provide services to you
- your employer or prospective employer, but only if you agree
- insurance companies that have issued or may issue an insurance policy for you
- government agencies reviewing your financial status for government benefits
- anyone else with a legitimate business need for the information, such as a potential landlord or a bank at which you are opening a checking account.

Credit bureaus also furnish reports if required by court orders or federal grand jury subpoenas. Upon your written request, they will also issue your report to a third party.

Does the Credit Bureau Decide Whether to Grant Me Credit?

No, credit bureaus do not make credit decisions. They provide credit reports to lenders who decide whether to grant you credit.

How Long Does Negative Information, Such as Late Payments, Stay on My Credit Report?

Generally, negative credit information stays on your credit report for seven years. If you have filed for personal bankruptcy, that fact stays on your report for ten years. Information about a lawsuit or an unpaid judgment against you can be reported for seven years or until the statute of limitations runs out, whichever is longer. Information about criminal convictions may stay on your credit report indefinitely.

What Can I Do If I Am Denied Credit, Insurance, or Employment Because of Something in My Credit Report? What Can I Do If I Receive Less Favorable Credit Terms than Other Consumers Because of Something in My Credit Report?

If you are denied credit, insurance, or employment—or some other adverse action is taken against you, such as lowering your credit limit on credit card account—because of information in your credit report, the lender, insurance company, or employer must notify you and provide you with the name, address, and phone number of the credit bureau that provided the credit report used to make the decision. You can get a free credit report from this credit bureau if you request it within sixty days after receiving the notice. This free report is in addition to your annual free report. In addition, lenders may use a credit report to set the terms of credit they offer you. If a lender offers you terms less favorable (for example, a higher rate) than the terms offered to consumers with better credit histories based on the information in your credit report, the lender may give you a notice with information about the credit bureau that provided the credit report used to make the decision. Again, you can get a free credit report (in addition to your annual free report) from this credit bureau if you request it within sixty days after receiving the notice.

If you receive one of these notices, it's a good idea to get your free credit report and review the information in it right away.

I've Been Receiving Unsolicited Credit Offers. Why? Can I Opt-Out of Receiving These Offers?

Credit bureaus may sell the names and addresses of consumers who meet specific credit criteria to creditors or insurers, who must then offer them credit or insurance. For example, a creditor could request from a credit bureau the names and addresses of consumers who have a credit score of 680 or higher and then offer credit to those consumers. You can have your name and address removed from these lists by opting-out of the listing. This will reduce the number of unsolicited offers you receive. To opt-out, call 888-5-OPTOUT (888-567-8688) or visit www.optoutprescreen.com. You will need to provide certain information in order to opt-out, such as your name, address, Social Security number, and date of birth. You have the ability to opt-out of receiving offers either for five years or permanently. If you want to opt-out permanently, you will need to fill out, sign, and mail in a form. The form is available by either calling the toll-free number or visiting the website. You can reverse your opt-out decision at any time to start receiving offers of credit and insurance again by calling the toll-free phone number or visiting the website.

Your Credit Score
What Is a Credit Score? How Is My Credit Score Calculated?

A credit score is a number that reflects the information in your credit report. The score summarizes your credit history and helps lenders predict how likely it is that you will repay a loan and make payments when they are due. Lenders may use credit scores in deciding whether to grant you credit, what terms you are offered, or the rate you will pay on a loan. Information used to calculate your credit score can include:

- The number and type of accounts you have (credit cards, auto loans, mortgages, etc.)
- Whether you pay your bills on time
- How much of your available credit you are currently using
- Whether you have any collection actions against you
- The amount of your outstanding debt
- The age of your accounts

What Can Cause My Credit Score to Change?

Because your credit score reflects the information in your credit report, changes to your credit report may cause your credit score to change. For instance, if you pay your bills late or incur more debt, your credit score may go down. However, if you pay down an outstanding balance on a credit card or mortgage or correct an error in your credit report, your credit score may go up.

How Can I Get My Credit Score?

In some cases, a lender may tell you your credit score for free when you apply for credit. For example, if you apply for a mortgage, you will receive the credit score or scores that were used to determine whether the lender would extend credit to you and on what terms. You may also

373

receive a free credit score or scores from lenders when you apply for other types of credit, such as an automobile loan or a credit card.

You may also purchase your credit score from any of the credit bureaus by calling them or visiting their websites.

- Equifax: Call 800-685-1111 or visit www.equifax.com/personal

- Experian: Call 888-397-3742 or visit www.experian.com/consumer-products/free-credit-report.html

- TransUnion: Call 800-493-2392 or visit www.transunion.com/credit-reports-disclosures/free-credit-report

Credit Report Errors
How Can I Correct Errors Found in My Credit Report?

If you find errors in your credit report, you may dispute the information and request that the information be deleted or corrected. To do so, you should contact either the credit bureau that provided the report or the company or person that provided the incorrect information to the credit bureau. To contact the credit bureau, call the toll-free number on your credit report or visit their website:

- Equifax (www.equifax.com/personal/education/credit/report)

- Experian (www.experian.com/disputes)

- TransUnion (www.transunion.com/credit-disputes/dispute-your-credit)

To contact the company or person that provided the incorrect information to the credit bureau, look on your credit report, in an account statement, or on the company's website for contact information for handling such disputes.

When disputing information on your credit report, you should:

- Provide information about yourself, such as your name, address, date of birth, and Social Security number

- Identify specific details about the information that is being disputed and explain the basis of your dispute

- Have a copy of your credit report that contains the disputed information available

- Provide supporting documentation, such as a copy of the relevant portion of the consumer report, a police report, a fraud or identity theft affidavit, or account statements.

What Happens Once I Send in Information to Correct Information in My Credit Report?

If you submit your dispute through a credit bureau or directly to the company or person that provided the incorrect information to the credit bureau, your dispute must be investigated, usually within thirty days. If you provide additional information during the thirty-day investigation, that investigation period may be extended an additional fifteen days in some circumstances. When the investigation is completed, either the credit bureau or the company or person that provided the incorrect information to the credit bureau must give you the written results of its investigation. If the information provider finds the disputed information is inaccurate, it must notify all three nationwide credit bureaus so they can correct the information in your credit report. You can get a free copy of your report if the dispute results in a change. This free report is in addition to your annual free report. If an item is changed or deleted, a credit bureau cannot put the disputed information back in your credit report unless the company or person that provided the incorrect information to the credit bureau verifies that the information is, indeed, accurate and complete. You can request that the credit bureau send notices of any correction to anyone who received your report in the past six months. A corrected copy of your report can be sent to anyone who received a copy during the past two years for employment purposes.

What If an Investigation Does Not Resolve My Dispute?

If an investigation does not resolve your dispute, you can ask that a statement of the dispute be included in your future credit reports. You also can ask the credit bureau to provide your statement to anyone who received a copy of your report in the recent past, but you may have to pay a fee for this service.

Your credit report contains information about where you live, how you pay your bills, and whether you've been sued or arrested, or have filed for bankruptcy. Credit reporting companies sell the information in your report to creditors, insurers, employers, and other businesses that use it to evaluate your applications for credit, insurance, employment, or renting a home. The federal Fair Credit Reporting Act (FCRA) promotes the accuracy and privacy of information in the files of the nation's credit reporting companies.

Some financial advisors and consumer advocates suggest that you review your credit report periodically. Why?

Because the information it contains affects whether you can get a loan—and how much you will have to pay to borrow money. To make sure the information is accurate, complete, and

---

up-to-date before you apply for a loan for a major purchase like a house or car, buy insurance, or apply for a job.

To help guard against identity theft. That's when someone uses your personal information—like your name, your Social Security number, or your credit card number—to commit fraud. Identity thieves may use your information to open a new credit card account in your name. Then, when they don't pay the bills, the delinquent account is reported on your credit report. Inaccurate information like that could affect your ability to get credit, insurance, or even a job.

(Source: "Disputing Errors on Credit Reports," Federal Trade Commission (FTC).)

Part Eight
If You Need More Information

Chapter 58

Online Money Management Tools

BizKid$

A companion site for the public TV series that teaches kids and teens about money and business.
Website: www.bizkids.com

College Savings Plans Network (CSPN)

A nonprofit association dedicated to making a college education affordable and accessible.
Website: www.collegesavings.org

Compound Interest Calculator

Determine how much your money can grow using the power of compound interest. You can find out if you're dealing with a registered investment professional with a free search on Investor.gov's homepage.
Website: www.investor.gov/additional-resources/free-financial-planning-tools/compound-interest-calculator

Cost of Raising a Child Calculator

With this calculator you can estimate how much it will annually cost to raise a child. This may help you plan better for overall expenses including food or to purchase adequate life insurance.
Website: www.cnpp.usda.gov/calculatorintro

Dollars from Sense

Funded by the FINRA Investor Education, this interactive site instructs young adults in the basics of personal finance and investing.
Website: www.dollarsfromsense.com

About This Chapter: The tools/resources listed in this chapter were excerpted from various sources deemed reliable. Inclusion does not constitute endorsement, and there is no implication associated with omission. All website information was verified and updated in October 2018.

Estimation Calculators

This tool helps approximate the future value of your savings bonds and show how much and how long it will take to reach your goals.
Website: www.treasurydirect.gov/indiv/tools/tools_estimationcalc.htm

FastWeb

Fastweb is one of the oldest and largest scholarship sites. It offers connection to scholarships, colleges, financial aid, and student loan options.
Website: www.fastweb.com

GenIRevolution

Developed for middle school and high school students, this online game gives students the chance to learn important personal finance skills as they play and compete against fellow classmates. Online personal finance game for high school students developed by the Council for Economic Education (CEE).
Website: www.genirevolution.org

Growth Calculator

Use this calculator to see how your savings add up.
Website: www.savingsbonds.gov/BC/SBCGrw

Investor.gov

The resources you need to learn the basics, protect yourself, and stay informed.
Website: www.investor.gov

IRS Withholding Calculator

This Withholding calculator works for most taxpayers. You can use your results from this calculator to help you complete a new Form W-4, Employee's Withholding Allowance Certificate.
Website: www.irs.gov/individuals/irs-withholding-calculator

Jumpstart Coalition for Personal Financial Literacy

Coalition of organizations dedicated to improve financial literacy of pre-K through college-age youth.
Website: www.jumpstart.org

The Mint

Money management tips, games, and tools for kids, teens, and parents.
Website: www.themint.org

Moneytopia

Online interactive game to help teens learn to save and manage money.
Website: apps.finra.org/moneytopia

National Foundation for Credit Counseling (NFCC)

It is a nonprofit organization dedicated to improving people's financial well-being. It connects the consumers with local credit counseling services.
Website: www.nfcc.org

Savings Bond Calculator

This calculator will price Series EE, Series E, and Series I savings bonds, and Savings Notes. Features include current interest rate, next accrual date, final maturity date, and year-to-date interest earned.
Website: www.savingsbonds.gov/indiv/tools/tools_savingsbondcalc.htm

Savings Planner

Use this planner to find out how you can reach your savings goals.
Website: www.savingsbonds.gov/BC/SBCPln

SBA Teen Business Link

Ideas and advice for teen entrepreneurs.
Website: www. sba.gov/teens

Tax Advantage Calculator

This calculator is used to see how tax advantages factor into your savings bond earnings.
Website: www.savingsbonds.gov/BC/SBCTax

Teens and Money: Money 101

Resources, games, and activities for sound money management from the FINRA Investor Education Foundation.
Website: www.saveandinvest.org/educate-youth

Treasury Direct Kids®

Excellent introduction to public debt, treasury securities, and saving money.
Website: www.treasurydirect.gov/kids/kids.htm

U.S. Mint for Kids

Fun money facts and activities for kids, also includes financial literacy links for parents and teachers.
Website: www.usmint.gov/learn/kids

Chapter 59

Resources for Financial Information

ACA International
P.O. Box 390106
Minneapolis, MN 55439
Phone: 952-926-6547
Website: www.acainternational.org

American Association of Individual Investors (AAII)
625 N. Michigan Ave.
Chicago, IL 60611
Toll-Free: 800-428-2244
Phone: 312-280-0170
Fax: 312-280-9883
Website: www.aaii.com
E-mail: techsupport@aaii.com

American Bankers Association (ABA)
1120 Connecticut Ave. N.W.
Washington, DC 20036
Toll-Free: 800-BANKERS (800-226-5377)
Website: www.aba.com
E-mail: cutserv@aba.com

About This Chapter: Resources in this chapter were compiled from several sources deemed reliable; all contact information was verified and updated in October 2018.

American Consumer Credit Counseling (ACCC)
130 Rumford Ave.
Ste. 202
Auburndale, MA 02466-1371
Toll-Free: 800-769-3571
Phone: 617-559-5700
Fax: 617-244-1116
Website: www.consumercredit.com
E-mail: info@consumercredit.com

American Council of Life Insurers (ACLI)
101 Constitution Ave. N.W.
Ste. 700
Washington, DC 20001-2133
Toll-Free: 877-674-4659
Phone: 202-624-2000
Website: www.acli.com
E-mail: webadmin@acli.com

American Financial Services Association (AFSA)
919 18th St. N.W.
Ste. 300
Washington, DC 20006
Website: www.afsaonline.org
E-mail: info@afsamail.org

American Institute of Certified Public Accountants (AICPA)
Personal Financial Planning Division
1455 Pennsylvania Ave. N.W.
Washington, DC 20004-1081
Toll-Free: 888-777-7077
Phone: 202-737-6600
Fax: 202-638-4512
Website: www.aicpa.org
E-mail: service@aicpa.org

Asset Builders of America
1213 N. Sherman Ave.
Ste. 195
Madison, WI 53704
Phone: 608-663-6332
Website: www.assetbuilders.org
E-mail: info@assetbuilders.org

Bankrate.com
Toll-Free: 855-733-0700
Website: www.bankrate.com

BetterInvesting
711 W. 13 Mile Rd.
Ste. 900
Madison Heights, MI 48071
Phone: 248-583-6242
Fax: 248-583-4880
Website: www.betterinvesting.org
E-mail: service@betterinvesting.org

Certified Financial Planner (CFP)
Board of Standards
1425 K St. N.W.
Ste. 800
Washington, DC 20005
Toll-Free: 800-487-1497
Phone: 202-379-2200
Fax: 202-379-2299
Website: www.cfp.net
E-mail: mail@cfpboard.org

Choose to Save®
Employee Benefit Research Institute's Education and Research Fund (EBRI-ERF)
1100 13th St. N.W.
Ste. 878
Washington, DC 20005
Phone: 202-659-0670
Fax: 202-775-6312
Website: www.choosetosave.org
E-mail: info@choosetosave.org

Consolidated Credit, Inc.

5701 W. Sunrise Blvd.
Fort Lauderdale, FL 33313
Toll-Free: 800-320-9929
Website: www.consolidatedcredit.org

Consumer Action

1170 Market St.
Ste. 500
San Francisco, CA 94102
Phone: 415-777-9635
Fax: 415-777-5267
Website: www.consumer-action.org

Consumer Federation of America (CFA)

1620 I St. N.W.
Ste. 200
Washington, DC 20006
Phone: 202-387-6121
Website: consumerfed.org
E-mail: cfa@consumerfed.org

Consumers' Checkbook

1625 K St. N.W.
Eighth Fl.
Washington, DC 20006
Toll-Free: 800-213-7283
Website: www.checkbook.org

Council for Economic Education (CEE)

122 E. 42nd St.
Ste. 2600
New York, NY 10168
Phone: 212-730-7007
Fax: 212-730-1793
Website: www.councilforeconed.org

Credit Union National Association (CUNA)
5710 Mineral Pt. Rd.
Madison, WI 53705
Toll-Free: 800-356-9655
Website: www.cuna.org
E-mail: hello@cuna.coop

Credit.org
4351 Latham St.
Riverside, CA 92501
Toll-Free: 800-431-8157
Website: www.credit.org
E-mail: ClientHelp@credit.org

CreditSmart
1551 Park Run Dr. MS D5O
McLean, VA 22102
Toll-Free: 800-FREDDIE (800-373-3343)
Website: www.freddiemac.com/creditsmart

CuraDebt
4000 Hollywood Blvd.
Ste. 555-S
Hollywood, FL 33021
Toll-Free: 877-850-3328
Fax: 754-333-5510
Website: www.curadebt.com
E-mail: counselors@curadebt.com

Debtors Anonymous (DA)
1116 Great Plain Ave.
Needham, MA 02492
Toll-Free: 800-421-2383
Phone: 781-453-2743
Fax: 781-453-2745
Website: debtorsanonymous.org

Dominion Bond Rating Service (DBRS)

333 W. Wacker Dr.
Ste. 1800
Chicago, IL 60606
Phone: 312-332-3429
Fax: 312-332-3492
Website: www.dbrs.com
E-mail: info@dbrs.com

Employee Benefit Research Institute (EBRI)

1100 13th St. N.W.
Ste. 878
Washington, DC 20005-4051
Phone: 202-659-0670
Fax: 202-775-6312
Website: ww.ebri.org
E-mail: info@ebri.org

Equifax, Inc.

P.O. Box 740241
Atlanta, GA 30374-0241
Toll-Free: 866-349-5191
Website: www.equifax.com/personal

Experian Information Solutions, Inc.

475 Anton Blvd.
Costa Mesa, CA 92626
Phone: 714-830-7000
Website: www.experian.com

Federal Deposit Insurance Corporation (FDIC)

Division of Finance
3501 N. Fairfax Dr. Bldg. E
Fifth Fl.
Arlington, VA 22226
Toll-Free: 800-759-6596
Website: www.fdic.gov
E-mail: assessments@fdic.gov

Federal Reserve Education

Board of Governors of the Federal Reserve System
20th St. and Constitution Ave. N.W.
Washington, DC 20551
Phone: 202-452-3000
TDD: 202-263-4869
Website: www.federalreserveeducation.org

Federal Trade Commission (FTC)

600 Pennsylvania Ave. N.W.
Washington, DC 20580
Phone: 202-326-2222
Website: www.ftc.gov
E-mail: webmaster@ftc.gov

Financial Planning Association (FPA)

7535 E. Hampden Ave., Ste. 600
Denver, CO 80231
Toll-Free: 800-322-4237
Phone: 303-759-4900
Website: www.onefpa.org
E-mail: info@onefpa.org

InCharge Debt Solutions

5750 Major Blvd.
Ste. 300
Orlando, FL 32819
Toll-Free: 877-906-5599
Website: www.incharge.org

Insurance Information Institute (III)

110 William St.
New York, NY 10038
Phone: 212-346-5500
Website: www.iii.org
E-mail: info@iii.org

389

Internal Revenue Service (IRS)
1111 Constitution Ave. N.W.
Washington, DC 20224
Phone: 267-941-1000
Fax: 267-466-1055
Website: www.irs.gov

Investment Company Institute (ICI)
1401 H St. N.W., Ste. 1200
Washington, DC 20005
Phone: 202-326-5800
Website: www.ici.org
E-mail: webmaster@ici.org

Investor Protection Trust (IPT)
1020 19th St. N.W.
Ste. 890
Washington, DC 20036-6123
Website: www.investorprotection.org
E-mail: iptinfo@investorprotection.org

Iowa State University (ISU) Cooperative Extension
2150 Beardshear Hall
Ames, IA 50011-2031
Toll-Free: 800-262-3804
Website: www.extension.iastate.edu

Jump$tart Coalition
1001 Connecticut Ave. N.W., Ste. 640
Washington, DC 20036
Phone: 202-846-6780
Website: www.jumpstart.org
E-mail: info@jumpstart.org

Junior Achievement USA®
One Education Way
Colorado Springs, CO 80906
Phone: 719-540-8000
Website: www.juniorachievement.org

Kiplinger

1100 13th St. N.W.
Ste. 750
Washington, DC 20005
Toll-Free: 800-544-0155
Phone: 202-887-6400
Website: www.kiplinger.com

Morningstar

22 W. Washington St.
Chicago, IL 60602
Phone: 312-696-6000
Website: www.morningstar.in
E-mail: productinfo@morningstar.com

Motley Fool

2000 Duke St.
Fourth Fl.
Alexandria, VA 22314
Fax: 703-254-1999
Website: www.fool.com

Nasdaq

One Liberty Plaza
165 Bdwy.
New York, NY 10006
Phone: 212-401-8700
Website: www.nasdaq.com

National Association of Personal Financial Advisors (NAPFA)

8700 W. Bryn Mawr Ave.
Ste. 700N
Chicago, IL 60631
Toll-Free: 888-FEE-ONLY (888-333-6659)
Phone: 847-483-5400
Website: www.napfa.org
E-mail: info@napfa.org

National Association of Professional Insurance Agents (PIA)
419 N. Lee St.
Alexandria, VA 22314
Phone: 703-836-9340
Fax: 703-836-1279
Website: pianet.com
E-mail: web@pianet.org

National Association of Real Estate Investment Trusts (NAREIT)
1875 I St. N.W., Ste. 600
Washington, DC 20006
Toll-Free: 800-362-7348
Phone: 202-739-9400
Fax: 202-739-9401
Website: www.reit.com/nareit

National Consumer Law Center, Inc. (NCLC)
7 Winthrop Sq.
Boston, MA 02110-1245
Phone: 617-542-8010
Fax: 617-542-8028
Website: www.nclc.org
E-mail: consumerlaw@nclc.org

National Consumers League (NCL)
1701 K St. N.W.
Ste. 1200
Washington, DC 20006
Phone: 202-835-3323
Website: www.nclnet.org
E-mail: info@nclnet.org

National Endowment for Financial Education (NEFE)
1331 17th St., Ste. 1200
Denver, CO 80202
Toll-Free: 866-460-5586
Phone: 303-741-6333
Website: www.nefe.org

National Futures Association (NFA)

300 S. Riverside Plaza, Ste. 1800
Chicago, IL 60606-6615
Toll-Free: 800-621-3570
Phone: 312-781-1300
Fax: 312-781-1467
Website: www.nfa.futures.org

National Institute of Food and Agriculture (NIFA)

U.S. Department of Agriculture (USDA)
1400 Independence Ave. S.W.
Washington, DC 20250
Toll-Free: 877-622-3056
Phone: 202-720-2791
Website: nifa.usda.gov

Navient Solutions, Inc.

P.O. Box 9500
Wilkes-Barre, PA 18773-9500
Phone: 570-821-6585
Website: www.navient.com

New York Stock Exchange, Inc. (NYSE)

Website: www.nyse.com

North American Securities Administrators Association (NASAA)

750 First St. N.E.
Ste. 1140
Washington, DC 20002
Phone: 202-737-0900
Fax: 202-783-3571
Website: www.nasaa.org

Plan Sponsor Council of America (PSCA)

200 S. Wacker Dr.
Ste. 3100
Chicago, IL 60606
Phone: 312-419-186
Fax: 703-516-9308
Website: www.psca.org
E-mail: psca@psca.org

Practical Money Skills
900 Metro Center Blvd.
MS-M1-11NE
Foster City, CA 94404-2172
Website: www.practicalmoneyskills.com
E-mail: info@practicalmoneyskills.com

Rutgers Cooperative Extension
New Jersey Agricultural Experiment Station (NJAES)
88 Lipman Dr.
New Brunswick, NJ 08901-8525
Phone: 848-932-9126
Website: njaes.rutgers.edu

Securities Industry and Financial Markets Association Foundation for Investor Education (SIFMA)
120 Bdwy.
35th Fl.
Phone: 212-313-1200
Website: www.sifma.org
E-mail: inquiry@sifma.org

Society of Financial Service Professionals (FSP)
3803 W. Chester Pike
Newtown Square, PA 19073-2334
Phone: 610-526-2500
Website: national.societyoffsp.org

TransUnion LLC
Website: www.transunion.com

TSX Inc.
TMX Group Limited
Toll-Free: 888-873-8392
Website: www.tmx.com
E-mail: businessdevelopment@tmx.com

USAA Educational Foundation (USAAEF)
9800 Fredericksburg Rd.
San Antonio, TX 78288-0026
Website: usaaef.org
E-mail: edfoundation_info@usaa.com

U.S. Commodity Futures Trading Commission (CFTC)
Three Lafayette Centre
1155 21st St. N.W.
Washington, DC 20581
Phone: 202-418-5000
Website: www.cftc.gov

U.S. Department of the Treasury (USDT)
1500 Pennsylvania Ave. N.W.
Washington, DC 20220
Toll-Free: 800-826-9434
Phone: 202-622-2000
Website: home.treasury.gov

U.S. Securities and Exchange Commission (SEC)
100 F St. N.E.
Washington, DC 20549
Toll-Free: 800-SEC-0330 (800-732-0330)
Phone: 202-551-6551
Website: www.sec.gov
E-mail: webmaster@sec.gov

U.S. Trustee Program
Website: www.justice.gov/ust

Index

Index

Page numbers that appear in *Italics* refer to tables or illustrations. Page numbers that have a small 'n' after the page number refer to citation information shown as Notes. Page numbers that appear in **Bold** refer to information contained in boxes within the chapters.

F

N

S